LOSE THE WHEAT, LOSE THE WEIGHT!

LOSE THE WHEAT, LOSE THE WEIGHT!

BANISH YOUR WHEAT BELLY, FEEL BETTER THAN EVER, AND TURBOCHARGE YOUR HEALTH

WILLIAM DAVIS, MD

RODALE.

Previously published as trade hardcover in August 2011 by Rodale Inc. under the title *Wheat Belly*. Exclusive direct mail hardcover edition published in January 2012.

Printed in the United States of America
Rodale Inc. makes every effort to use acid-free ♾, recycled paper ♻.

Book design by Joanna Williams

Library of Congress Cataloging-in-Publication Data

Davis, William, M.D.
    Lose the wheat, lose the weight! : banish your wheat belly, feel better than ever, and turbocharge your health / William Davis.
        p. cm.
    Includes bibliographical references and index.
    ISBN 978–1–60961–740–0 direct hardcover
    1. Wheat-free diet.   I. Title.
    RM237.87.D36   2012
    613.2′6—dc23   201200229

2   4   6   8   10   9   7   5   3   hardcover

We inspire and enable people to improve their lives and the world around them.

For more of our products, visit rodalestore.com or call 800-848-4735.

For Dawn, Bill, Lauren, and Jacob,
my companions on this wheat-free journey

CONTENTS

INTRODUCTION

FLIP THROUGH YOUR parents' or grandparents' family albums and you're likely to be struck by how *thin* everyone looks. The women probably wore size-four dresses and the men sported 32-inch waists. Overweight was something measured only by a few pounds; obesity rare. Overweight children? Almost never. Any 42-inch waists? Not here. Two-hundred-pound teenagers? Certainly not.

Why were the June Cleavers of the fifties and sixties, the stay-at-home housewives as well as other people of that era, so much skinnier than the modern people we see at the beach, mall, or in our own mirrors? While women of that era typically weighed in at 110 or 115 pounds, men at 150 or 165 pounds, today we carry 50, 75, even 200 pounds *more*.

The women of that world didn't exercise much at all. (It was considered unseemly, after all, like having impure thoughts at church.) How many times did you see your mom put on her jogging shoes to go out for a three-mile run? Exercise for my mother was vacuuming the stairs. Nowadays I go outdoors on any nice day and see dozens of women jogging, riding their bicycles, power walking—things we'd virtually *never* see 40 or 50 years ago. And yet, we're getting fatter and fatter every year.

My wife is a triathlete and triathlon instructor, so I observe a few of these extreme exercise events every year. Triathletes train intensively for months to years before a race to complete a 1- to 2½-mile open water swim, a 56- to 112-mile bike ride, and finish with a 13- to 26-mile run. Just completing a race is a feat in itself, since the event requires up to several thousand calories and spectacular endurance. The majority of triathletes adhere to fairly healthy eating habits.

Then why are a third of these dedicated men and women athletes overweight? I give them even greater credit for having to cart around the extra thirty, forty, or fifty pounds. But, given their extreme level of sustained activity and demanding training schedule, how can they still be overweight?

If we follow conventional logic, overweight triathletes need to *exercise more* or *eat less* to lose weight. I believe that is a downright ridiculous notion. I am going to argue that the problem with the diet and health of most Americans is not fat, not sugar, not the rise of the Internet and the demise of the agrarian lifestyle. It's *wheat*—or what we are being sold that is called "wheat."

You will see that what we are eating, cleverly disguised as a bran muffin or onion ciabatta, is not really wheat at all but the transformed product of genetic research conducted during the latter half of the twentieth century. Modern wheat is no more real wheat than a chimpanzee is an approximation of a human. While our hairy primate relatives share 99 percent of all genes found in humans, with longer arms, full body hair, and lesser capacity to win the jackpot at Jeopardy, I trust you can readily tell the difference that that 1 percent makes. Compared to its ancestor of only forty years ago, modern wheat isn't even that close.

I believe that the increased consumption of grains—or more accurately, the increased consumption of this genetically altered thing called modern wheat—explains the contrast between slender, sedentary people of the fifties and overweight twenty-first-century people, triathletes included.

I recognize that declaring wheat a malicious food is like declaring that Ronald Reagan was a Communist. It may seem absurd, even unpatriotic, to demote an iconic dietary staple to the status of public health hazard. But I will make the case that the world's most popular grain is also the world's most destructive dietary ingredient.

Documented peculiar effects of wheat on humans include appetite stimulation, exposure to brain-active *exorphins* (the counterpart of internally derived endorphins), exaggerated blood sugar surges that trigger cycles of satiety alternating with heightened appetite, the process of *glycation* that underlies disease and aging, inflammatory and pH effects that erode cartilage and damage bone, and activation of disordered immune responses. A complex range of diseases results from consumption of wheat, from celiac disease—the devastating intestinal disease that develops from exposure to wheat gluten—to an assortment of neurological disorders, diabetes, heart disease, arthritis, curious rashes, and the paralyzing delusions of schizophrenia.

If this thing called wheat is such a problem, then removing it should yield outsize and unexpected benefits. Indeed, that is the case. As a cardiologist who sees and treats thousands of patients at risk for heart disease, diabetes, and the myriad destructive effects of obesity, I have personally observed protuberant, flop-over-the-belt belly fat *vanish* when my patients eliminated wheat from their diets, with typical weight loss totaling 20, 30, or 50 pounds just within the first few months. Rapid and effortless weight loss is usually followed by health benefits that continue to amaze me even today after having witnessed this phenomenon thousands of times.

I've seen dramatic turnarounds in health, such as the thirty-eight-year-old woman with ulcerative colitis facing colon removal who was *cured* with wheat elimination—colon intact. Or the twenty-six-year-old man, incapacitated and barely able to walk because of joint pain, who experienced complete relief and walked and ran freely again after taking wheat off the menu.

Extraordinary as these results may sound, there is ample scientific research to implicate wheat as the root cause of these conditions—and to indicate that removal of wheat can reduce or relieve symptoms entirely. You will see that we have unwittingly traded convenience, abundance, and low cost for health with wheat bellies, bulging thighs, and double chins to prove it. Many of the arguments I make in the chapters that follow have been proven in scientific studies that are available for one and all to review. Incredibly, many of the lessons I've learned were demonstrated in clinical studies *decades* ago, but somehow never percolated to the surface of medical or public consciousness. I've simply put two and two together to come up with some conclusions that you may find startling.

IT'S NOT YOUR FAULT

In the movie *Good Will Hunting*, Matt Damon's character, possessing uncommon genius but harboring demons of past abuse, breaks down in sobs when psychologist Sean Maguire (Robin Williams) repeats "It's not your fault" over and over again.

Likewise, too many of us, stricken with an unsightly wheat belly, blame ourselves: too many calories, too little exercise, too little restraint. But it's more accurate to say that the advice we've been given to eat more "healthy whole grains" has deprived us of control over appetites and impulses, making us fat and unhealthy despite our best efforts and good intentions.

I liken the widely accepted advice to eat healthy whole grains to telling an alcoholic that, if a drink or two won't hurt, nine or ten may be even better. Taking this advice has disastrous repercussions on health.

It's not your fault.

If you find yourself carrying around a protuberant, uncomfortable wheat belly; unsuccessfully trying to squeeze into last year's jeans; reassuring your doctor that, no, you haven't been eating badly, but you're still overweight and prediabetic with high blood pressure and cholesterol; or desperately trying to conceal a pair of humiliating man breasts, consider saying goodbye to wheat.

Eliminate the wheat, eliminate the problem.

What have you got to lose except your wheat belly, your man breasts, or your bagel butt?

PART ONE

WHEAT: THE *UNHEALTHY* WHOLE GRAIN

CHAPTER 1

WHAT BELLY?

The scientific physician welcomes the establishment of a standard loaf of bread made according to the best scientific evidence. . . . Such a product can be included in diets both for the sick and for the well with a clear understanding of the effect that it may have on digestion and growth.

Morris Fishbein, MD,
editor, *Journal of the American Medical Association,* 1932

IN CENTURIES PAST, a prominent belly was the domain of the privileged, a mark of wealth and success, a symbol of not having to clean your own stables or plow your own field. In this century, you don't have to plow your own field. Today, obesity has been democratized: *Everybody* can have a big belly. Your dad called his rudimentary mid-twentieth-century equivalent a beer belly. But what are soccer moms, kids, and half of your friends and neighbors who don't drink beer doing with a beer belly?

I call it wheat belly, though I could have just as easily called this condition pretzel brain or bagel bowel or biscuit face since there's not an organ system unaffected by wheat. But wheat's impact on the waistline is its most visible and defining character-istic, an outward expression of the grotesque distortions humans experience with consumption of this grain.

A wheat belly represents the accumulation of fat that results from years of consuming foods that trigger insulin, the hormone of fat storage. While some people store fat in their buttocks and thighs, most people collect ungainly fat around the middle. This "central" or "visceral" fat is unique: Unlike fat in other body areas, it provokes inflammatory phenomena, distorts insulin responses, and issues abnormal metabolic signals to the rest of the body. In the unwitting wheat-bellied male, visceral fat also produces estrogen, creating "man breasts."

The consequences of wheat consumption, however, are not just manifested on the body's surface; wheat can also reach deep down into virtually every organ of the body, from the intestines, liver, heart, and thyroid gland all the way up to the brain. In fact, there's hardly an organ that is *not* affected by wheat in some potentially damaging way.

PANTING AND SWEATING IN THE HEARTLAND

I practice preventive cardiology in Milwaukee. Like many other midwestern cities, Milwaukee is a good place to live and raise a family. City services work pretty well, the libraries are first-rate, my kids go to quality public schools, and the population is just large enough to enjoy big-city culture, such as an excellent sym-phony and art museum. The people living here are a fairly friendly bunch. But . . . they're *fat*.

I don't mean a little bit fat. I mean really, really fat. I mean panting-and-sweating-after-one-flight-of-stairs fat. I mean 240-pound 18-year-old women, SUVs tipped sharply to the driver's side, double-wide wheelchairs, hospital equipment unable to accommodate patients who tip the scales at 350 pounds or more. (Not only can't they fit into the CT scanner or other imaging device, you wouldn't be able to *see* anything even if they could. It's like trying to determine whether the image in the murky ocean water is a flounder or a shark.)

Once upon a time, an individual weighing 250 pounds or more was a rarity; today it's a common sight among the men and women walking the mall, as humdrum as selling jeans at the Gap. Retired people are overweight or obese, as are middle-aged adults, young adults, teenagers, even children. White-collar workers are fat, blue-collar workers are fat. The sedentary are fat and so are athletes. White people are fat, black people are fat, Hispanics are fat, Asians are fat. Carnivores are fat, vegetarians are fat. Americans are plagued by obesity on a scale never before seen in the human experience. No demographic has escaped the weight gain crisis.

Ask the USDA or the Surgeon General's office and they will tell you that Americans are fat because they drink too many soft drinks, eat too many potato chips, drink too much beer, and don't exercise enough. And those things may indeed be true. But that's hardly the whole story.

Many overweight people, in fact, are quite health conscious. Ask anyone tipping the scales over 250 pounds: What do you think happened to allow such incredible weight gain? You may be surprised at how many do *not* say "I drink Big Gulps, eat Pop-Tarts, and watch TV all day." Most will say something like "I don't get it. I exercise five days a week. I've cut my fat and increased my healthy whole grains. Yet I can't seem to stop gaining weight!"

HOW DID WE GET HERE?

The national trend to reduce fat and cholesterol intake and increase carbohydrate calories has created a peculiar situation in which products made from wheat have not just increased their presence in our diets; they have come to *dominate* our diets. For most Americans, every single meal and snack contains foods made with wheat flour. It might be the main course, it might be the side dish, it might be the dessert—and it's probably *all* of them.

Wheat has become the national icon of health: "Eat more healthy whole grains," we're told, and the food industry happily jumped on board, creating "heart healthy" versions of all our favorite wheat products chock-full of whole grains.

The sad truth is that the proliferation of wheat products in the American diet parallels the expansion of our waists. Advice to cut fat and cholesterol intake and replace the calories with whole grains that was issued by the National Heart, Lung, and Blood Institute through its National Cholesterol Education Program in 1985 coincides precisely with the start of a sharp upward climb in body weight for men and women. Ironically, 1985 also marks the year when the Centers for Disease Control and Prevention (CDC) began tracking body weight statistics, tidily documenting the explosion in obesity and diabetes that began that very year.

Of all the grains in the human diet, why only pick on wheat? Because wheat, by a considerable margin, is the dominant source of gluten protein in the human diet. Unless they're Euell Gibbons, most people don't eat much rye, barley, spelt, triticale, bulgur, kamut, or other less common gluten sources; wheat consumption overshadows consumption of other gluten-containing grains by more than a hundred to one. Wheat also has unique attributes those other grains do not, attributes that make it especially destructive to our health, which I will cover in later chapters. But I focus on wheat because, in the vast majority of American diets, gluten exposure can be used interchangeably with wheat exposure. For that reason, I often use wheat to signify all gluten-containing grains.

The health impact of *Triticum aestivum*, common bread wheat, and its genetic brethren ranges far and wide, with curious effects from mouth to anus, brain to pancreas, Appalachian housewife to Wall Street arbitrageur.

If it sounds crazy, bear with me. I make these claims with a clear, wheat-free conscience.

NUTRI-GROAN

Like most children of my generation, born in the middle of the twentieth century and reared on Wonder Bread and Devil Dogs, I have a long and close personal relationship with wheat. My sisters and I were veritable connoisseurs of breakfast cereal, making our own individual blends of Trix, Lucky Charms, and Froot Loops and eagerly drinking the sweet, pastel-hued milk that remained at the bottom of the bowl. The Great American Processed Food Experience didn't end at breakfast, of course. For school lunch my mom usually packed peanut butter or bologna sandwiches, the prelude to cellophane-wrapped Ho Hos and Scooter Pies. Sometimes she would throw in a few Oreos or Vienna Fingers, too. For supper, we loved the TV dinners that came packaged in their own foil plates, allowing us to consume our battered chicken, corn muffin, and apple brown betty while watching *Get Smart*.

My first year of college, armed with an all-you-can-eat dining room ticket, I gorged on waffles and pancakes for breakfast, fettuccine Alfredo for lunch, pasta with Italian bread for dinner. Poppy seed muffin or angel food cake for dessert? You bet! Not only did I gain a hefty spare tire around the middle at age nineteen, I felt exhausted all the time. For the next twenty years, I battled this effect, drinking gallons of coffee, struggling to shake off the pervasive stupor that persisted no matter how many hours I slept each night.

Yet none of this really registered until I caught sight of a photo my wife snapped of me while on vacation with our kids, then ages ten, eight, and four, on Marco Island, Florida. It was 1999.

In the picture, I was fast asleep on the sand, my flabby abdomen splayed to either side, my second chin resting on my crossed flabby arms.

That's when it really hit me: I didn't just have a few extra pounds to lose, I had a good thirty pounds of accumulated weight around my middle. What must my patients be thinking when I counseled them on diet? I was no better than the doctors of the sixties puffing on Marlboros while advising their patients to live healthier lives.

Why did I have those extra pounds under my belt? After all, I jogged three to five miles every day, ate a sensible, balanced diet that didn't include excessive quantities of meats or fats, avoided junk foods and snacks, and instead concentrated on getting plenty of healthy whole grains. What was going on here?

Sure, I had my suspicions. I couldn't help but notice that on the days when I'd eat toast, waffles, or bagels for breakfast, I'd stumble through several hours of sleepiness and lethargy. But eat a three-egg omelet with cheese, feel fine. Some basic laboratory work, though, really stopped me in my tracks. Triglycerides: 350 mg/dl; HDL ("good") cholesterol: 27 mg/dl. And I was diabetic, with a fasting blood sugar of 161 mg/dl. Jogging nearly every day but I was overweight and diabetic? Something had to be fundamentally wrong with my diet. Of all the changes I had made in my diet in the name of health, boosting my intake of healthy whole grains had been the most significant. Could it be that the grains were actually making me fatter?

That moment of flabby realization began the start of a journey, following the trail of crumbs back from being overweight and all the health problems that came with it. But it was when I observed even greater effects on a larger scale beyond my own personal experience that I became convinced that there really was something interesting going on.

LESSONS FROM A WHEAT-FREE EXPERIMENT

An interesting fact: Whole wheat bread (glycemic index 72) increases blood sugar as much as or *more than* table sugar, or sucrose (glycemic index 59). (Glucose increases blood sugar to 100, hence a glycemic index of 100. The extent to which a particular food increases blood sugar relative to glucose determines that food's glycemic index.) So when I was devising a strategy to help my overweight, diabetes-prone patients reduce blood sugar most efficiently, it made sense to me that the quickest and simplest way to get results would be to eliminate the foods that caused their blood sugar to rise most pro-foundly: in other words, not sugar, but wheat. I provided a simple handout detailing how to replace wheat-based foods with other low-glycemic whole foods to create a healthy diet.

After three months, my patients returned to have more blood work done. As I had anticipated, with only rare exceptions, blood sugar (glucose) had indeed often dropped from diabetic range (126 mg/dl or greater) to normal. Yes, diabetics became *non*diabetics. That's right: Diabetes in many cases can be cured—not simply man-aged—by removal of carbohydrates, especially wheat, from the diet. Many of my patients had also lost twenty, thirty, even forty pounds.

But it's what I *didn't* expect that astounded me.

They reported that symptoms of acid reflux disappeared and the cyclic cramping and diarrhea of irritable bowel syndrome were gone. Their energy improved, they had greater focus, sleep was deeper. Rashes disappeared, even rashes that had been pres-ent for many years. Their rheumatoid arthritis pain improved or disappeared, enabling them to cut back, even eliminate, the nasty medications used to treat it. Asthma symptoms improved or resolved completely, allowing many to throw away their inhalers. Athletes reported more consistent performance.

Thinner. More energetic. Clearer thinking. Better bowel, joint, and lung health. Time and time again. Surely these results were reason enough to forgo wheat.

What convinced me further were the many instances in which people removed wheat, then permitted themselves a wheat indulgence: a couple of pretzels, a canapé at a cocktail party. Within minutes, many would experience diarrhea, joint swelling and pain, or wheezing. On again, off again, the phenomenon would repeat itself.

What started out as a simple experiment in reducing blood sugars exploded into an insight into multiple health conditions and weight loss that continues to amaze me even today.

A RADICAL WHEAT-ECTOMY

For many, the idea of removing wheat from the diet is, at least psychologically, as painful as the thought of having a root canal without anesthesia. For some, the process can indeed have uncomfortable side effects akin to withdrawal from cigarettes or alcohol. But this procedure *must* be performed to permit the patient to recover.

Lose the Wheat, Lose the Weight explores the proposition that the health problems of Americans, from fatigue to arthritis to gastrointestinal distress to obesity, originate with the innocent-looking bran muffin or cinnamon raisin bagel you down with your coffee every morning.

The good news: There is a cure for this condition called wheat belly—or, if you prefer, pretzel brain, bagel bowel, or biscuit face.

The bottom line: Elimination of this food, part of human culture for more centuries than Larry King was on the air, will make you sleeker, smarter, faster, and happier. Weight loss, in particular, can proceed at a pace you didn't think possible. And you can selectively lose the most visible, insulin-opposing, diabetes-creating, inflammation-producing, embarrassment-causing fat: belly fat. It is a process accomplished with virtually no hunger or deprivation, with a wide spectrum of health benefits.

So why eliminate wheat rather than, say, sugar, or all grains in general? The next chapter will explain why wheat is unique among modern grains in its ability to convert quickly to blood sugar. In addition, it has a poorly understood and understudied genetic makeup and addictive properties that actually cause us to overeat even *more*; has been linked to literally dozens of debilitating ailments beyond those associated with overweight; and has infiltrated almost every aspect of our diet. Sure, cutting out refined sugar is probably a good idea, as it provides little or no nutritional benefit and will also impact your blood sugar in a negative way. But for the most bang for your buck, eliminating wheat is the easiest and most effective step you can take to safeguard your health and trim your waistline.

Test Results So Good, He Thought His Doctor Had the Wrong File

Just like most of the country, John bought into the healthy whole grains idea as a way to lower his heart risk, but it wasn't working. "After being a diehard Ezekiel Bread toast and old-fashioned oatmeal breakfast aficionado my entire adult life, I could not understand why my blood lipids were so out of whack," he says. After years of frustration, the fifty-seven-year-old man was looking for another way to lower his lipid profile. What made him decide to try this as opposed to other plans? "Simple," he says. "It was commonsense advice."

John says the program is low cost, does not require prescriptions, insurance, or co-pays, and his own doctor agreed with many philosophies advocated by Dr. Davis. "While I did not have a wheat belly, I did have many lipid-related maladies associated with wheat consumption which statins do not help with." Since starting the wheat belly diet, his coronary calcium score dropped 10.63 percent, his Lp(a) went from 21 to 3 (Lipoprotein(a) is a marker for high-risk for heart disease), and he moved from Pattern B to Pattern A (meaning the small and *really* bad LDL cholesterol particles were decreased or eliminated, thereby reducing his risk for heart attack and extra growth of coronary plaque) in just one year. "I was shocked! I even questioned my doctor if the test results got mixed up with someone else's," he says.

This new wheat-free diet, in addition to severely improving his health measures, resulted in a seven-pound weight loss for John, who was not even looking to lose. Now he says, he's exactly where he wants to be weight-wise. And he quickly discovered that it wasn't just the diet keeping him healthy, but his ability to exercise right along with it. "I could go for a long run or bike ride and not have to eat a bunch of carbs to keep fueled and from bonking," he said.

Today, John feels very clear headed because he sleeps like a rock every night—another things he credits to a lack of wheat. And he's very determined to stick with the wheat belly diet. "Because it is just so easy to do!" he says.

CHAPTER 2

NOT YOUR GRANDMA'S MUFFINS: THE CREATION OF MODERN WHEAT

He is as good as good bread.
Miguel de Cervantes,
Don Quixote

WHEAT, MORE THAN any other foodstuff (including sugar, fat, and salt), is woven into the fabric of the American food experience, a trend that began even before Ozzie met Harriet. It has become such a ubiquitous part of the American diet in so many ways that it seems essential to our lifestyle. What would a plate of eggs be without toast, lunch without sandwiches, beer without pretzels, picnics without hot dog buns, dip without crackers, hummus without pita, lox without bagels, apple pie without the crust?

IF IT'S TUESDAY, IT MUST BE WHEAT

I once measured the length of the bread aisle at my local super-market: sixty-eight feet.

That's sixty-eight feet of white bread, whole wheat bread, multigrain bread, seven-grain bread, rye bread, pumpernickel bread, sourdough bread, Italian bread, French bread, bread sticks, white bagels, raisin bagels, cheese bagels, garlic bagels, oat bread, flax bread, pita bread, dinner rolls, Kaiser rolls, poppy seed rolls, hamburger buns, and fourteen varieties of hot dog buns. That's not even counting the bakery and the additional forty feet of shelves packed with a variety of "artisanal" wheat products.

And then there's the snack aisle with forty-some brands of crackers and twenty-seven brands of pretzels. The baking aisle has bread crumbs and croutons. The dairy case has dozens of those tubes you crack open to bake rolls, Danish, and crescents.

Breakfast cereals fill a world unto themselves, usually enjoying a monopoly over an entire supermarket aisle, top to bottom shelf.

There's much of an aisle devoted to boxes and bags of pasta and noodles: spaghetti, lasagna, penne, elbows, shells, whole wheat pasta, green spinach pasta, orange tomato pasta, egg noodles, tiny-grained couscous to three-inch-wide pasta sheets.

How about frozen foods? The freezer has hundreds of noodle, pasta, and wheat-containing side dishes to accompany the meat loaf and roast beef au jus.

In fact, apart from the detergent and soap aisle, there's barely a shelf that *doesn't* contain wheat products. Can you blame Americans if they've allowed wheat to dominate their diets? After all, it's in practically everything.

Wheat as a crop has succeeded on an unprecedented scale, exceeded only by corn in acreage of farmland planted. It is, by a long stretch, among the most consumed grains on earth, consti-tuting 20 percent of all calories consumed.

And wheat has been an undeniable financial success. How many other ways can a manufacturer transform a nickel's worth of raw material into $3.99 worth of glitzy, consumer-friendly product, topped off with endorsements from the American Heart Association? In most cases, the cost of marketing these products exceeds the cost of the ingredients themselves.

Foods made partly or entirely of wheat for breakfast, lunch, dinner, and snacks have become the rule. Indeed, such a regimen would make the USDA, the Whole Grains Council, the Whole Wheat Council, the American Dietetic Association, the American Diabetes Association, and the American Heart Association happy, knowing that their message to eat more "healthy whole grains" has gained a wide and eager following.

So why has this seemingly benign plant that sustained generations of humans suddenly turned on us? For one thing, it is not the same grain our forebears ground into their daily bread. Wheat naturally evolved to only a modest degree over the centuries, but it has changed dramatically in the past fifty years under the influence of agricultural scientists. Wheat strains have been hybridized, crossbred, and introgressed to make the wheat plant resistant to environmental conditions, such as drought, or pathogens, such as fungi. But most of all, genetic changes have been induced to increase *yield per acre*. The average yield on a modern North American farm is more than tenfold greater than farms of a century ago. Such enormous strides in yield have required drastic changes in genetic code, including reducing the proud "amber waves of grain" of yesteryear to the rigid, eighteen-inch-tall high-production "dwarf" wheat of today. Such fundamental genetic changes, as you will see, have come at a price.

Even in the few decades since your grandmother survived Prohibition and danced the Big Apple, wheat has undergone countless transformations. As the science of genetics has progressed over the past fifty years, permitting human intervention at a much more rapid rate than nature's slow, year-by-year breeding influence, the pace of change has increased exponentially. The genetic backbone of your high-tech poppy seed muffin has achieved its current condition by a process of evolutionary acceleration that makes us look like *Homo habilis* trapped somewhere in the early Pleistocene.

FROM NATUFIAN PORRIDGE TO DONUT HOLES

"Give us this day our daily bread."

It's in the Bible. In Deuteronomy, Moses describes the Promised Land as "a land of wheat and barley and vineyards." Bread is central to religious ritual. Jews celebrate Passover with unleavened matzo to commemorate the flight of the Israelites from Egypt. Christians consume wafers representing the body of Christ. Muslims regard unleavened naan as sacred, insisting it be stored upright and never thrown away in public. In the Bible, bread is a metaphor for bountiful harvest, a time of plenty, freedom from starvation, even salvation.

Don't we break bread with friends and family? Isn't something new and wonderful "the best thing since sliced bread"? "Taking the bread out of someone's mouth" is to deprive that person of a fundamental necessity. Bread is a nearly universal diet staple: chapati in India, tsoureki in Greece, pita in the Middle East, aebleskiver in Denmark, naan bya for breakfast in Burma, glazed donuts any old time in the United States.

The notion that a foodstuff so fundamental, so deeply ingrained in the human experience, can be bad for us is, well, unsettling and counter to long-held cultural views of wheat and bread. But today's bread bears little resemblance to the loaves that emerged from our forebears' ovens. Just as a modern Napa Cabernet Sauvignon is a far cry from the crude ferment of fourth-century bc Georgian winemakers who buried wine urns in underground mounds, so has wheat changed. Bread and other foods made of wheat have sustained humans for centuries, but the wheat of our ancestors is not the same as modern commercial wheat that reaches your breakfast, lunch, and dinner table. From the original strains of wild grass harvested by early humans, wheat has exploded to more than 25,000 varieties, virtually all of them the result of human intervention.

In the waning days of the Pleistocene, around 8500 bc, millennia before any Christian, Jew, or Muslim walked the earth, before the Egyptian, Greek, and Roman empires, the Natufians led a semi-nomadic life roaming the Fertile Crescent (now Syria, Jordan, Lebanon, Israel, and Iraq), supplementing their hunting and gathering by harvesting indigenous plants. They harvested the ancestor of modern wheat, einkorn, from fields that flourished wildly in open plains. Meals of gazelle, boar, fowl, and ibex were rounded out with dishes of wild-growing grain and fruit. Relics like those excavated at the Tell Abu Hureyra settlement in what is now central Syria suggest skilled use of tools such as sickles and mortars to harvest and grind grains, as well as storage pits for stockpiling harvested food. Remains of harvested wheat have been found at archaeological digs in Tell Aswad, Jericho, Nahal Hemar, Navali Cori, and other locales. Wheat was ground by hand, then eaten as porridge. The modern concept of bread leavened by yeast would not come along for several thousand years.

Natufians harvested wild einkorn wheat and may have purposefully stored seeds to sow in areas of their own choosing the next season. Einkorn wheat eventually became an essential component of the Natufian diet, reducing the need for hunting and gathering. The shift from harvesting wild grain to cultivating it was a fundamental change that shaped their subsequent migratory behavior, as well as the development of tools, language, and culture. It marked the beginning of agriculture, a lifestyle that required long-term commitment to more or less permanent settlement, a turning point in the course of human civilization. Growing grains and other foods yielded a surplus of food that allowed for occupational specialization, government, and all the elaborate trappings of culture (while, in contrast, the *absence* of agriculture arrested cultural development at something resembling Neolithic life).

Over most of the ten thousand years that wheat has occupied a prominent place in the caves, huts, and adobes and on the tables of humans, what started out as harvested einkorn, then emmer, followed by cultivated *Triticum aestivum*, changed gradually and only in small fits and starts. The wheat of the seventeenth century was the wheat of the eighteenth century, which in turn was much the same as the wheat of the nineteenth century and the first half of the twentieth century. Riding your oxcart through the countryside during any of these centuries, you'd see fields of four-foot-tall "amber waves of grain" swaying in the breeze. Crude human wheat breeding efforts yielded hit-and-miss, year-over-year incremental modifications, some successful, most not, and even a discerning eye would be hard pressed to tell the difference between the wheat of early twentieth century farming from its many centuries of predecessors.

During the nineteenth and early twentieth centuries, as in many preceding centuries, wheat changed little. The Pillsbury's Best XXXX flour my grandmother used to make her famous sour cream muffins in 1940 was little different from the flour of her great-grandmother sixty years earlier or, for that matter, from that of a relative two centuries before that. Grinding of wheat had become more mechanized in the twentieth century, yielding finer flour on a larger scale, but the basic composition of the flour remained much the same.

That all ended in the latter part of the twentieth century, when an upheaval in hybridization methods transformed this grain. What now passes for wheat has changed, not through the forces of drought or disease or a Darwinian scramble for survival, but through human intervention. As a result, wheat has undergone a more drastic transformation than Joan Rivers, stretched, sewed, cut, and stitched back together to yield something entirely unique, nearly unrecognizable when compared to the original and yet still called by the same name: wheat.

Modern commercial wheat production has been intent on delivering features such as increased yield, decreased production costs, and large-scale production of a consistent commodity. All the while, virtually no questions have been asked about whether these features are compatible with human health. I submit that, somewhere along the way during wheat's history, perhaps five thousand years ago but more likely fifty years ago, wheat changed.

The result: A loaf of bread, biscuit, or pancake of today is different than its counterpart of a thousand years ago, different even from what our grandmothers made. They might look the same, even taste much the same, but there are biochemical differences. Small changes in wheat protein structure can spell the difference between a devastating immune response to wheat protein versus no immune response at all.

WHEAT *BEFORE* GENETICISTS GOT HOLD OF IT

Wheat is uniquely adaptable to environmental conditions, growing in Jericho, 850 feet below sea level, to Himalayan mountainous regions 10,000 feet above sea level. Its latitudinal range is also wide, ranging from as far north as Norway, 65° north latitude, to Argentina, 45° south latitude. Wheat occupies sixty million acres of farmland in the United States, an area equal to the state of Ohio. Worldwide, wheat is grown on an area ten times that figure, or twice the total acreage of Western Europe.

The first wild, then cultivated, wheat was einkorn, the great-granddaddy of all subsequent wheat. Einkorn has the simplest genetic code of all wheat, containing only fourteen chromosomes. Circa 3300 bc, hardy, cold-tolerant einkorn wheat was a popular grain in Europe. This was the age of the Tyrolean Iceman, fondly known as Ötzi. Examination of the intestinal contents of this naturally mummified Late Neolithic hunter, killed by attackers and left to freeze in the mountain glaciers of the Italian Alps, revealed the partially digested remains of einkorn wheat consumed as unleavened flatbread, along with remains of plants, deer, and ibex meat.[1]

Shortly after the cultivation of the first einkorn plant, the emmer variety of wheat, the natural offspring of parents einkorn and an unrelated wild grass, *Aegilops speltoides* or goatgrass, made its appearance in the Middle East.[2] Goatgrass added its genetic code to that of einkorn, resulting in the more complex twenty-eight-chromosome emmer wheat. Plants such as wheat have the ability to retain the *sum* of the genes of their forebears. Imagine that, when your parents mated to create you, rather than mixing chromosomes and coming up with forty-six chromosomes to create their offspring, they *combined* forty-six chromosomes from Mom with forty-six chromosomes from Dad, totaling ninety-two chromosomes in you. This, of course, doesn't happen in higher species. Such additive accumulation of chromosomes in plants is called polyploidy.

Einkorn and its evolutionary successor emmer wheat remained popular for several thousand years, sufficient to earn their place as food staples and religious icons, despite their relatively poor yield and less desirable baking characteristics compared to modern wheat. (These denser, cruder flours would have yielded lousy ciabattas or bear claws.) Emmer wheat is probably what Moses referred to in his pronouncements, as well as the *kussemeth* mentioned in the Bible, and the variety that persisted up until the dawn of the Roman Empire.

Sumerians, credited with developing the first written language, left us tens of thousands of cuneiform tablets. Pictographic characters scrawled on several tablets, dated to 3000 bc, describe recipes for breads and pastries, all made by taking mortar and pestle or a hand-pushed grinding wheel to emmer wheat. Sand was often added to the mixture to hasten the laborious grinding process, leaving bread-eating Sumerians with sand-chipped teeth.

Emmer wheat flourished in ancient Egypt, its cycle of growth suited to the seasonal rise and fall of the Nile. Egyptians are credited with learning how to make bread "rise" by the addition of yeast. When the Jews fled Egypt, in their hurry they failed to take the leavening mixture with them, forcing them to consume unleavened bread made from emmer wheat.

Sometime in the millennia predating Biblical times, twenty-eight-chromosome emmer wheat (*Triticum turgidum*) mated naturally with another grass, *Triticum tauschii*, yielding primordial forty-two-chromosome *Triticum aestivum*, genetically closest to what we now call wheat. Because it contains the sum total of the chromosomal content of three unique plants with forty-two chromosomes, it is the most genetically complex. It is therefore the most genetically "pliable," an issue that will serve future genetics researchers well in the millennia to come.

Over time, the higher yielding and more baking-compatible *Triticum aestivum* species gradually overshadowed its parents einkorn and emmer wheat. For many ensuing centuries, *Triticum aestivum* wheat changed little. By the mid-eighteenth century, the great Swedish botanist and biological cataloguer, Carolus Linnaeus, father of the Linnean system of the categorization of species, counted five different varieties falling under the *Triticum* genus.

Wheat did not evolve naturally in the New World, but was introduced by Christopher Columbus, whose crew first planted a few grains in Puerto Rico in 1493. Spanish explorers accidentally brought wheat seeds in a sack of rice to Mexico in 1530, and later introduced it to the American southwest. The namer of Cape Cod and discoverer of Martha's Vineyard, Bartholomew Gosnold, first brought wheat to New England in 1602, followed shortly thereafter by the Pilgrims, who transported wheat with them on the *Mayflower*.

The *Real* Wheat

What was the wheat grown ten thousand years ago and harvested by hand from wild fields like? That simple question took me to the Middle East—or more precisely, to a small organic farm in western Massachusetts.

There I found Elisheva Rogosa. Eli is not only a science teacher but an organic farmer, advocate of sustainable agriculture, and founder of the Heritage Wheat Conservancy (www.growseed.org), an organization devoted to preserving ancient food crops and cultivating them using organic principles. After living in the Middle East for ten years and working with the Jordanian, Israeli, and Palestinian GenBank project to collect nearly extinct ancient wheat strains, Eli returned to the United States with seeds descended from the original wheat plants of ancient Egypt and Canaan. She has since devoted herself to cultivating the ancient grains that sustained her ancestors.

My first contact with Ms. Rogosa began with an exchange of e-mails that resulted from my request for two pounds of einkorn wheat grain. She couldn't stop herself from educating me about her unique crop, which was not just any old wheat grain, after all. Eli described the taste of einkorn bread as "rich, subtle, with more complex flavor," unlike bread made from modern wheat flour, which she claimed tasted like cardboard.

Eli bristles at the suggestion that wheat products might be unhealthy, citing instead the yield-increasing, profit-expanding agricultural practices of the past few decades as the source of adverse health effects of wheat. She views einkorn and emmer as the solution, restoring the original grasses, grown under organic conditions, to replace modern industrial wheat.

And so it went, a gradual expansion of the reach of wheat plants with only modest and gradual evolutionary selection at work.

Today einkorn, emmer, and the original wild and cultivated strains of *Triticum aestivum* have been replaced by thousands of modern human-bred offspring of *Triticum aestivum*, as well as *Triticum durum* (pasta) and *Triticum compactum* (very fine flours used to make cupcakes and other products). To find einkorn or emmer today, you'd have to look for the limited wild collections or modest human plantings scattered around the Middle East, southern France, and northern Italy. Courtesy of modern human-designed hybridizations, *Triticum* species of today are hundreds, perhaps thousands, of genes apart from the original einkorn wheat that bred naturally.

Triticum wheat of today is the product of breeding to generate greater yield and characteristics such as disease, drought, and heat resistance. In fact, wheat has been modified by humans to such a degree that modern strains are unable to survive in the wild without human support such as nitrate fertilization and pest control.[3] (Imagine this bizarre situation in the world of domesticated animals: an animal able to exist only with human assistance, such as special feed, or else it would die.)

Differences between the wheat of the Natufians and what we call wheat in the twenty-first century would be evident to the naked eye. Original einkorn and emmer wheat were "hulled" forms, in which the seeds clung tightly to the stem. Modern wheats are "naked" forms, in which the seeds depart from the stem more readily, a characteristic that makes threshing (separating the edible grain from the inedible chaff) easier and more efficient, determined by mutations at the Q and Tg (*tenacious glume*) genes.[4] But other differences are even more obvious. Modern wheat is much shorter. The romantic notion of tall fields of wheat grain gracefully waving in the wind has been replaced by "dwarf" and "semi-dwarf" varieties that stand barely a foot or two tall, yet another product of breeding experiments to increase yield.

SMALL IS THE NEW BIG

For as long as humans have practiced agriculture, farmers have strived to increase yield. Marrying a woman with a dowry of several acres of farmland was, for many centuries, the primary means of increasing crop yield, arrangements often accompanied by several goats and a sack of rice. The twentieth century introduced mechanized farm machinery, which replaced animal power and increased efficiency and yield with less manpower, providing another incremental increase in yield per acre. While production in the United States was usually sufficient to meet demand (with distribution limited more by poverty than by supply), many other nations worldwide were unable to feed their populations, resulting in widespread hunger.

In modern times, humans have tried to increase yield by creating new strains, crossbreeding different wheats and grasses and generating new genetic varieties in the laboratory. Hybridization efforts involve techniques such as introgression and "back-crossing," in which offspring of plant breeding are mated with their parents or with different strains of wheat or even other grasses. Such efforts, though first formally described by Austrian priest and botanist Gregor Mendel in 1866, did not begin in earnest until the mid-twentieth century, when concepts such as heterozygosity and gene dominance were better understood. Since Mendel's early efforts, geneticists have developed elaborate techniques to obtain a desired trait, though much trial and error is still required.

Much of the current world supply of purposefully bred wheat is descended from strains developed at the International Maize and Wheat Improvement Center (IMWIC), located east of Mexico City at the foot of the Sierra Madre Oriental mountains. IMWIC began as an agricultural research program in 1943 through a collaboration of the Rockefeller Foundation and the Mexican government to help Mexico achieve agricultural self-sufficiency. It grew into an impressive worldwide effort to increase the yield of corn, soy, and wheat, with the admirable goal of reducing world hunger. Mexico provided an efficient proving ground for plant hybridization, since the climate allows two growing seasons per year, cutting the time required to hybridize strains by half. By 1980, these efforts had produced thousands of new strains of wheat, the most high-yielding of which have since been adopted worldwide, from

Third World countries to modern industrialized nations, including the United States.

One of the practical difficulties solved during IMWIC's push to increase yield is that, when large quantities of nitrogen-rich fertilizer are applied to wheat fields, the seed head at the top of the plant grows to enormous proportions. The top-heavy seed head, however, buckles the stalk (what agricultural scientists call "lodging"). Buckling kills the plant and makes harvesting problematic. University of Minnesota–trained geneticist Norman Borlaug, working at IMWIC, is credited with developing the exceptionally high-yielding dwarf wheat that was shorter and stockier, allowing the plant to maintain erect posture and resist buckling under the large seed head. Tall stalks are also inefficient; short stalks reach maturity more quickly, which means a shorter growing season with less fertilizer required to generate the otherwise useless stalk.

Dr. Borlaug's wheat-hybridizing accomplishments earned him the title of "Father of the Green Revolution" in the agricultural community, as well as the Presidential Medal of Freedom, the Congressional Gold Medal, and the Nobel Peace Prize in 1970. On his death in 2009, the *Wall Street Journal* eulogized him: "More than any other single person, Borlaug showed that nature is no match for human ingenuity in setting the real limits to growth." Dr. Borlaug lived to see his dream come true: His high-yield dwarf wheat did indeed help solve world hunger, with the wheat crop yield in China, for example, increasing eightfold from 1961 to 1999.

Dwarf wheat today has essentially replaced most other strains of wheat in the United States and much of the world thanks to its extraordinary capacity for high yield. According to Allan Fritz, PhD, professor of wheat breeding at Kansas State University, dwarf and semi-dwarf wheat now comprise more than 99 percent of all wheat grown worldwide.

BAD BREEDING

The peculiar oversight in the flurry of breeding activity, such as that conducted at IMWIC, was that, despite dramatic changes in the genetic makeup of wheat and other crops, no animal or human safety testing was conducted on the new genetic strains that were created. So intent were the efforts to increase yield, so confident were plant geneticists that hybridization yielded safe products for human consumption, so urgent was the cause of world hunger, that these products of agricultural research were released into the food supply without human safety concerns being part of the equation.

It was simply assumed that, because hybridization and breeding efforts yielded plants that remained essentially "wheat," new strains would be perfectly well tolerated by the consuming public. Agricultural scientists, in fact, scoff at the idea that hybridization has the potential to generate hybrids that are unhealthy for humans. After all, hybridization techniques have been used, albeit in cruder form, in crops, animals, even humans for centuries. Mate two varieties of tomatoes, you still get tomatoes, right? What's the problem? The question of animal or human safety testing is never raised. With wheat, it was likewise assumed that variations in gluten content and structure, modifications of other enzymes and proteins, qualities that confer susceptibility or resistance to various plant diseases, would all make their way to humans without consequence.

Judging by research findings of agricultural geneticists, such assumptions may be unfounded and just plain wrong. Analyses of proteins expressed by a wheat hybrid compared to its two parent strains have demonstrated that, while approximately 95 percent of the proteins expressed in the offspring are the same, 5 percent are unique, found in *neither* parent.[5] Wheat gluten proteins, in particular, undergo considerable structural change with hybridization. In one hybridization experiment, *fourteen* new gluten proteins were

A Good Grain Gone Bad?

Given the genetic distance that has evolved between modern-day wheat and its evolutionary predecessors, is it possible that ancient grains such as emmer and einkorn can be eaten without the unwanted effects that attach to other wheat products?

I decided to put einkorn to the test, grinding two pounds of whole grain to flour, which I then used to make bread. I also ground conventional organic whole wheat flour from seed. I made bread from both the einkorn and conventional flour using only water and yeast with no added sugars or flavorings. The einkorn flour looked much like conventional whole wheat flour, but once water and yeast were added, differences became evident: The light brown dough was less stretchy, less pliable, and stickier than a traditional dough, and lacked the moldability of conventional wheat flour dough. The dough smelled different, too, more like peanut butter rather than the standard neutral smell of dough. It rose less than modern dough, rising just a little, compared to the doubling in size expected of modern bread. And, as Eli Rogosa claimed, the final bread product did indeed taste different: heavier, nutty, with an astringent aftertaste. I could envision this loaf of crude einkorn bread on the tables of third century BC Amorites or Mesopotamians.

I have a wheat sensitivity. So, in the interest of science, I conducted my own little experiment: four ounces of einkorn bread on day one versus four ounces of modern organic whole wheat bread on day two. I braced myself for the worst, since in the past my reactions have been rather unpleasant.

identified in the offspring that were not present in either parent wheat plant.[6] Moreover, when compared to century-old strains of wheat, modern strains of *Triticum aestivum* express a higher quantity of genes for gluten proteins that are associated with celiac disease.[7]

Multiply these alterations by the tens of thousands of hybridizations to which wheat has been subjected and you have the potential for dramatic shifts in genetically determined traits such as gluten structure. And note that the genetic modifications created by hybridization for the wheat plants themselves

Beyond simply observing my physical reaction, I also performed fingerstick blood sugars after eating each type of bread. The differences were striking.

Blood sugar at the start: 84 mg/dl. Blood sugar after consuming einkorn bread: 110 mg/dl. This was more or less the expected response to eating some carbohydrate. Afterwards, though, I felt no perceptible effects—no sleepiness, no nausea, nothing hurt. In short, I felt fine. Whew!

The next day, I repeated the procedure, substituting four ounces of conventional organic whole wheat bread. Blood sugar at the start: 84 mg/dl. Blood sugar after consuming conventional bread: 167 mg/dl. Moreover, I soon became nauseated, nearly losing my lunch. The queasy effect persisted for thirty-six hours, accompanied by stomach cramps that started almost immediately and lasted for many hours. Sleep that night was fitful, though filled with vivid dreams. I couldn't think straight, nor could I understand the research papers I was trying to read the next morning, having to read and reread paragraphs four or five times; I finally gave up. Only a full day and a half later did I start feeling normal again.

I survived my little wheat experiment, but I was impressed with the difference in responses to the ancient wheat and the modern wheat in my whole wheat bread. Surely something odd was going on here.

My personal experience, of course, does not qualify as a clinical trial. But it raises some questions about the potential differences that span a distance of ten thousand years: ancient wheat that predates the changes introduced by human genetic intervention versus modern wheat.

were essentially fatal, since the thousands of new wheat breeds were helpless when left to grow in the wild, relying on human assistance for survival.[8]

The new agriculture of increased wheat yield was initially met with skepticism in the Third World, with objections based mostly on the perennial "That's not how we used to do it" variety. Dr. Borlaug, hero of wheat hybridization, answered critics of high-yield wheat by blaming explosive world population growth, making high-tech agriculture a "necessity." The marvelously increased yields enjoyed in hunger-plagued India, Pakistan, China, Colombia, and other countries quickly quieted naysayers. Yields improved exponentially, turning shortages into surplus and making wheat products cheap and accessible.

Can you blame farmers for preferring high-yield dwarf hybrid strains? After all, many small farmers struggle financially. If they can increase yield-per-acre up to tenfold, with a shorter growing season and easier harvest, why wouldn't they?

In the future, the science of genetic modification has the potential to change wheat even further. No longer do scientists need to breed strains, cross their fingers, and hope for just the right mix of chromosomal exchange. Instead, single genes can be purposefully inserted or removed, and strains bred for disease resistance, pesticide resistance, cold or drought tolerance, or any number of other genetically determined characteristics. In particular, new strains can be genetically tailored to be compatible with specific fertilizers or pesticides. This is a financially rewarding process for big agribusiness, and seed and farm chemical producers such as Cargill, Monsanto, and ADM, since specific strains of seed can be patent protected and thereby command a premium and boost sales of the compatible chemical treatments.

Genetic modification is built on the premise that a single gene can be inserted in just the right place without disrupting the genetic expression of other characteristics. While the concept seems sound, it doesn't always work out that cleanly. In the first decade of genetic modification, no animal or safety testing was required for genetically modified plants, since the practice was considered no different than the assumed-to-be-benign practice of hybridization. Public pressure has, more recently, caused regulatory agencies, such as the food-regulating branch of the FDA, to require testing prior to a genetically modified product's release into the market. Critics of genetic modification, however, have cited studies that identify potential problems with genetically modified crops. Test animals fed glyphosate-tolerant soybeans (known as Roundup Ready, these beans are genetically bred to allow the farmer to freely spray the weed killer Roundup without harming the crop) show alterations in liver, pancreatic, intestinal, and testicular tissue compared to animals fed conventional soybeans. The difference is believed to be due to unexpected DNA rearrangement near the gene insertion site, yielding altered proteins in food with potential toxic effects.[9]

It took the introduction of gene modification to finally bring the notion of safety testing for genetically altered plants to light. Public outcry has prompted the international agricultural community to develop guidelines, such as the 2003 Codex Alimentarius, a joint effort by the Food and Agricultural Organization of the United Nations and the World Health Organization, to help determine what new genetically modified crops should be subjected to safety testing, what kinds of tests should be conducted, and what should be measured.

But no such outcry was raised years earlier as farmers and geneticists carried out tens of thousands of hybridization experiments. There is no question that unexpected genetic rearrangements that might generate some desirable property, such as greater drought resistance or better dough properties, can be accompanied by changes in proteins that are not evident to the eye, nose, or tongue, but little effort has focused on these side effects. Hybridization efforts continue, breeding new "synthetic" wheat. While hybridization falls short of the precision of gene modification techniques, it still possesses the potential to inadvertently "turn on" or "turn off" genes unrelated to the intended effect, generating unique characteristics, not all of which are presently identifiable.[10]

Thus, the alterations of wheat that could potentially result in undesirable effects on humans are *not* due to gene insertion or deletion, but are due to the hybridization experiments that predate genetic modification. As a result, over the past fifty years, thousands of new strains have made it to the human commercial food supply without a single effort at safety testing. This is a development with such enormous implications for human health

that I will repeat it: Modern wheat, despite all the genetic alterations to modify hundreds, if not thousands, of its genetically
determined characteristics, made its way to the worldwide
human food supply with nary a question surrounding its suitability
for human consumption.

Because hybridization experiments did not require the documentation of animal or human testing, pinpointing where, when,
and how the precise hybrids that might have amplified the ill
effects of wheat is an impossible task. Nor is it known whether
only *some* or *all* of the hybrid wheat generated has potential for
undesirable human health effects.

The incremental genetic variations introduced with each
round of hybridization can make a world of difference. Take
human males and females. While men and women are, at their
genetic core, largely the same, the differences clearly make for
interesting conversation, not to mention romantic dalliances. The
crucial differences between human men and women, a set of differences that originate with just a single chromosome, the diminu-
tive male Y chromosome and its few genes, set the stage for
thousands of years of human life and death, Shakespearean drama,
and the chasm separating Homer from Marge Simpson.

And so it goes with this human-engineered grass we still call
"wheat." Genetic differences generated via thousands of human-
engineered hybridizations make for substantial variation in composition, appearance, and qualities important not just to chefs and
food processors, but also potentially to human health.

CHAPTER 3

WHEAT DECONSTRUCTED

WHETHER IT'S A LOAF OF organic high-fiber multigrain bread or a Twinkie, what exactly are you eating? We all know that the Twinkie is just a processed indulgence, but conventional advice tells us that the former is a better health choice, a source of fiber and B vitamins, and rich in "complex" carbohydrates.

Ah, but there's always another layer to the story. Let's peer inside the contents of this grain and try to understand why—regardless of shape, color, fiber content, organic or not—it potentially does odd things to humans.

WHEAT: SUPERCARBOHYDRATE

The transformation of the domesticated wild grass of Neolithic times into the modern Cinnabon, French crullers, or Dunkin' Donuts requires some serious sleight of hand. These modern configurations were not possible with the dough of ancient wheat.

An attempt to make a modern jelly donut with einkorn wheat, for example, would yield a crumbly mess that would not hold its filling, and it would taste, feel, and look like, well, a crumbly mess. In addition to hybridizing wheat for increased yield, plant geneticists have also sought to generate hybrids that have properties best suited to become, for instance, a chocolate sour cream cupcake or a seven-tiered wedding cake.

Modern *Triticum aestivum* wheat flour is, on average, 70 percent carbohydrate by weight, with protein and indigestible fiber each comprising 10 to 15 percent. The small remaining weight of *Triticum* wheat flour is fat, mostly phospholipids and polyunsaturated fatty acids.[1] (Interestingly, ancient wheat has higher protein content. Emmer wheat, for instance, contains 28 percent or more protein.[2])

Wheat starches are the complex carbohydrates that are the darlings of dietitians. "Complex" means that the carbohydrates in wheat are composed of polymers (repeating chains) of the simple sugar, glucose, unlike simple carbohydrates such as sucrose, which are one- or two-unit sugar structures. (Sucrose is a two-sugar molecule, glucose + fructose.) Conventional wisdom, such as that from your dietitian or the USDA, says we should all reduce our consumption of simple carbohydrates in the form of candy and soft drinks, and increase our consumption of complex carbohydrates.

Of the complex carbohydrate in wheat, 75 percent is the chain of branching glucose units, *amylopectin*, and 25 percent is the linear chain of glucose units, *amylose*. In the human gastrointestinal tract, both amylopectin and amylose are digested by the salivary and stomach enzyme amylase. Amylopectin is efficiently digested by amylase to glucose, while amylose is much less efficiently digested, some of it making its way to the colon undigested. Thus, the complex carbohydrate amylopectin is rapidly converted to glucose and absorbed into the bloodstream and, because it is most efficiently digested, is mainly responsible for wheat's blood-sugar-increasing effect.

Other carbohydrate foods also contain amylopectin, but not the same kind of amylopectin as wheat. The branching structure of amylopectin varies depending on its source.[3] Amylopectin from legumes, so-called amylopectin C, is the least digestible—hence the schoolkid's chant, "Beans, beans, they're good for your heart, the more you eat 'em, the more you. . . ." Undigested amylopectin makes its way to the colon, whereupon the symbiotic bacteria happily dwelling there feast on the undigested starches and generate gases such as nitrogen and hydrogen, making the sugars unavailable for you to digest.

Amylopectin B is the form found in bananas and potatoes and, while more digestible than bean amylopectin C, still resists digestion to some degree. The *most* digestible form of amylopectin, amylopectin A, is the form found in wheat. Because it is the most digestible, it is the form that most enthusiastically increases blood sugar. This explains why, gram for gram, wheat increases blood sugar to a greater degree than, say, kidney beans or potato chips. The amylopectin A of wheat products, complex or no, might be regarded as a supercarbohydrate, a form of highly digestible carbohydrate that is more efficiently converted to blood sugar than nearly all other carbohydrate foods, simple or complex.

This means that not all complex carbohydrates are created equal, with amylopectin A–containing wheat increasing blood sugar more than other complex carbohydrates. But the uniquely digestible amylopectin A of wheat also means that the complex carbohydrate of wheat products, on a gram-for-gram basis, are no better, and are often worse, than even simple carbohydrates such as sucrose.

People are usually shocked when I tell them that whole wheat bread increases blood sugar to a higher level than sucrose.[4] Aside from some extra fiber, eating two slices of whole wheat bread is really little different, and often worse, than drinking a can of sugar-sweetened soda or eating a sugary candy bar.

This information is not new. A 1981 University of Toronto study launched the concept of the glycemic index, i.e., the comparative blood sugar effects of carbohydrates: the higher the blood sugar after consuming a specific food compared to glucose, the higher the glycemic index (GI). The original study showed that the GI of white bread was 69, while the GI of whole grain bread was 72 and Shredded Wheat cereal was 67, while that of sucrose (table sugar) was 59.[5] Yes, the GI of whole grain bread is higher than that of sucrose. Incidentally, the GI of a Mars bar—nougat, chocolate, sugar, caramel, and all—is 68. That's *better* than whole grain bread. The GI of a Snickers bar is 41—*far* better than whole grain bread.

In fact, the degree of processing, from a blood sugar standpoint, makes little difference: Wheat is wheat, with various forms of processing or lack of processing, simple or complex, high-fiber or low-fiber, all generating similarly high blood sugars. Just as "boys will be boys," amylopectin A will be amylopectin A. In healthy, slender volunteers, two medium-sized slices of whole wheat bread increase blood sugar by 30 mg/dl (from 93 to 123 mg/dl), no different from white bread.[6] In people with diabetes, both white and whole grain bread increase blood sugar 70 to 120 mg/dl over starting levels.[7]

One consistent observation, also made in the original University of Toronto study as well as in subsequent efforts, is that pasta has a lower two-hour GI, with whole wheat spaghetti showing a GI of 42 compared to white flour spaghetti's GI of 50. Pasta stands apart from other wheat products, likely due, in part, to the compression of the wheat flour that occurs during the extruding process, slowing digestion by amylase. (Rolled fresh pasta, such as fettuccine, has similar glycemic properties to extruded pastas.) Pastas are also usually made from *Triticum durum* rather than *aestivum*, putting them genetically closer to emmer. But even the favorable GI rating of pasta is misleading, since it is only a two-hour observation and pasta has the curious ability to generate high blood sugars for periods of four to six hours after consumption, sending blood sugars up by 100 mg/dl for sustained periods in people with diabetes.[8,9]

These irksome facts have not been lost on agricultural and food scientists, who have been trying, via genetic manipulation, to increase the content of so-called resistant starch (starch that does not get fully digested) and reduce the amount of amylopectin. Amylose is the most common resistant starch, comprising as much as 40 to 70 percent by weight in some purposefully hybridized varieties of wheat.[10]

Therefore, wheat products elevate blood sugar levels more than virtually any other carbohydrate, from beans to candy bars. This has important implications for body weight, since glucose is unavoidably accompanied by insulin, the hormone that allows entry of glucose into the cells of the body, converting the glucose to fat. The higher the blood glucose after consumption of food, the greater the insulin level, the more fat is deposited. This is why, say, eating a three-egg omelet that triggers no increase in glucose does not add to body fat, while two slices of whole wheat bread increases blood glucose to high levels, triggering insulin and growth of fat, particularly abdominal or deep visceral fat.

There's even more to wheat's curious glucose behavior. The amylopectin A–induced surge in glucose and insulin following wheat consumption is a 120-minute-long phenomenon that produces the "high" at the glucose peak, followed by the "low" of the inevitable glucose drop. The surge and drop creates a two-hour roller coaster ride of satiety and hunger that repeats itself throughout the day. The glucose "low" is responsible for stomach growling at 9 a.m., just two hours after a bowl of wheat cereal or an English muffin breakfast, followed by 11 a.m. prelunch cravings, as well as the mental fog, fatigue, and shakiness of the hypoglycemic glucose nadir.

Trigger high blood sugars repeatedly and/or over sustained periods, and more fat accumulation results. The consequences of glucose-insulin-fat deposition are especially visible in the abdomen— resulting in, yes, wheat belly. The bigger your wheat belly, the poorer your response to insulin, since the deep visceral fat of the wheat belly is associated with poor responsiveness, or "resistance," to insulin, demanding higher and higher insulin levels, a situation that cultivates diabetes. Moreover, the bigger the wheat belly in males, the more estrogen is produced by fat tissue, and the larger the breasts. The bigger your wheat belly, the more inflammatory responses that are triggered: heart disease and cancer.

Because of wheat's morphine-like effect (discussed in the next chapter) and the glucose-insulin cycle that wheat amylopectin A generates, wheat is, in effect, an appetite *stimulant*. Accordingly, people who eliminate wheat from their diet consume fewer calories, something I will discuss later in the book.

If glucose-insulin-fat provocation from wheat consumption is a major phenomenon underlying weight gain, then *elimination* of wheat from the diet should reverse the phenomenon. And that is exactly what happens.

For years, wheat-related weight loss has been observed in patients with celiac disease, who must eliminate all foods containing gluten from their diets to halt an immune response gone awry, which in celiac patients essentially destroys the small intestine. As it happens, wheat-free, gluten-free diets are also amylopectin A–free.

However, the weight loss effects of wheat elimination are not immediately clear from clinical studies. Many celiac sufferers are diagnosed after years of suffering and begin the diet change in a severely malnourished state due to prolonged diarrhea and impaired nutrient absorption. Underweight, malnourished celiac sufferers may actually *gain* weight with wheat removal thanks to improved digestive function.

But if we look only at overweight people who are not severely malnourished at the time of diagnosis who remove wheat from their diet, it becomes clear that this enables them to lose a substantial amount of weight. A Mayo Clinic/University of Iowa study of 215 obese celiac patients showed 27.5 pounds of weight loss in the first six months of a wheat-free diet.[11] In another study, wheat elimination slashed the number of people classified as obese (body mass index, or BMI, 30 or greater) in half within a year.[12] Oddly, investigators performing these studies usually attribute the weight loss of wheat- and gluten-free diets to lack of food variety. (Food variety, incidentally, can still be quite wide and wonderful after wheat is eliminated, as I will discuss.)

Advice to consume more healthy whole grains therefore causes increased consumption of the amylopectin A form of wheat carbohydrate, a form of carbohydrate that, for all practical purposes, is little different, and in some ways worse, than dipping your spoon into the sugar bowl.

GLUTEN: WE HARDLY KNOW YA!

If you were to add water to wheat flour, knead the mixture into dough, then rinse the glob under running water to wash away starches and fiber, you'd be left with a protein mixture called gluten.

Wheat is the principal source of gluten in the diet, both because wheat products have come to dominate and because most Americans do not make a habit of consuming plentiful quantities of barley, rye, bulgur, kamut, or triticale, the other sources of gluten. For all practical purposes, therefore, when I discuss gluten, I am primarily referring to wheat.

While wheat is, by weight, mostly carbohydrate as amylopectin A, gluten protein is what makes wheat "wheat." Gluten is the unique component of wheat that makes dough "doughy": stretchable, rollable, spreadable, twistable, baking gymnastics that cannot be achieved with rice flour, corn flour, or any other grain. Gluten allows the pizza maker to roll and toss dough and mold it into the characteristic flattened shape; it allows the dough to stretch and rise when yeast fermentation causes it to fill with air pockets. The distinctive doughy quality of the simple mix of wheat flour and water, properties food scientists call viscoelasticity and cohesiveness, are due to gluten. While wheat is mostly carbohydrate and only 10 to 15 percent protein, 80 percent of that protein is gluten. Wheat *without* gluten would lose the unique qualities that transform dough into bagels, pizza, or focaccia.

Here's a quick lesson in this thing called gluten (a lesson that you might categorize under "Know thine enemy"). Glutens are the storage proteins of the wheat plant, a means of storing carbon and nitrogen for germination of the seed to form new wheat plants. Leavening, the "rising" process created by the marriage of wheat with yeast, does not occur without gluten, and is therefore unique to wheat flour.

The term "gluten" encompasses two primary families of proteins, the gliadins and the glutenins. The gliadins, the protein group that most vigorously triggers the immune response in celiac disease, has three subtypes: α/β-gliadins, γ-gliadins, and ω-gliadins. Like amylopectin, glutenins are large repeating structures, or polymers, of more basic structures. The strength of dough is due to the large polymeric glutenins, a genetically programmed characteristic purposefully selected by plant breeders.[13]

Gluten from one wheat strain can be quite different in structure from that of another strain. The gluten proteins produced by einkorn wheat, for example, are distinct from the gluten proteins of emmer, which are, in turn, different from the gluten proteins of *Triticum aestivum*.[14,15] Because fourteen-chromosome einkorn, containing the so-called A genome (set of genes), has the smallest chromosomal set, it codes for the fewest number and variety of glutens. Twenty-eight-chromosome emmer, containing the A genome with the added B genome, codes for a larger variety of gluten. Forty-two-chromosome *Triticum aestivum*, with the A, B, and D genomes, has the greatest gluten variety, even before any human manipulation of its breeding. Hybridization efforts of the past fifty years have generated numerous additional changes in gluten-coding genes in *Triticum aestivum*, most of them purposeful modifications of the D genome that confer baking and aesthetic characteristics on flour.[16] Indeed, genes located in the D genome are those most frequently pinpointed as the source of the glutens that trigger celiac disease.[17]

It is therefore the D genome of modern *Triticum aestivum* that, having been the focus of all manner of genetic shenanigans by plant geneticists, has accumulated substantial change in genetically determined characteristics of gluten proteins. It is also potentially the source for many of the odd health phenomena experienced by consuming humans.

IT'S NOT *ALL* ABOUT GLUTEN

Gluten isn't the only potential villain lurking in wheat flour.

Beyond gluten, the other 20 percent or so of nongluten proteins in wheat include albumins, prolamins, and globulins, each of which can also vary from strain to strain. In total, there are more than a thousand other proteins that are meant to serve such functions as protecting the grain from pathogens, providing water resistance, and providing reproductive functions. There are agglutinins, peroxidases, α-amylases, serpins, and acyl CoA oxidases, not to mention five forms of glycerinaldehyde-3-phosphate dehydrogenases. I shouldn't neglect to mention β-purothionin, puroindolines a and b, and starch synthases. Wheat ain't just gluten, any more than southern cooking is just grits.

As if this protein/enzyme smorgasbord weren't enough, food manufacturers have also turned to fungal enzymes, such as cellulases, glucoamylases, xylanases, and β-xylosidases, to enhance leavening and texture in wheat products. Many bakers also add soy flour to their dough to enhance mixing and whiteness, introducing yet another collection of proteins and enzymes.

In celiac disease, the one conventionally accepted (though much underdiagnosed) example of wheat-related intestinal illness, gluten protein, specifically α-gliadin, provokes an immune response that inflames the small intestine, causing incapacitating abdominal cramps and diarrhea. Treatment is simple: complete avoidance of anything containing gluten.

Beyond celiac disease, though, there are allergic or anaphylactic (a severe reaction resulting in shock) reactions to nongluten proteins, including α-amylases, thioredoxin, and glycerinaldehyde-3-phosphate dehydrogenase, along with about a dozen others.[18] Exposure in susceptible individuals triggers asthma, rashes (atopic dermatitis and urticaria), and a curious and dangerous condition called wheat-dependent exercise-induced anaphylaxis (WDEIA), in which rash, asthma, or anaphylaxis are provoked during exercise. WDEIA is most commonly associated with wheat (it can also occur with shellfish) and has been attributed to various ω-gliadins and glutenins.

In short, wheat is not just a complex carbohydrate with gluten and bran. Wheat is a complex collection of biochemically unique compounds that vary widely according to genetic code. Just by looking at a poppy seed muffin, for instance, you would be unable to discern the incredible variety of gliadins, other gluten proteins, and nongluten proteins contained within it, many of them unique to the modern dwarf wheat that was your muffin's source. On taking your first bite, you would enjoy the immediate sweetness of the muffin's amylopectin A as it sends your blood sugar skyward.

Let's next explore the incredible wide-ranging health effects of your muffin and other wheat-containing foods.

PART TWO

WHEAT AND ITS HEAD-TO-TOE DESTRUCTION OF HEALTH

CHAPTER 4

HEY, MAN, WANNA BUY SOME EXORPHINS? THE ADDICTIVE PROPERTIES OF WHEAT

ADDICTION. WITHDRAWAL. Delusions. Hallucinations. I'm not describing mental illness or a scene from *One Flew Over the Cuckoo's Nest*. I'm talking about this food you invite into your kitchen, share with friends, and dunk in your coffee.

I will discuss why wheat is unique among foods for its curious effects on the brain, effects shared with opiate drugs. It explains why some people experience incredible difficulty removing wheat from their diet. It's not just a matter of inadequate resolve, inconvenience, or breaking well-worn habits; it's about severing a relationship with something that gains hold of your psyche and emotions, not unlike the hold heroin has over the desperate addict.

While you knowingly consume coffee and alcohol to obtain specific mind effects, wheat is something you consume for "nutrition," not for a "fix." Like drinking the Kool-Aid at the Jim Jones revival meeting, you may not even be aware that this thing, endorsed by all "official" agencies, is fiddling with your mind.

People who eliminate wheat from their diet typically report improved mood, fewer mood swings, improved ability to concentrate, and deeper sleep within just days to weeks of their last bite of bagel or baked lasagna. These sorts of "soft" subjective experiences on our brains, however, are tough to quantify. They are also subject to the placebo effect—i.e., people just *think* they're feeling better. I am, however, impressed with how consistent these observations are, experienced by the majority of people once the initial withdrawal effects of mental fog and fatigue subside. I've personally experienced these effects and also witnessed them in thousands of people.

It is easy to underestimate the psychological pull of wheat. Just how dangerous can an innocent bran muffin be, after all?

"BREAD IS MY CRACK!"

Wheat is the Haight-Ashbury of foods, unparalleled for its potential to generate entirely unique effects on the brain and nervous system. There is no doubt: For some people, wheat is addictive. And, in some people, it is addictive to the point of obsession.

Some people with wheat addiction just *know* they have a wheat addiction. Or perhaps they identify it as an addiction to some wheat-containing food, such as pasta or pizza. They already understand, even before I tell them, that their wheat-food-addiction-of-choice provides a little "high." I still get shivers when a well-dressed, suburban soccer mom desperately confesses to me, "Bread is my crack. I just can't give it up!"

Wheat can dictate food choice, calorie consumption, timing of meals and snacks. It can influence behavior and mood. It can even come to dominate thoughts. A number of my patients, when presented with the suggestion of removing it from their diets, report obsessing over wheat products to the point of thinking about them, talking about them, salivating over them constantly for weeks. "I can't stop thinking about bread. I *dream* about bread!" they tell me, leading some to succumb to a wheat-consuming frenzy and give up within days after starting.

There is, of course, a flip side to addiction. When people divorce themselves from wheat-containing products, 30 percent experience something that can only be called withdrawal.

I've personally witnessed hundreds of people report extreme fatigue, mental fog, irritability, inability to function at work or school, even depression in the first several days to weeks after eliminating wheat. Complete relief is achieved by a bagel or cupcake (or, sadly, more like four bagels, two cupcakes, a bag of pretzels, two muffins, and a handful of brownies, followed the next morning by a nasty case of wheat remorse). It's a vicious circle: Abstain from a substance and a distinctly unpleasant experience ensues; resume it, the unpleasant experience ceases—that sounds a lot like addiction and withdrawal to me.

People who haven't experienced these effects pooh-pooh it all, thinking it strains credibility to believe that something as pedestrian as wheat can affect the central nervous system much as nicotine or crack cocaine do.

There is a scientifically plausible reason for both the addiction and withdrawal effects. Not only does wheat exert effects on the normal brain, but also on the vulnerable abnormal brain, with results beyond simple addiction and withdrawal. Studying the effects of wheat on the abnormal brain can teach us some lessons on why and how wheat can be associated with such phenomena.

WHEAT AND THE SCHIZOPHRENIC MIND

The first important lessons on the effects wheat has on the brain came through studying its effects on people with schizophrenia.

Schizophrenics lead a difficult life. They struggle to differentiate reality from internal fantasy, often entertaining delusions of persecution, even believing their minds and actions are controlled by external forces. (Remember "Son of Sam" David Berkowitz, the New York City serial killer who stalked his victims on instructions received from his dog? Thankfully, violent behavior is unusual in schizophrenics, but it illustrates the depth of pathology possible.) Once schizophrenia is diagnosed, there is little hope of leading a normal life of work, family, and children. A life of institutionalization, medications with awful side effects, and a constant struggle with dark internal demons lies ahead.

So what are the effects of wheat on the vulnerable schizophrenic mind?

The earliest formal connection of the effects of wheat on the schizophrenic brain began with the work of psychiatrist F. Curtis Dohan. whose observations ranged as far as Europe and New Guinea. Dr. Dohan journeyed down this line of investigation because he observed that, during World War II, the men and women of Finland, Norway, Sweden, Canada, and the United States required fewer hospitalizations for schizophrenia when food shortages made bread unavailable, only to require an increased number of hospitalizations when wheat consumption resumed after the war was over.[1]

Dr. Dohan observed a similar pattern in the hunter-gatherer Stone Age culture of New Guinea. Prior to the introduction of Western influence, schizophrenia was virtually unknown, diagnosed in only 2 of 65,000 inhabitants. As Western eating habits infiltrated the New Guinean population and cultivated wheat products, beer made from barley, and corn were introduced, Dr. Dohan watched the incidence of schizophrenia skyrocket *sixty-five-fold*.[2] On this background, he set out to develop the observations that established whether or not there was a cause-and-effect relationship between wheat consumption and schizophrenia.

In the mid-sixties, while working at the Veterans Administration Hospital in Philadelphia, Dr. Dohan and his colleagues decided to remove all wheat products from meals provided to schizophrenic patients without their knowledge or permission. (This was in the era before informed consent of participants was required, and before the infamous Tuskegee syphilis experiment became publicized, which triggered public outrage and led to legislation requiring fully informed participant consent.) Lo and behold, four weeks sans wheat and there were distinct and measurable improvements in the hallmarks of the disease: a reduced number of auditory hallucinations, fewer delusions, less detachment from reality. Psychiatrists then added the wheat products back into their patients' diets and the hallucinations, delusions, and social detachment rushed right back. Remove wheat again, patients and symptoms got better; add it back, they got worse.[3]

The Philadelphia observations in schizophrenics were corroborated by psychiatrists at the University of Sheffield in England, with similar conclusions.[4] There have since even been reports of complete remission of the disease, such as the seventy-year-old schizophrenic woman described by Duke University doctors, suffering with delusions, hallucinations, and suicide attempts with sharp objects and cleaning solutions over a period of fifty-three years, who experienced complete relief from psychosis and suicidal desires within eight days of stopping wheat.[5]

While it seems unlikely that wheat exposure *caused* schizophrenia in the first place, the observations of Dr. Dohan and others suggest that wheat is associated with measurable worsening of symptoms.

Another condition in which wheat may exert effects on a vulnerable mind is autism. Autistic children suffer from impaired ability to interact socially and communicate. The condition has increased in frequency over the past forty years, from rare in the mid-twentieth century to 1 in 150 children in the twenty-first.[6] Initial small samples have demonstrated improvement in autistic behaviors with wheat gluten removal.[7,8] The most comprehensive clinical trial to date involved fifty-five autistic Danish children, with formal measures of autistic behavior showing improvement with gluten elimination (along with elimination of casein from dairy).[9]

While it remains a topic of debate, a substantial proportion of children and adults with attention deficit/hyperactivity disorder (ADHD) may also respond to elimination of wheat. However, responses are often muddied due to sensitivities to other components of diet, such as sugars, artificial sweeteners, additives, and dairy.[10]

It is unlikely that wheat exposure was the initial *cause* of autism or ADHD but, as with schizophrenia, wheat appears to be associated with worsening of the symptoms characteristic of the conditions.

Though the laboratory rat treatment of the unsuspecting schizophrenic patients in the Philadelphia VA Hospital may send chills down our spines from the comfort of our fully informed and consenting twenty-first century, it is nevertheless a graphic illustration of wheat's effect on mental function. But why in the world are schizophrenia, autism, and ADHD exacerbated by wheat? What is in this grain that worsens psychosis and other abnormal behaviors?

Investigators at the National Institutes of Health (NIH) set out to find some answers.

EXORPHINS: THE WHEAT-MIND CONNECTION

Dr. Christine Zioudrou and her colleagues at the NIH subjected gluten, the main protein of wheat, to a simulated digestive process to mimic what happens after we eat bread or other wheat-containing products.[11] Exposed to pepsin (a stomach enzyme) and hydrochloric acid (stomach acid), gluten is degraded to a mix of polypeptides. The dominant polypeptides were then isolated and administered to laboratory rats. These polypeptides were discovered to have the peculiar ability to penetrate the blood-brain barrier that separates the bloodstream from the brain. This barrier is there for a reason: The brain is highly sensitive to the wide variety of substances that gain entry to the blood, some of which can provoke undesirable effects should they cross into your amygdala, hippocampus, cerebral cortex, or other brain structure. Once having gained entry into the brain, wheat polypeptides bind to the brain's morphine receptor, the very same receptor to which opiate drugs bind.

Zioudrou and her colleagues dubbed these polypeptides "exorphins," short for exogenous morphine-like compounds, distinguishing them from endorphins, the endogenous (internally sourced) morphine-like compounds that occur, for instance, during a "runner's high." They named the dominant polypeptide that crossed the blood-brain barrier "gluteomorphin," or morphine-like compound from gluten (though the name sounds to me more like a morphine shot in the butt). The investigators speculated that exorphins might be the active factors derived from wheat that account for the deterioration of schizophrenic symptoms seen in the Philadelphia VA Hospital and elsewhere.

Even more telling, the brain effect of gluten-derived polypeptides is blocked by administration of the drug naloxone.

Let's pretend you're an inner-city heroin addict. You get knifed during a drug deal gone sour and get carted to the nearest trauma emergency room. Because you're high on heroin, you kick and scream at the ER staff trying to help you. So these nice people strap you down and inject you with a drug called naloxone, and you are instantly *not* high. Through the magic of chemistry, naloxone immediately reverses the action of heroin or any other opiate drug such as morphine or oxycodone.

In lab animals, administration of naloxone blocks the binding of wheat exorphins to the morphine receptor of brain cells. Yes, opiate-blocking naloxone prevents the binding of wheat-derived exorphins to the brain. The very same drug that turns off the heroin in a drug-abusing addict also blocks the effects of wheat exorphins.

In a World Health Organization study of thirty-two schizophrenic people with active auditory hallucinations, naloxone was shown to reduce hallucinations.[12] Unfortunately, the next logical step—administering naloxone to schizophrenics eating a "normal" wheat-containing diet compared to schizophrenics administered naloxone on a wheat-free diet—has not been studied. (Clinical studies that might lead to conclusions that don't support drug use are often not performed. In this case, had naloxone shown benefit in wheat-consuming schizophrenics, the unavoidable conclusion would have been to eliminate wheat, not prescribe the drug.)

The schizophrenia experience shows us that wheat exorphins have the potential to exert distinct effects on the brain. Those of us without schizophrenia don't experience auditory hallucinations from exorphins resulting from an onion bagel, but these compounds are still there in the brain, no different than in a schizophrenic. It also highlights how wheat is truly unique among grains, since other grains such as millet and flax do not generate exorphins (since they lack gluten), nor do they cultivate obsessive behavior or withdrawal in people with normal brains or people with abnormal brains.

So this is your brain on wheat: Digestion yields morphine-like compounds that bind to the brain's opiate receptors. It induces a form of reward, a mild euphoria. When the effect is blocked or no exorphin-yielding foods are consumed, some people experience a distinctly unpleasant withdrawal.

What happens if normal (i.e., nonschizophrenic) humans are given opiate-blocking drugs? In a study conducted at the Psychiatric Institute of the University of South Carolina, wheat-consuming participants given naloxone consumed 33 percent fewer calories at lunch and 23 percent fewer calories at dinner (a total of approximately 400 calories less over the two meals) than participants given a placebo.[13] At the University of Michigan, binge eaters were confined to a room filled with food for one hour. (There's an idea for a new TV show: *The Biggest Gainer.*) Participants consumed 28 percent less wheat crackers, bread sticks, and pretzels with administration of naloxone.[14]

In other words, block the euphoric reward of wheat and calorie intake goes down, since wheat no longer generates the favorable feelings that encourage repetitive consumption. (Predictably, this strategy is being pursued by the pharmaceutical industry to commercialize a weight loss drug that contains naltrexone, an oral equivalent to naloxone. The drug is purported to block the mesolimbic reward system buried deep within the human brain that is responsible for generating pleasurable feelings from heroin, morphine, and other substances. Pleasurable feelings can be replaced by feelings of dysphoria, or unhappiness. Naltrexone will therefore be combined with the antidepressant and smoking cessation drug bupropion.)

From withdrawal effects to psychotic hallucinations, wheat is party to some peculiar neurological phenomena. To recap:

- Common wheat, upon digestion, yields polypeptides that possess the ability to cross into the brain and bind to opiate receptors.
- The action of wheat-derived polypeptides, the so-called exorphins such as gluteomorphin, can be short-circuited with the opiate-blocking drugs naloxone and naltrexone.
- When administered to normal people or people with uncontrollable appetite, opiate-blocking drugs yield reductions in appetite, cravings, and calorie intake, as well as dampen mood, and the effect seems particularly specific to wheat-containing products.

Wheat, in fact, nearly stands alone as a food with potent central nervous system effects. Outside of intoxicants such as ethanol (like that in your favorite merlot or chardonnay), wheat is one of the few foods that can alter behavior, induce pleasurable effects, and generate a withdrawal syndrome upon its removal. And it required observations in schizophrenic patients to teach us about these effects.

Night Cravings Conquered

For as long as he could remember, Larry struggled with weight.

It never made sense to him: He exercised, often to extremes. A 50-mile bike ride was not unusual, nor was a 15-mile walk in the woods or desert. As part of his work, Larry enjoyed the terrain of many different areas of the United States. His travel often took him to the southwest, where he hiked for up to six hours. He also prided himself on following a healthy diet: limiting his red meat and oils and eating plenty of vegetables and fruit and, yes, an abundance of "healthy whole grains."

I met Larry because of a heart rhythm problem, an issue we dealt with easily. But his blood work was another issue. In short, it was a disaster: blood glucose in the low diabetic range, triglycerides too high at 210 mg/dl, HDL too low at 37 mg/dl, and 70 percent of his LDL particles were the small heart disease–causing type. Blood pressure was an important issue with systolic ("top") values ranging up to 170 mmHg and diastolic ("bottom") values of 90 mmHg. Larry was also, at 5 feet 8 inches and 243 pounds, about 80 pounds overweight.

"I don't get it. I exercise like nobody you know. I really *like* exercise. But I just cannot—*cannot*—lose the weight, no matter what I do." Larry recounted his diet escapades that included an all-rice diet, protein drink programs, "detox" regimens, even hypnosis. They all resulted in a few

WHEAT: APPETITE STIMULANT

Crackheads and heroin addicts shooting up in the dark corners of an inner-city drug house have no qualms about ingesting substances that mess with their minds. But how about law-abiding citizens like you and your family? I'll bet your idea of mind bending is going for the strong brew rather than the mild stuff at Starbucks, or hoisting one too many Heinekens on the weekend. But ingesting wheat means you have been unwittingly ingesting the most common dietary mind-active food known.

In effect, wheat is an appetite *stimulant*: It makes you want more—more cookies, cupcakes, pretzels, candy, soft drinks. More bagels, muffins, tacos, submarine sandwiches, pizza. It makes you

pounds lost, only to be promptly regained. He did admit to one peculiar excess: "I really struggle with my appetite at night. After dinner, I can't resist the urge to graze. I try to graze on the good stuff, like whole wheat pretzels and these multigrain crackers I have with a yogurt dip. But I'll sometimes eat all night from dinner until I go to bed. I don't know why, but something happens at night and I just can't stop."

I counseled Larry on the need to remove the number one most powerful appetite stimulant in his diet: wheat. Larry gave me that "not another kooky idea!" look. After a big sigh, he agreed to give it a go. With four teenagers in the house, clearing the shelves of all things wheat was quite a task, but he and his wife did it.

Larry returned to my office six weeks later. He reported that, within three days, his nighttime cravings had disappeared entirely. He now ate dinner and was satisfied with no need to graze. He also noticed that his appetite was much smaller during the day and his desire for snacks virtually disappeared. He also admitted that, now that his craving for food was much less, his calorie intake and portion size was a fraction of its former level. With no change in his exercise habits, he'd lost "only" eleven pounds. But, more than that, he also felt that he'd regained control over appetite and impulse, a feeling he thought he'd lost years earlier.

want both wheat-containing and non-wheat-containing foods. And, on top of that, for some people wheat is a drug, or at least yields peculiar drug-like neurological effects that can be reversed with medications used to counter the effects of narcotics.

If you balk at the notion of being dosed with a drug such as naloxone, you might ask, "What happens if, rather than blocking the brain effect of wheat chemically, you simply remove the wheat altogether?" Well, that's the very same question I have been asking. Provided you can tolerate the withdrawal (while unpleasant, the withdrawal syndrome is generally harmless aside from the rancor you incur from your irritated spouse, friends, and coworkers), hunger and cravings diminish, calorie intake decreases, mood and well-being increase, weight goes down, wheat belly shrinks.

Understanding that wheat, specifically exorphins from gluten, have the potential to generate euphoria, addictive behavior, and appetite stimulation means that we have a potential means of weight control: Lose the wheat, lose the weight.

CHAPTER 5

YOUR WHEAT BELLY IS SHOWING: THE WHEAT/ OBESITY CONNECTION

PERHAPS YOU'VE EXPERIENCED this scenario:

You encounter a friend you haven't seen in some time and exclaim with delight: *"Elizabeth! When are you due?"*

Elizabeth: [Pause.] *"Due? I'm not sure what you mean."*

You: Gulp . . .

Yes, indeed. Wheat belly's abdominal fat can do a darn good imitation of a baby bump.

Why does wheat cause fat accumulation specifically in the abdomen and not, say, on the scalp, left ear, or backside? And, beyond the occasional "I'm not pregnant" mishap, why does it matter?

And why would elimination of wheat lead to loss of abdominal fat?

Let's explore the unique features of the wheat belly habitus.

WHEAT BELLY, LOVE HANDLES, MAN BOOBS, AND "FOOD BABIES"

These are the curious manifestations of consuming the modern grain we call wheat. Dimpled or smooth, hairy or hairless, tense or flaccid, wheat bellies come in as many shapes, colors, and sizes as there are humans. But all share the same underlying metabolic cause.

I'd like to make the case that foods made with or containing wheat make you fat. I'd go as far as saying that overly enthusiastic wheat consumption is the *main* cause of the obesity and diabetes crisis in the United States. It's a big part of the reason why Jillian Michaels needs to badger *Biggest Loser* contestants. It explains why modern athletes, such as baseball players and triathletes, are fatter than ever. Blame wheat when you are being crushed in your airline seat by the 280-pound man next to you.

Sure, sugary soft drinks and sedentary lifestyles add to the problem. But for the great majority of health-conscious people who don't indulge in these obvious weight-gaining behaviors, the principal trigger for increasing weight is wheat.

In fact, the incredible financial bonanza that the proliferation of wheat in the American diet has created for the food and drug industries can make you wonder if this "perfect storm" was somehow man-made. Did a group of powerful men convene a secret Howard Hughesian meeting in 1955, map out an evil plan to mass-produce high-yield, low-cost dwarf wheat, engineer the release of government-sanctioned advice to eat "healthy whole grains," lead the charge of corporate Big Food to sell hundreds of billions of dollars worth of processed wheat food products—all leading to obesity and the "need" for billions of dollars of drug treatments for diabetes, heart disease, and all the other health consequences of obesity? It sounds ridiculous, but in a sense that's exactly what happened. Here's how.

Wheat Belly Diva

Celeste no longer felt "cool."

At age sixty-one, Celeste reported that she'd gradually gained weight from her normal range of 120 to 135 pounds in her twenties and thirties. Something happened starting in her mid-forties, and even without substantial changes in habits, she gradually ballooned up to 182 pounds. "This is the heaviest I have *ever* been," she groaned.

As a professor of modern art, Celeste hung around with a fairly urbane crowd and her weight made her feel even more self-conscious and out of place. So I got an attentive ear when I explained my diet approach that involved elimination of all wheat products.

Over the first three months she lost twenty-one pounds, more than enough to convince her that the program worked. She was already having to reach to the back of her closet to find clothes she hadn't been able to wear for the past five years.

Celeste stuck to the diet, admitting to me that it had quickly become second nature with no cravings, a rare need to snack, just a comfortable cruise through meals that kept her satisfied. She noted that, from time to time, work pressures kept her from being able to have lunch or dinner, but the prolonged periods without something to eat proved effortless. I reminded her that healthy snacks such as raw nuts, flaxseed crackers, and cheese readily fit into her program. But she simply found that snacks weren't necessary most of the time.

Fourteen months after adopting the Lose the Wheat, Lose the Weight diet, Celeste couldn't stop smiling when she returned to my office at 127 pounds—a weight she'd last seen in her thirties. She'd lost fifty-five pounds from her high, including twelve inches off her waist, which shrank from thirty-nine inches to twenty-seven. Not only could she fit into size 6 dresses again, she no longer felt uncomfortable mingling with the artsy set. No more need to conceal her sagging wheat belly under loose-fitting tops or layers. She could wear her tightest Oscar de la Renta cocktail dress proudly, no wheat belly bulge in sight.

WHOLE GRAINS, HALF-TRUTHS

In nutrition circles, whole grain is the dietary darling du jour. In fact, this USDA-endorsed, "heart healthy" ingredient, the stuff that purveyors of dietary advice agree you should eat more of, makes us hungry and fat, hungrier and fatter than any other time in human history.

Hold up a current picture of ten random Americans against a picture of ten Americans from the early twentieth century, or any preceding century where photographs are available, and you'd see the stark contrast: Americans are now fat. According to the CDC, 34.4 percent of adults are now overweight (BMI of 25 to 29.9) and another 33.9 percent are obese (BMI 30 or greater), leaving less than one in three normal weight.[1] Since 1960, the ranks of the obese have grown the most rapidly, nearly tripling over those fifty years.[2]

Few Americans were overweight or obese during the first two centuries of the nation's history. (Most data collected on BMI that we have for comparison prior to the twentieth century come from body weight and height tabulated by the US military. The average male in the military in the late nineteenth century had a BMI of <23.2, regardless of age; by the 1990s, the average military BMI was well into the overweight range.[3] We can easily presume that, if it applies to military recruits, it's worse in the civilian population.) Weight grew at the fastest pace once the USDA and others got into the business of telling Americans what to eat. Accordingly, while obesity grew gradually from 1960, the real upward acceleration of obesity started in the mid-eighties.

Studies conducted during the eighties and since have shown that, when processed white flour products are replaced with whole grain flour products, there is a reduction in colon cancer, heart disease, and diabetes. That is indeed true and indisputable.

According to accepted dietary wisdom, if something that is bad for you (white flour) is replaced by something *less* bad (whole wheat), then lots of that less-bad thing must be great for you. By that logic, if high-tar cigarettes are bad for you and low-tar cigarettes are less bad, then lots of low-tar cigarettes should be good for you. An imperfect analogy, perhaps, but it illustrates the flawed rationale used to justify the proliferation of grains in our diet. Throw into the mix the fact that wheat has undergone extensive agricultural genetics-engineered changes, and you have devised the formula for creating a nation of fat people.

The USDA and other "official" opinion makers say that more than two-thirds of Americans are overweight or obese because we're inactive and gluttonous. We sit on our fat behinds watching too much reality TV, spend too much time online, and don't exercise. We drink too much sugary soda and eat too much fast food and junk snacks. Betcha can't eat just one!

Certainly these are poor habits that will eventually take their toll on one's health. But I meet plenty of people who tell me that they follow "official" nutritional guidelines seriously, avoid junk foods and fast foods, exercise an hour every day, all while continuing to gain and gain and gain. Many follow the guidelines set by the USDA food pyramid (six to eleven servings of grain per day, of which four or more should be whole grain), the American Heart Association, the American Dietetic Association, or the American Diabetes Association. The cornerstone of all these nutritional directives? "Eat more healthy whole grains."

Are these organizations in cahoots with the wheat farmers and seed and chemical companies? There's more to it than that. "Eat more healthy whole grains" is really just the corollary of the "Cut the fat" movement embraced by the medical establishment in the sixties. Based on epidemiologic observations that suggested that higher dietary fat intakes are associated with higher cholesterol levels and risk for heart disease, Americans were advised to reduce total and saturated fat intake. Grain-based foods came to replace the calorie gap left by reduced fat consumption. The whole-grain-is-better-than-white argument further fueled the transition. The low-fat, more-grain message also proved enormously profitable for the processed food industry. It triggered an explosion of processed food products, most requiring just a few pennies worth of basic materials. Wheat flour, cornstarch, high-fructose corn syrup, sucrose, and food coloring are now the main ingredients of products that fill the interior aisles of any modern supermarket. (Whole ingredients such as vegetables, meats, and dairy tend to be at the perimeter of these same stores.) Revenues for Big Food companies swelled. Kraft alone now generates $48.1 *billion* in annual revenues, an 1,800 percent increase since the late eighties, a substantial portion of which comes from wheat- and corn-based snacks.

Just as the tobacco industry created and sustained its market with the addictive property of cigarettes, so does wheat in the diet make for a helpless, hungry consumer. From the perspective of the seller of food products, wheat is a perfect processed food ingredient: The more you eat, the more you want. The situation for the food industry has been made even better by the glowing endorsements provided by the US government urging Americans to eat more "healthy whole grains."

GRAB MY LOVE HANDLES: THE UNIQUE PROPERTIES OF VISCERAL FAT

Wheat triggers a cycle of insulin-driven satiety and hunger, paralleled by the ups and downs of euphoria and withdrawal, distortions of neurological function, and addictive effects, all leading to fat deposition.

The extremes of blood sugar and insulin are responsible for growth of fat specifically in the visceral organs. Experienced over and over again, visceral fat accumulates, creating a fat liver, two fat kidneys, a fat pancreas, fat large and small intestines, as well as its familiar surface manifestation, a wheat belly. (Even your heart gets fat, but you can't see this through the semi-rigid ribs.)

So the Michelin tire encircling your or your loved one's waistline represents the surface manifestation of visceral fat contained within the abdomen and encasing abdominal organs, resulting from months to years of repeated cycles of high blood sugar and high blood insulin, followed by insulin-driven fat deposition. Not fat deposition in the arms, buttocks, or thighs, but the saggy ridge encircling the abdomen created by bulging fatty internal organs. (Exactly why disordered glucose-insulin metabolism preferentially causes visceral fat accumulation in the abdomen and not your left shoulder or the top of your head is a question that continues to stump medical science.)

Buttock or thigh fat is precisely that: buttock or thigh fat—no more, no less. You sit on it, you squeeze it into your jeans, you lament the cellulite dimples it creates. It represents excess calories over caloric expenditure. While wheat consumption adds to buttock and thigh fat, the fat in these regions is comparatively quiescent, metabolically speaking.

Visceral fat is different. While it might be useful as "love handles" grasped by your partner, it is also uniquely capable of triggering a universe of inflammatory phenomena. Visceral fat filling and encircling the abdomen of the wheat belly sort is a unique, twenty-four-hour-a-day, seven-day-a-week metabolic factory. And what it produces is inflammatory signals and abnormal cytokines, or cell-to-cell hormone signal molecules, such as leptin, resistin, and tumor necrosis factor.[4,5] The more visceral fat present, the greater the quantities of abnormal signals released into the bloodstream.

All body fat is capable of producing another cytokine, adiponectin, a protective molecule that reduces risk for heart disease, diabetes, and hypertension. However, as visceral fat increases, its capacity to produce protective adiponectin diminishes (for reasons unclear).[6] The combination of lack of adiponectin along with increased leptin, tumor necrosis factor, and other inflammatory products underlies abnormal insulin responses, diabetes, hypertension, and heart disease.[7] The list of other health conditions triggered by visceral fat is growing and now includes dementia, rheumatoid arthritis, and colon cancer.[8] This is why waist circumference is proving to be a powerful predictor of all these conditions, as well as of mortality.[9]

Visceral fat not only produces abnormally high levels of inflammatory signals but is also *itself* inflamed, containing boun-

"I Am Looking Forward to My 35th High School Reunion!"

When David was in his twenties, his total cholesterol level was already well over 250—due to what he thought was genetics, having had a grandfather die of a heart attack at a young age. But years of watching what he ate, including what he thought were "healthy" whole grains, and hitting the pavement on regular runs didn't change his cholesterol numbers. "For over twenty years I ate whole grain cereal for breakfast and rarely had eggs," he said.

Then came the big news: At just forty-eight years old, David was diagnosed with severe heart disease. Shortly afterward he received six stents to open his coronary arteries because three major arteries had been blocked up to 90 percent. Tired of doing all the right things yet seeing no improvements in his health, David started to search for alternative ways to fix his cholesterol when he found my program.

In just five months of going wheat free, David found himself twenty pounds lighter (having dropped about a pound a week), and his cholesterol has decreased significantly. David did have what he called his "wheat belly," which is bad for anyone, but particularly dangerous for anyone with heart problems. But within just two weeks of his following my advice, people complimented him on his smaller waistline. "Today I physically feel and look great," said David. "In fact, I am looking forward to my thirty-fifth high school reunion in July . . . and I don't need to lose weight, because I am already there!"

He craved some wheat products when he cut them out cold turkey, but in just a month the cravings subsided—and David's health balanced out. "No wheat has meant normal body weight and a better lipid profile," he said. "And I look better!"

And while he appreciates the cosmetic benefits of going wheat-free, David has found some other surprising changes. As an avid runner for thirty years, David says dropping wheat has helped him sleep better and has given him more energy. "Even with heart disease, I am running faster at fifty-two than I did when I was in my late thirties!"

tiful collections of inflammatory white blood cells (macrophages).[10] The endocrine and inflammatory molecules produced by visceral fat empty (via the portal circulation draining blood from the intestinal tract) directly into the liver, which then responds by producing yet another sequence of inflammatory signals and abnormal proteins.

In other words, in the human body, all fat is not equal. Wheat belly fat is a *special* fat. It is not just a passive repository for excess pizza calories; it is, in effect, an endocrine gland much like your thyroid gland or pancreas, albeit a very large and active endocrine gland. (Ironically, Grandma was correct forty years ago when she labeled an overweight person as having a "gland" problem.) Unlike other endocrine glands, the visceral fat endocrine gland does not play by the rules, but follows a unique playbook that works against the body's health.

So a wheat belly is not just unsightly, it's also dreadfully unhealthy.

GETTING HIGH ON INSULIN

Why is wheat so much worse for weight than other foods?

The essential phenomenon that sets the growth of the wheat belly in motion is high blood sugar (glucose). High blood sugar, in turn, provokes high blood insulin. (Insulin is released by the pancreas in response to the blood sugar: The higher the blood sugar, the more insulin must be released to move the sugar into the body's cells, such as those of the muscle and liver.) When the pancreas' ability to produce insulin in response to blood sugar rises is exceeded, diabetes develops. But you don't have to be diabetic to experience high blood sugar and high insulin: Nondiabetics can easily experience the high blood sugars required to cultivate their very own wheat belly, particularly because foods made from wheat so readily convert to sugar.

High blood insulin provokes visceral fat accumulation, the

body's means of storing excess energy. When visceral fat accumulates, the flood of inflammatory signals it produces causes tissues such as muscle and liver to respond less to insulin. This so-called insulin resistance means that the pancreas must produce greater and greater quantities of insulin to metabolize the sugars. Eventually, a vicious circle of increased insulin resistance, increased insulin production, increased deposition of visceral fat, increased insulin resistance, etc., etc., ensues.

Nutritionists established the fact that wheat increases blood sugar more profoundly than table sugar thirty years ago. As we've discussed, the glycemic index, or GI, is the nutritionist's measure of how much blood sugar levels increase in the 90 to 120 minutes after a food is consumed. By this measure, whole wheat bread has a GI of 72, while plain table sugar has a GI of 59 (though some labs have gotten results as high as 65). In contrast, kidney beans have a GI of 51, grapefruit comes in at 25, while noncarbohydrate foods such as salmon and walnuts have GIs of essentially zero: Eating these foods has no effect on blood sugar. In fact, with few exceptions, *few foods have as high a GI as foods made from wheat.* Outside of dried sugar-rich fruits such as dates and figs, the only other foods that have GIs as high as wheat products are dried, pulverized starches such as cornstarch, rice starch, potato starch, and tapioca starch. (It is worth noting that these are the very same carbohydrates often used to make "gluten-free" food. More on this later.)

Because wheat carbohydrate, the uniquely digestible amylopectin A, causes a greater spike in blood sugar than virtually any other food—more than a candy bar, table sugar, or ice cream—it also triggers greater insulin release. More amylopectin A means higher blood sugar, higher insulin, more visceral fat deposition . . . bigger wheat belly.

Throw in the inevitable drop in blood sugar (hypoglycemia) that is the natural aftermath of high insulin levels and you see why irresistible hunger so often results, as the body tries to protect you from the dangers of low blood sugar. You scramble for something to eat to increase blood sugar, and the cycle is set in motion again, repeating every two hours.

Now factor in your brain's response to the euphoric exorphin effects induced by wheat (and the attendant potential for withdrawal if your next "fix" is missed), and it's no wonder the wheat belly encircling your waist continues to grow and grow.

MEN'S LINGERIE IS ON THE SECOND FLOOR

Wheat belly is not just a cosmetic issue, but a phenomenon with real health consequences. In addition to producing inflammatory hormones such as leptin, visceral fat is also a factory for estrogen production in both sexes, the very same estrogen that confers female characteristics on girls beginning at puberty, such as widening of the hips and growth of the breasts.

Until menopause, adult females have high levels of estrogen. Surplus estrogen, however, produced by visceral fat adds considerably to breast cancer risk, since estrogen at high levels stimulates breast tissue.[11] Thus, increased visceral fat on a female has been associated with an increased risk for breast cancer as high as fourfold. Breast cancer risk in postmenopausal women with the visceral fat of a wheat belly is double that of slender, non-wheat-belly-bearing postmenopausal females.[12] Despite the apparent connection, no study—incredibly—has examined the results of a wheat-free, lose-the-visceral-fat-wheat-belly diet and its effect on the incidence of breast cancer. If we simply connect the dots, a marked reduction in risk would be predicted.

Males, having only a tiny fraction of the estrogen of females, are sensitive to anything that increases estrogen. The bigger the wheat belly in males, the more estrogen that is produced by visceral fat tissue. Since estrogen stimulates growth of breast tissue, elevated estrogen levels can cause men to develop larger breasts—

those dreaded "man boobs," "man cans," or, for you professional types, gynecomastia.[13] Levels of the hormone prolactin are also increased as much as sevenfold by visceral fat.[14] As the name suggests (prolactin means "stimulating lactation"), high prolactin levels stimulate breast tissue growth and milk production.

Enlarged breasts on a male are therefore not just the embarrassing body feature that your annoying nephew snickers at, but B-cup evidence that estrogen and prolactin levels are increased due to the inflammatory and hormonal factory hanging around your waist.

An entire industry is growing to help men embarrassed by their enlarged breasts. Male breast reduction surgery is booming, growing nationwide at double-digit rates. Other "solutions" include special clothing, compression vests, and exercise programs. (Maybe *Seinfeld*'s Kramer wasn't so crazy when he invented the mansierre.)

Increased estrogen, breast cancer, man boobs . . . all from the bag of bagels shared at the office.

CELIAC DISEASE: A WEIGHT LOSS LABORATORY

As noted earlier, the one ailment to which wheat has been conclusively linked is celiac disease. Celiac sufferers are counseled to remove wheat products from their diet, lest all manner of nasty complications of their disease develop. What can their experience teach us about the effects of wheat elimination? In fact, there are unclaimed gems of important weight loss lessons to be gleaned from clinical studies of people with celiac disease who remove wheat gluten–containing foods.

The lack of appreciation of celiac disease among physicians, coupled with its many unusual presentations (for example, fatigue or migraine headaches without intestinal symptoms), means an average delay of *eleven years* from symptom onset to diagnosis.[15,16] Celiac sufferers may therefore develop a severely malnourished state due to impaired nutrient absorption at the time of their diagnosis. This is especially true for children with celiac disease, who are often both underweight and underdeveloped for their age.[17]

Some celiac sufferers become positively emaciated before the cause of their illness is determined. A 2010 Columbia University study of 369 people with celiac disease enrolled 64 participants (17.3 percent) with an incredible body mass index of 18.5 or less.[18] (A BMI of 18.5 in a 5-foot-4 female would equate to a weight of 105 pounds, or 132 pounds for a 5-foot-10 male.) Years of poor nutrient and calorie absorption, worsened by frequent diarrhea, leave many celiac sufferers underweight, malnourished, and struggling just to maintain weight.

Elimination of wheat gluten removes the offensive agent that destroys the intestinal lining. Once the intestinal lining regenerates, better absorption of vitamins, minerals, and calories becomes possible, and weight begins to increase due to improved nutrition. Such studies document the weight *gain* with wheat removal experienced by underweight, malnourished celiac sufferers.

For this reason, celiac disease has traditionally been regarded as a plague of children and emaciated adults. However, celiac experts have observed that, over the past thirty to forty years, newly diagnosed patients with celiac disease are more and more often overweight or obese. One such recent ten-year tabulation of newly diagnosed celiac patients showed that 39 percent started overweight (BMI 25 to 29.9) and 13 percent started obese (BMI ≥ 30).[19] By this estimate, more than half the people now diagnosed with celiac disease are therefore overweight or obese.

If we focus only on overweight people who are not severely malnourished at time of diagnosis, celiac sufferers actually *lose* a substantial quantity of weight when they eliminate wheat gluten. A Mayo Clinic/University of Iowa study tracked 215 celiac patients after wheat gluten elimination and tabulated 27.5 pounds of weight loss in the first six months in those who started obese.[20] In the Columbia University study cited above, wheat elimination cut the frequency of obesity *in half* within a year, with more than 50 percent of the participants with a starting BMI in the overweight range of 25 to 29.9 losing an average of 26 pounds.[21] Dr. Peter Green, lead gastroenterologist in the study and professor of clinical medicine at Columbia, speculates that "it is unclear whether it is reduced calories or another factor in diet" responsible for the weight loss of the gluten-free diet. With all you've learned, isn't it clear that it's the elimination of wheat that accounts for the extravagant weight loss?

Similar observations have been made in children. Kids with celiac disease who eliminate wheat gluten gain muscle and resume normal growth, but also have less fat mass compared to kids without celiac disease.[22] (Tracking weight changes in kids is complicated by the fact that they are growing.) Another study showed that 50 percent of obese children with celiac disease approached normal BMI with wheat gluten elimination.[23]

What makes this incredible is that, beyond gluten removal, the diet in celiac patients is not further restricted. These were not purposeful weight loss programs, just wheat and gluten elimination. No calorie counting was involved, nor portion control, exercise, or any other means of losing weight . . . just losing the wheat. There are no prescriptions for carbohydrate or fat content, just removal of wheat gluten. It means that some people incorporate "gluten-free" foods, such as breads, cupcakes, and cookies, that cause weight *gain*, sometimes dramatic. (As we will discuss later, if you have a goal of weight loss, it will be important not to substitute one weight-increasing food, wheat, with yet another collection of weight-increasing foods, gluten-free items.) In many gluten-free programs, gluten-free foods are actually *encouraged*. Despite this flawed diet prescription, the fact remains: Overweight celiac sufferers experience marked weight loss with elimination of wheat gluten.

Investigators performing these studies, though suspecting "other factors," never offer the possibility that weight loss is from elimination of a food that causes extravagant weight gain—i.e., wheat.

Interestingly, these patients have substantially lower caloric intake once on a gluten-free diet, compared to people not on a gluten-free diet, even though other foods are not restricted. Calorie intake measured 14 percent less per day on gluten-free diets.[24] Another study found that celiac patients who strictly adhered to gluten elimination consumed 418 calories less per day than celiac patients who were noncompliant and permitted wheat gluten to remain in their diets.[25] For someone whose daily calorie intake is 2,500 calories, this would represent a 16.7 percent reduction in calorie intake. Guess what that does to weight?

Symptomatic of the bias of conventional nutritional dogma, the investigators in the first study labeled the diet followed by participants recovered from celiac disease "unbalanced," since the gluten-free diet contained no pasta, bread, or pizza but included more "wrong natural foods" (yes, they actually said this) such as meat, eggs, and cheese. In other words, the investigators proved the value of a wheat-free diet that reduces appetite and requires calorie replacement with real food without intending to or, indeed, even realizing they had done so. A recent thorough review of celiac disease, for instance, written by two highly regarded celiac disease experts, makes no mention of weight loss with gluten elimination.[26] But it's right there in the data, clear as day: Lose the wheat, lose the weight. Investigators in these studies also tend to dismiss the weight loss that results from wheat-free, gluten-free diets as due to the lack of food variety with wheat elimination, rather than wheat elimination itself. (As you will see later, there is no lack of variety with elimination of wheat; there is plenty of great food remaining in a wheat-free lifestyle.)

It might be the lack of exorphins, reduction of the insulin-glucose cycle that triggers hunger, or some other factor, but elimination of wheat reduces total daily calorie intake by 350 to

400 calories—with no further restrictions on calories, fats, carbohydrates, or portion sizes. No smaller plates, prolonged chewing, or frequent small meals. Just banishing wheat from your table.

There's no reason to believe that weight loss with wheat elimination is peculiar to celiac disease sufferers. It's true for people *with* gluten sensitivity and for people *without* gluten sensitivity.

So when we extrapolate wheat elimination to people who don't have celiac disease, as I have done in thousands of patients, we see the same phenomenon: dramatic and immediate weight loss, similar to that seen in the obese celiac population.

LOSE THE WHEAT BELLY

Ten pounds in fourteen days. I know: It sounds like another TV infomercial boasting the latest "lose weight fast" gimmick.

But I've seen it time and time again: Eliminate wheat in all its myriad forms and pounds melt away, often as much as a pound a day. No gimmicks, no subscription meals, no special formulas, no "meal replacement" drinks or "cleansing" regimens required.

Obviously, weight loss at this rate can be maintained for only so long, or you'd end up a pile of dust. But the initial pace of weight loss can be shocking, equaling what you might achieve with an outright fast. I find this phenomenon fascinating: Why would elimination of wheat yield weight loss as rapid as *starvation*? I suspect it is a combination of halting the glucose-insulin-fat-deposition cycle and the natural reduction in calorie intake that results. But I have seen it happen time and time again in my practice.

Wheat elimination is often part of low-carbohydrate diets. Clinical studies are accumulating that demonstrate the weight loss advantages of low-carb diets.[27,28] In fact, the success of low-carb diets, in my experience, originates largely from the elimination of

Down 104 Pounds . . . 20 More to Go

When I first met Geno, he had that familiar look: gray pallor, tired, almost inattentive. At 5 feet 10, his 322 pounds included a considerable wheat belly flowing over his belt. Geno came to me for an opinion regarding a coronary prevention program, triggered by concern over an abnormal heart scan "score," an indicator of coronary atherosclerotic plaque and potential risk for heart attack.

Not unexpectedly, Geno's girth was accompanied by multiple abnormal metabolic measures, including high blood sugars well into the range defined as diabetes, high triglycerides, low HDL cholesterol, and several others, all contributors to his coronary plaque and heart disease risk.

I somehow got through to him, despite his seemingly indifferent demeanor. I believe it helped that I enlisted the assistance of his chief cook and grocery shopper, Geno's wife. He was at first puzzled by the idea of eliminating all "healthy whole grains," including his beloved pasta, and replacing them with all the foods that he had regarded as no-no's such as nuts, oils, eggs, cheese, and meats.

Six months later, Geno came back to my office. I don't think it would be an exaggeration to say that he was transformed. Alert, attentive, and smiling, Geno told me that his life had changed. He had not only lost an incredible sixty-four pounds and fourteen inches off his waist in those six months, he had regained the energy of his youth, again wanting to socialize with friends and travel with his wife, walking and biking outdoors, sleeping more deeply, along with a newly rediscovered optimism. And he had laboratory values that matched: blood sugars were in the normal range, HDL cholesterol had *doubled*, triglycerides dropped from several hundred milligrams to a perfect range.

Another six months later, Geno had lost forty more pounds, now tipping the scale at 218—a total of 104 pounds lost in one year.

"My goal is 198 pounds, the weight I had when I got married," Geno told me. "Only twenty more pounds to go." And he said it with a smile.

wheat. Cut carbs and, by necessity, you cut wheat. Because wheat dominates the diets of most modern adults, removing wheat removes the biggest problem source. (I've also witnessed low-carb diets *fail* because the only remaining carbohydrate source in the diet was wheat-containing products.)

Sugar and other carbohydrates do indeed count, too. In other words, if you eliminate wheat but drink sugary sodas and eat candy bars and corn chips every day, you will negate most of the weight loss benefit of eliminating wheat. But most rational adults already know that avoiding Big Gulps and Ben & Jerry's is a necessary part of weight loss. It's the wheat that seems counterintuitive.

Wheat elimination is a vastly underappreciated strategy for rapid and profound weight loss, particularly from visceral fat. I've witnessed the wheat belly weight loss effect thousands of times: Eliminate wheat and weight drops rapidly, effortlessly, often as much as fifty, sixty, a hundred or more pounds over a year, depending on the degree of excess weight to start. Just among the last thirty patients who eliminated wheat in my clinic, the average weight loss was 26.7 pounds over 5.6 months.

The amazing thing about wheat elimination is that removing this food that triggers appetite and addictive behavior forges a brand-new relationship with food: You eat food because you need it to supply your physiologic energy needs, not because you have some odd food ingredient pushing your appetite "buttons," increasing appetite and the impulse to eat more and more. You will find yourself barely interested in lunch at noon, easily bypassing the bakery counter at the grocery store, turning down the donuts in the office breakroom without a blink. You will divorce yourself from the helpless, wheat-driven desire for more and more and more.

It makes perfect sense: If you eliminate foods that trigger exaggerated blood sugar and insulin responses, you eliminate the cycle of hunger and momentary satiety, you eliminate the dietary source of addictive exorphins, you are more satisfied with *less*. Excess weight dissolves and you revert back to physiologically appropriate weight. You lose the peculiar and unsightly ring around your abdomen: Kiss your wheat belly goodbye.

BE GLUTEN-FREE BUT DON'T EAT "GLUTEN-FREE"

Say what?

Gluten is the main protein of wheat, and as I have explained, it is responsible for some, though not all, of the adverse effects of wheat consumption. Gluten is the culprit underlying inflammatory damage to the intestinal tract in celiac disease. People with celiac disease must meticulously avoid food containing gluten. This means the elimination of wheat, as well as gluten-containing grains such as barley, rye, spelt, triticale, kamut, and perhaps oats. People with celiac disease often seek out "gluten-free" foods that mimic wheat-containing products. An entire industry has developed to meet their gluten-free desires, from gluten-free bread to gluten-free cakes and desserts.

However, many gluten-free foods are made by replacing wheat flour with cornstarch, rice starch, potato starch, or tapioca starch (starch extracted from the root of the cassava plant). This is especially hazardous for anybody looking to drop twenty, thirty, or more pounds, since gluten-free foods, though they do not trigger the immune or neurological response of wheat gluten, still trigger the glucose-insulin response that causes you to gain weight. Wheat products increase blood sugar and insulin more than most other foods. But remember: Foods made with cornstarch, rice starch, potato starch, and tapioca starch are among the few foods that increase blood sugar even *more* than wheat products.

So gluten-free foods are not *problem*-free. Gluten-free foods are the likely explanation for the overweight celiac sufferers who eliminate wheat and fail to lose weight. In my view, there is no role for gluten-free foods beyond the occasional indulgence, since the metabolic effect of these foods is little different from eating a bowl of jelly beans.

Thus, wheat elimination is not just about eliminating gluten.

Eliminating wheat means eliminating the amylopectin A of wheat, the form of complex carbohydrate that actually increases blood sugar higher than table sugar and candy bars. But you don't want to replace wheat's amylopectin A with the rapidly absorbed carbohydrates of powdered rice starch, cornstarch, potato starch, and tapioca starch. In short, don't replace wheat calories with rapidly absorbed carbohydrates of the sort that trigger insulin and visceral fat deposition. And avoid gluten-free foods if you are gluten-free.

Later in the book, I will discuss the ins and outs of wheat removal, how to navigate everything from choosing healthy replacement foods to wheat withdrawal. I provide a view from the trenches, having witnessed thousands of people do it successfully.

But before we get to the details of wheat elimination, let's talk about celiac disease. Even if you do *not* suffer from this devastating disease, understanding its causes and cures provides a useful framework for thinking about wheat and its role in the human diet. Beyond teaching us lessons about weight loss, celiac disease can provide other useful health insights to those of us without this condition.

So put down that Cinnabon and let's talk about celiac.

CHAPTER 6

HELLO, INTESTINE. IT'S ME, WHEAT. WHEAT AND CELIAC DISEASE

YOUR POOR, UNSUSPECTING intestine. There it is, doing its job every day, pushing along the partially digested remains of your last meal through twenty-some feet of small intestine, four feet of large intestine, eventually yielding the stuff that dominates the conversations of most retired people. It never stops for a rest but just does its thing, never asking for a raise or health care benefits. Deviled eggs, roast chicken, or spinach salad are all transformed into the familiar product of digestion, the bilirubin-tinted, semisolid waste that, in our modern society, you just flush away, no questions asked.

Enter an intruder that can disrupt the entire happy system: wheat gluten.

After *Homo sapiens* and our immediate predecessors spent millions of years eating from the limited menu of hunting and gathering, wheat entered the human diet, a practice that developed only during the past ten thousand years. This relatively brief time—300 generations—was insufficient to allow all humans to make the adaptation to this unique plant. The most dramatic evidence of failed adaptation to wheat is celiac disease, the disruption of small intestinal health by wheat gluten. There are other examples of failed adaptation to foods, such as lactose intolerance, but celiac disease stands alone in the severity of the response and its incredibly varied expression.

Even if you don't have celiac disease, I urge you to read on. *Lose Wheat, Lose the Weight* is not a book about celiac disease. But it is impossible to talk about the effects of wheat on health without talking about celiac disease. Celiac disease is the prototype for wheat intolerance, a standard against which we compare all other forms of wheat intolerance. Celiac disease is also on the rise, increasing fourfold over the past fifty years, a fact that, I believe, reflects the changes that wheat itself has undergone. Not having celiac disease at age twenty-five does not mean you cannot develop it at age forty-five, and it is increasingly showing itself in a variety of new ways besides disruption of intestinal function. So, even if you have happy intestinal health and can match success stories of regularity with your grandmother, you can't be sure that some other body system is not being affected in a celiac-like way.

Flowery descriptions of the characteristic diarrheal struggles of celiac sufferers started with the ancient Greek physician Aretaeus in ad 100, who advised celiac patients to fast. No lack of theories issued over the ensuing centuries to try to explain why celiac sufferers had intractable diarrhea, cramping, and malnutrition. It led to useless treatments such as castor oil, frequent enemas, and eating bread only if toasted. There were even treatments that enjoyed some degree of success, including Dr. Samuel Gee's use of the mussel-only diet in the 1880s and Dr. Sidney Haas's eight-bananas-a-day diet.[1]

The connection between celiac disease and wheat consumption was first made in 1953 by Dutch pediatrician Dr. Willem-Karel Dicke. It was the chance observation of the mother of a celiac child, who observed that her son's rash improved when she did not feed him bread, that first sparked his suspicion. During food shortages toward the end of World War II, bread became scarce and Dicke witnessed improvements of celiac symptoms in children, only to witness deterioration when Swedish relief planes dropped bread into the Netherlands. Dr. Dicke subsequently made meticulous measurements of children's growth and stool fat content that finally confirmed that the gluten of wheat, barley, and rye was the source of the life-threatening struggles. Gluten elimination yielded dramatic cures, major improvements over the banana and mussel regimens.[2]

While celiac disease is not the most common expression of wheat intolerance, it provides a vivid and dramatic illustration of what wheat is capable of doing when it encounters the unprepared human intestine.

CELIAC DISEASE: BEWARE THE MIGHTY BREAD CRUMB

Celiac disease is serious stuff. It's truly incredible that a disease so debilitating, potentially fatal, can be triggered by something as small and seemingly innocent as a bread crumb or a crouton.

About 1 percent of the population is unable to tolerate wheat gluten, even in small quantities. Feed gluten to these people, and the lining of the small intestine, the delicate barrier separating incipient fecal matter from the rest of you, breaks down. It leads to cramping, diarrhea, and yellow-colored stools that float in the toilet bowl because of undigested fats. If this is allowed to progress over years, the celiac sufferer becomes unable to absorb nutrients, loses weight, and develops nutritional deficiencies, such as deficiencies of protein, fatty acids, and vitamins B_{12}, D, E, K, folate, iron, and zinc.[3]

The broken-down intestinal lining allows various components of wheat to gain entry to places they don't belong, such as the bloodstream, a phenomenon that is used to diagnose the condition:

Antibodies against wheat gliadin, one of the components of gluten, can be found in the blood. It also causes the body to generate antibodies against components of the disrupted intestinal lining itself, such as transglutaminase and endomysium, two proteins of intestinal muscle that also provide the basis for the two other antibody tests for diagnosis of celiac, transglutaminase and endomysium antibodies. Otherwise "friendly" bacteria that normally inhabit the intestinal tract are also permitted to send their products into the bloodstream, initiating another range of abnormal inflammatory and immune responses.[4]

Until a few years ago, celiac was believed to be rare, affecting only one per several thousand people. As the means to diagnose the disease have improved, the number of people with it has expanded to 1 per 133. Immediate relatives of people with celiac disease have a 4.5 percent likelihood of also developing it. Those with suggestive intestinal symptoms have as high as 17 percent likelihood.[5]

As we shall see, not only has more celiac disease been uncovered by better diagnostic testing, but the incidence of the disease itself has increased. Nonetheless, celiac disease is a well-kept secret. In the United States, 1 in 133 equates to just over two million people who have celiac disease, yet less than 10 percent of them know it. One of the reasons 1,800,000 Americans don't know that they have celiac disease is that it is "The Great Imitator" (an honor previously bestowed on syphilis), expressing itself in so many varied ways. While 50 percent will experience the classic cramping, diarrhea, and weight loss over time, the other half show anemia, migraine headaches, arthritis, neurological symptoms, infertility, short stature (in children), depression, chronic fatigue, or a variety of other symptoms and disorders that, at first glance, seem to have nothing to do with celiac disease.[6] In others, it may cause no symptoms whatsoever but shows up later in life as neurological impairment, incontinence, dementia, or gastrointestinal cancer.

The ways that celiac disease shows itself are also changing. Until the mid-eighties, children were usually diagnosed with symptoms of "failure to thrive" (weight loss, poor growth), diarrhea, and abdominal distention before age two. More recently, children are more likely to be diagnosed because of anemia, chronic abdominal pain, or with no symptoms at all, and not until age eight or older.[7,8,9] In one large clinical study at the Stollery Children's Hospital in Edmonton, Alberta, the number of children diagnosed with celiac disease increased elevenfold from 1998 to 2007.[10] Interestingly, 53 percent of children at the hospital who were diagnosed with antibody testing yet displayed no symptoms of celiac nonetheless reported feeling better with gluten elimination.

Parallel changes in celiac have been observed in adults, with fewer complaining of "classic" symptoms of diarrhea and abdominal pain, more being diagnosed with anemia, more complaining of skin rashes such as dermatitis herpetiformis and allergies, and more showing no symptoms at all.[11]

Researchers have failed to agree on why celiac disease may have changed or why it is on the rise. The most popular theory currently: More mothers are breastfeeding. (Yeah, I laughed, too.)

Much of the changing face of celiac disease can certainly be attributed to earlier diagnosis aided by the widely available antibody blood tests. But there also seems to be a fundamental change in the disease. Could the changing face of celiac disease be due to a change in wheat itself? It might cause dwarf wheat's developer, Dr. Norman Borlaug, to roll over in his grave, but there is data suggesting that something in wheat itself indeed changed sometime during the past fifty years.

A fascinating study performed at the Mayo Clinic provides a unique snapshot of celiac incidence in US residents from half a century ago, the closest we will come to having a time machine to answer our question. The researchers acquired blood samples drawn fifty years ago for a streptococcal infection study, and kept frozen since. The frozen samples were collected during the period from 1948 to 1954 from more than 9,000 male recruits at Warren Air Force Base (WAFB) in Wyoming. After establishing the reliability of the long-frozen samples, they tested them for celiac markers (transglutaminase and endomysium antibodies) and compared

Name That Antibody

Three groups of antibody blood tests are now widely available to diagnose celiac disease, or at least strongly suggest that an immune response against gluten has been triggered.

Antigliadin antibodies. The short-lived IgA antibody and the longer-lived IgG antigliadin antibodies are often used to screen people for celiac. While widely available, they are less likely to make the diagnosis in all people with the disease, failing to diagnose approximately 20 to 50 percent of true celiac sufferers.[12]

Transglutaminase antibody. Gluten damage to the intestinal lining uncovers muscle proteins that trigger antibody formation. Transglutaminase is one such protein. The antibody against this protein can be measured in the bloodstream and used to gauge the ongoing autoimmune response. Compared to intestinal biopsy, the transglutaminase antibody test identifies approximately 86 to 89 percent of celiac cases.[13,14]

Endomysium antibody. Like the transglutaminase antibody test, the endomysium antibody identifies another intestinal tissue protein that triggers an antibody response. Introduced in the mid-nineties, this test is emerging as the most accurate antibody test, identifying more than 90 percent of celiac cases.[15,16]

If you have already divorced yourself from wheat, note that these tests can turn negative within a few months, and almost certainly negative or reduced after six months. So the tests have value only for people currently consuming wheat products or only for those recently having stopped consuming wheat products. Fortunately, there are some other tests available.

HLA DQ2, HLA DQ8. These are not antibodies, but genetic markers for human leukocyte antigens, or HLA, that, if present, make the bearer more likely to develop celiac disease. More than 90 percent of people who have celiac disease diagnosed by intestinal biopsy have either of these two HLA markers, most commonly the DQ2.[17]

A dilemma: Forty percent of the population have one of the HLA markers and/or antibody markers that predispose them to celiac, yet express no symptoms or other evidence of an immune system gone awry. However, this latter group has been shown to experience better health when wheat gluten is eliminated.[18] It means that a very substantial portion of the population is potentially sensitive to wheat gluten.

Rectal challenge. Not a new TV game show, but a test involving the placement of a sample of gluten into the rectum to see whether an inflammatory response is triggered. While quite accurate, the logistical challenges of this four-hour test limit its usefulness.[19]

Small intestine biopsy. Biopsy of the jejunum, the uppermost part of the small intestine, performed via an endoscope, is the "gold standard" by which all other tests are measured. The positive: The diagnosis can be made confidently. Negatives: An endoscopy and biopsies are required. Most gastroenterologists advise a small intestinal biopsy to confirm the diagnosis if suggestive symptoms, such as chronic cramping and diarrhea, are present and antibody tests suggest celiac disease. However, some experts have argued (and I agree) that the increasing reliability of antibody tests, such as the endomysium antibody test, potentially make intestinal biopsy less necessary, perhaps unnecessary.

Most celiac disease experts advocate starting with an endomysium and/or transglutaminase antibody test, followed by intestinal biopsy if the antibody test is positive. In the occasional situation in which symptoms are highly suggestive of celiac disease but antibody tests are negative, intestinal biopsy might still be considered.

Conventional wisdom holds that, if one or more antibody tests are abnormal but intestinal biopsy is negative for celiac, then gluten elimination is not necessary. I believe this is dead wrong, since many of these so-called gluten-sensitive or latent celiac disease sufferers will either develop celiac disease over time, or will develop some other manifestation of celiac disease, such as neurological impairment or rheumatoid arthritis.

Another perspective: If you are committed to this notion of removing wheat from your diet, along with other sources of gluten such as rye and barley, then testing may be unnecessary. The only time testing is a necessity is when serious symptoms or potential signs of wheat intolerance are present and documentation would be useful to help eliminate the possibility of other causes. Knowing that you harbor the markers for celiac might also increase your resolve to be meticulously gluten-free.

results to samples from two modern groups. A modern "control" group was chosen that consisted of 5,500 men with similar birth years to the military recruits, with samples obtained starting in 2006 (mean age 70 years). A second modern control group consisted of 7,200 men of similar age (mean age 37 years) at the time of the blood draw of the Air Force recruits.[20]

While abnormal celiac antibody markers were identified in 0.2 percent of the WAFB recruits, 0.8 percent of men with similar birth ages and 0.9 percent of modern young men had abnormal celiac markers. It suggests that the incidence of celiac increased *fourfold* since 1948 in men as they age, and has increased fourfold in modern young men. (The incidence is likely to be even higher in females, since women outnumber men in celiac disease, but all the recruits enrolled in the original study were male.) Recruits with positive celiac markers were also four times more likely to die, usually from cancer, over the fifty years since providing blood samples.

I asked Dr. Joseph Murray, lead researcher in the study, if he expected to find the marked increase in the incidence of celiac disease. "No. My initial assumption was that celiac disease was there all along and we just weren't finding it. While that was partly true, the data taught me otherwise: It really *is* increasing. Other studies showing that celiac disease occurs for the first time in elderly patients back up the imputation that something is affecting the population at *any* age, not just infant feeding patterns."

A similarly constructed study was conducted by a group in Finland, part of a larger effort to chronicle health changes over time. Some 7,200 male and female Finns over age 30 provided blood samples for celiac markers from 1978 to 1980. Twenty years later, in 2000–01, another 6,700 male and female Finns, also over 30, provided blood samples. Measuring transglutaminase and endomysial antibody levels in both groups, the frequency of abnormal celiac markers increased from 1.05 percent in the earlier participants to 1.99 percent, a near doubling.[21]

We therefore have good evidence that the apparent increase in celiac disease (or at least the immune markers to gluten) is not just due to better testing: The disease itself has increased in frequency, fourfold over the past fifty years, doubling in just the past twenty years. To make matters worse, the increase in celiac disease has been paralleled by an increase in type 1 diabetes, autoimmune diseases such as multiple sclerosis and Crohn's disease, and allergies.[22]

Emerging evidence suggests that the greater exposure to gluten that now occurs with modern wheat may underlie at least part of the explanation for the increased incidence of celiac disease. A study from the Netherlands compared thirty-six modern strains of wheat with fifty strains representative of wheat grown up until a century ago. By looking for the gluten protein structures that trigger celiac, researchers found that celiac-triggering gluten proteins were expressed to higher levels in modern wheat, while non-celiac-triggering proteins were expressed less.[23]

In short, while celiac disease is usually diagnosed in people complaining of weight loss, diarrhea, and abdominal pain, in the twenty-first century you can be fat and constipated, or even thin and regular, and still have the disease. And you are more likely to have the disease than your grandparents were.

While twenty to fifty years may be a long time in terms of wine or mortgages, it is far too little time for humans to have changed genetically. The timing of the two studies chronicling the increasing incidence of celiac antibodies, one in 1948 and the other in 1978, also parallel changes in the type of wheat that now populates most of the world's farms, namely dwarf wheat.

ZONULINS: HOW WHEAT INVITES ITSELF INTO THE BLOODSTREAM

The gliadin protein of wheat gluten, present in all forms of wheat from spongy Wonder Bread to the coarsest organic multigrain loaf, has the unique ability to make your intestine permeable.

Intestines are not meant to be freely permeable. You already know that the human intestinal tract is home to all manner of odd things, many of which you observe during your morning ritual on the toilet. The wondrous transformation of ham sandwich or pepperoni pizza into the components of your body, the remainder discarded, is truly fascinating. But the process needs to be tightly regulated, allowing entry of only selected components of ingested foods and liquids into the bloodstream.

So what happens if various obnoxious compounds mistakenly gain entry into the bloodstream? One of the undesirable effects is autoimmunity—i.e., the body's immune response is "tricked" into activation and attacks normal organs such as the thyroid gland or joint tissue. This can lead to autoimmune conditions such as Hashimoto's thyroiditis and rheumatoid arthritis.

Regulating intestinal permeability is therefore a fundamental function of the cells lining the fragile intestinal wall. Recent research has fingered wheat gliadin as a trigger of intestinal release of a protein called zonulin, a regulator of intestinal permeability.[24] Zonulins have the peculiar effect of disassembling tight junctions, the normally secure barrier between intestinal cells. When gliadin triggers zonulin release, intestinal tight junctions are disrupted, and unwanted proteins such as gliadin and other wheat protein fractions gain entry to the bloodstream. Immune-activating lymphocytes, such as T-cells, are then triggered to begin an inflammatory process against various "self" proteins, thus initiating wheat gluten– and gliadin-initiated conditions such as celiac disease, thyroid disease, joint diseases, and asthma. Gliadin wheat proteins are akin to being able to pick the lock on any door, allowing unwanted intruders to gain entry into places they don't belong.

Outside of gliadin, few things share such a lock-picking, intestinal-disrupting talent. Other factors that trigger zonulin and disrupt intestinal permeability include the infectious agents that cause cholera and dysentery.[25] The difference, of course, is that you contract cholera or amoebic dysentery by ingesting feces-contaminated food or water; you contract diseases of wheat by eating some nicely packaged pretzels or devil's food cupcakes.

MAYBE YOU'LL WISH FOR DIARRHEA

After you read about some of the potential long-term effects of celiac disease, you just might find yourself *wishing* for diarrhea.

Traditional notions of celiac disease revolve around the presence of diarrhea: no diarrhea, no celiac. Not true. Celiac disease is more than an intestinal condition with diarrhea. It can extend beyond the intestinal tract and show itself in many other varied ways.

The range of diseases associated with celiac is truly astonishing, from childhood (type 1) diabetes to dementia to scleroderma. These associations are also among the least understood. It is therefore not clear whether *anticipation* of gluten sensitivity with removal of all gluten will, for instance, reduce or eliminate the development of childhood diabetes—certainly a tantalizing prospect. These conditions, like celiac disease, test positive for the various celiac antibody markers and are triggered by the immune and inflammatory phenomena set in motion by genetic predisposition (presence of the HLA DQ2 and HLA DQ8 markers) and exposure to wheat gluten.

One of the most bothersome aspects of the conditions associated with celiac disease is that intestinal symptoms of celiac may not be expressed. In other words, the celiac sufferer might have neurological impairment, such as loss of balance and dementia, yet be spared the characteristic cramping, diarrhea, and weight loss. Lack of telltale intestinal symptoms also means that the correct diagnosis is rarely made.

Rather than calling it celiac disease without the intestinal expression of the condition, it would be more accurate to speak

Is It Celiac Disease or Not?
A True Story

Let me tell you about Wendy.

For more than ten years, Wendy struggled unsuccessfully with ulcerative colitis. A thirty-six-year-old grade school teacher and mother of three, she lived with constant cramping, diarrhea, and frequent bleeding, necessitating occasional blood transfusions. She endured several colonoscopies and required the use of three prescription medications to manage her disease, including the highly toxic methotrexate, a drug also used in cancer treatment and medical abortions.

I met Wendy for an unrelated minor complaint of heart palpitations that proved to be benign, requiring no specific treatment. However, she told me that, because her ulcerative colitis was failing to respond to medications, her gastroenterologist advised colon removal with creation of an ileostomy. This is an artificial orifice for the small intestine (ileum) at the abdominal surface, the sort to which you affix a bag to catch the continually emptying stool.

After hearing Wendy's medical history, I urged her to try wheat elimination. "I really don't know if it's going to work," I told her, "but since you're facing colon removal and ileostomy, I think you should give it a try."

"But why?" she asked. "I've already been tested for celiac and my doctor said I don't have it."

"Yes, I know. But you've got nothing to lose. Try it for four weeks. You'll know if you're responding."

about *immune-mediated gluten intolerance*. But because these non-intestinal conditions of gluten sensitivity were first identified because they share the same HLA and immune markers with intestinal celiac disease, the convention is to speak about "latent" celiac disease or celiac disease without intestinal involvement. I predict that, as the medical world begins to better recognize that immune-mediated gluten intolerance is much more than celiac disease, we will be calling it something like immune-mediated gluten intolerance, of which celiac disease will be a subtype.

Wendy was skeptical but agreed to try.

She returned to my office three months later, no ileostomy bag in sight. "What happened?" I asked.

"Well, first I lost thirty-eight pounds." She ran her hand over her abdomen to show me. "And my ulcerative colitis is nearly gone. No more cramps or diarrhea. I'm off everything except my Asacol." (Asacol is a derivative of aspirin often used to treat ulcerative colitis.) "I really feel great."

In the year since, Wendy has meticulously avoided wheat and gluten and has also eliminated the Asacol, with no return of symptoms. Cured. Yes, *cured*. No diarrhea, no bleeding, no cramps, no anemia, no more drugs, no ileostomy.

So if Wendy's colitis tested negative for celiac antibodies, but responded to—indeed, was *cured* by—wheat gluten elimination, what should we label it? Should we call it antibody-negative celiac disease? Antibody-negative wheat intolerance?

There is great hazard in trying to pigeonhole conditions such as Wendy's into something like celiac disease. It nearly caused her to lose her colon and suffer the lifelong health difficulties associated with colon removal, not to mention the embarrassment and inconvenience of wearing an ileostomy bag.

There is not yet any neat name to fit conditions such as Wendy's, despite its extraordinary response to the elimination of wheat gluten. Wendy's experience highlights the many unknowns in this world of wheat sensitivities, many of which are as devastating as the cure is simple.

Conditions associated with celiac disease—i.e., immune-mediated gluten intolerance—include the following:

- **Dermatitis herpetiformis**—This characteristic rash is among the more common manifestations of celiac disease or immune-mediated gluten intolerance. Dermatitis herpetiformis is an itchy, bumpy rash that usually occurs over the elbows, knees, or back. The rash disappears upon gluten removal.[26]
- **Liver disease**—Liver diseases associated with celiac can

assume many forms, from mild abnormalities on liver tests to chronic active hepatitis to primary biliary cirrhosis to biliary cancer.[27] Like other forms of immune-mediated gluten intolerance, intestinal involvement and symptoms such as diarrhea are often not present, despite the fact that the liver is part of the gastrointestinal system.

- **Autoimmune diseases**—Diseases associated with immune attacks against various organs, known as autoimmune diseases, are more common in people with celiac. People with celiac disease are more likely to develop rheumatoid arthritis, Hashimoto's thyroiditis, connective tissue diseases such as lupus, asthma, inflammatory bowel diseases such as ulcerative colitis and Crohn's disease, as well as other inflammatory and immune disorders. Rheumatoid arthritis, a painful, disfiguring joint arthritis treated with anti-inflammatory agents, has been shown to improve, and occasionally remit entirely, with gluten removal.[28] The risk for autoimmune inflammatory bowel disease, ulcerative colitis, and Crohn's disease is especially high; incidence is sixty-eight-fold compared to nonceliacs.[29]

- **Insulin-dependent diabetes**—Children with insulin-dependent type 1 diabetes have an unusually high likelihood of having positive antibody markers for celiac disease, with up to twenty-fold greater risk for developing it.[30] It is not clear whether wheat gluten is the *cause* of diabetes, but investigators have speculated that a subgroup of type 1 diabetics develop the disease triggered by gluten exposure.[31]

- **Neurological impairment**—There are neurological conditions associated with gluten exposure that we will consider in greater detail later in the book. There is a curiously high incidence (50 percent) of celiac markers among people who develop otherwise unexplained loss of balance and coordination (ataxia) or loss of feeling and muscle control in the legs (peripheral neuropathy).[32] There is even a frightening condition called gluten encephalopathy, characterized by brain impairment with headaches, ataxia, and dementia, eventually fatal; abnormalities are seen in the white matter of the brain by MRI.[33]

- **Nutritional deficiencies**—Iron-deficiency anemia is unusually common among celiac sufferers, affecting up to 69 percent. Deficiencies of vitamin B_{12}, folic acid, zinc, and fat-soluble vitamins A, D, E, and K are also common.[34]

Beyond those listed above, there are literally hundreds of conditions that have been associated with celiac disease and/or immune-mediated gluten intolerance, though less commonly. Gluten-mediated reactions have been documented to affect every organ in the human body, sparing none. Eyes, brain, sinuses, lungs, bones . . . you name it, gluten antibodies have been there.

In short, the reach of gluten consumption consequences is mind-bogglingly wide. It can affect any organ at any age, showing itself in more ways than Tiger Woods had mistresses. Thinking of celiac disease as just diarrhea, as is often the case in many doctors' offices, is an enormous, and potentially fatal, oversimplification.

WHEAT AND BUNGEE JUMPING

Eating wheat, like ice climbing, mountain boarding, and bungee jumping, is an extreme sport. It is the only common food that carries its own long-term mortality rate.

Some foods, such as shellfish and peanuts, have the potential to provoke acute allergic reactions (e.g., hives or anaphylaxis) that can be dangerous in the susceptible, even fatal in rare instances. But wheat is the only common food that has its own measurable mortality rate when observed over years of consumption. In one large analysis over 8.8 years, there was up to

29.1 percent increased likelihood of death in people with celiac disease or who were antibody-positive without celiac disease, compared to the broad population.[35] The greatest mortality from wheat gluten exposure was observed in the twenty-year-old and younger age group, followed by the twenty to thirty-nine group. Mortality also increased across all age groups since 2000; mortality in people with positive antibodies to wheat gluten but *without* celiac has more than doubled compared to mortality prior to 2000.

Green peppers don't result in long-term mortality, nor do pumpkin, blueberries, or cheese. Only wheat. And you don't have to have symptoms of celiac disease for this to happen.

Yet wheat is the food our own USDA encourages us to eat. I personally don't believe that it would be a stretch for the FDA (which now regulates tobacco) to require a warning on wheat-containing products, much as they require for cigarettes.

Imagine:

Surgeon General's Warning: Wheat consumption in all forms poses potentially serious threats to health.

In June 2010, the FDA passed a regulation requiring tobacco manufacturers to remove the deceptive "light," "mild," and "low" descriptors from cigarette packages, since they are all every bit as bad as any other cigarette. Wouldn't it be interesting to see similar regulation highlighting that *wheat is wheat*, regardless of "whole grain," "multigrain," or "high-fiber"?

Our friends across the Atlantic published an extraordinary analysis of eight million residents of the United Kingdom, identifying more than 4,700 people with celiac disease, and comparing them to five control subjects for every celiac participant. All participants were then observed for three and a half years for the appearance of various cancers. Over the observation period, participants with celiac disease showed 30 percent greater likelihood of developing some form of cancer, with an incredible one of every thirty-three celiac participants developing cancer despite the relatively short period of observation. Most of the cancers were gastrointestinal malignancies.[36]

Observation of more than 12,000 Swedish celiac sufferers showed a similar 30 percent increased risk for gastrointestinal cancers. The large number of participants revealed the broad variety of gastrointestinal cancers that can develop, including malignant small intestinal lymphomas and cancers of the throat, esophagus, large intestine, hepatobiliary system (liver and bile ducts), and pancreas.[37] Over a period of up to thirty years, the investigators tabulated a doubling of mortality compared to Swedes without celiac disease.[38]

You'll recall that "latent" celiac disease means having one or more positive antibody tests for the disease but without evidence of intestinal inflammation observed via endoscopy and biopsy—what I call immune-mediated gluten intolerance. Observation of 29,000 people with celiac disease over approximately eight years showed that, of those with "latent" celiac disease, there was 30 to 49 percent increased risk for fatal cancers, cardiovascular disease, and respiratory diseases.[39] It may be latent, but it ain't dead. It's very much alive.

If celiac disease or immune-mediated gluten intolerance goes undiagnosed, non-Hodgkin's lymphoma of the small intestine can result, a difficult-to-treat and often fatal condition. Celiac sufferers are exposed to as much as forty-fold increased risk for this cancer compared to nonceliacs. Risk reverts to normal after five years of gluten removal. Celiac sufferers who fail to avoid gluten can experience as much as seventy-seven-fold increased risk for lymphoma and twenty-two-fold greater risk for cancers of the mouth, throat, and esophagus.[40]

Let's think about this: Wheat causes celiac disease and/or immune-mediated gluten intolerance, which is underdiagnosed by an incredibly large margin, since only 10 percent of celiac sufferers know they have the disease. That leaves the remaining 90 percent ignorant. Cancer is a not-uncommon result. Yes, indeed, wheat causes cancer. And it often causes cancer in the unsuspecting.

At least when you bungee jump off a bridge and hang at the end of a 200-foot cord, you know that you're doing something stupid. But eating "healthy whole grains" . . . who would guess that it makes bungee jumping look like hopscotch?

DON'T EAT COMMUNION WAFERS WITH LIPSTICK ON

Even knowing the painful and potentially severe consequences of eating gluten foods, celiac sufferers struggle to avoid wheat products, although it seems like an easy thing to do. Wheat has become ubiquitous, often added to processed foods, prescription drugs, even cosmetics. Wheat has become the rule, not the exception.

Try to eat breakfast and you discover that breakfast foods are a land mine of wheat exposure. Pancakes, waffles, French toast, cereal, English muffins, bagels, toast . . . what's left? Look for a snack, you'll be hard pressed to find anything without wheat— certainly not pretzels, crackers, or cookies. Take a new drug and you may experience diarrhea and cramping from the tiny quantity of wheat in one small pill. Unwrap a stick of chewing gum and the flour used to keep the gum from sticking may trigger a reaction. Brush your teeth and you may discover there is flour in the toothpaste. Apply lipstick and you can inadvertently ingest hydrolyzed wheat protein by licking your lips, followed by throat irritation or abdominal pain. At church, taking the sacrament means a wafer of . . . wheat!

For some people, the teensy-weensy quantity of wheat gluten contained in a few bread crumbs or the gluten-containing hand cream collected under your fingernails is enough to trigger diarrhea and cramps. Being sloppy about gluten avoidance can have dire long-term consequences, such as small intestinal lymphoma.

So the celiac sufferer ends up making a nuisance of herself at restaurants, grocery stores, and pharmacies, having to inquire constantly if products are gluten-free. Too often, the minimum-wage salesclerk or overworked pharmacist has no idea. The nineteen-year-old waitress serving your breaded eggplant usually doesn't know or care what gluten-free is. Friends, neighbors, and family will see you as a fanatic.

The celiac sufferer therefore has to navigate the world constantly on the lookout for anything containing wheat or other gluten sources such as rye and barley. To the dismay of the celiac community, the number of foods and products containing wheat has *increased* over the past several years, reflective of the lack of appreciation of the severity and frequency of this condition and the growing popularity of "healthy whole grains."

The celiac community offers several resources to help the celiac sufferer succeed. The Celiac Society (www.celiacsociety .com) provides a listing and search feature for gluten-free foods, restaurants, and manufacturers. The Celiac Disease Foundation (www.celiac.org) is a good resource for emerging science. One danger: Some celiac disease organizations obtain revenue from promotion of gluten-free products, a potential diet hazard that, while gluten-free, can act as "junk carbohydrates." Nonetheless, much of the resources and information provided by these organizations can be helpful. The Celiac Sprue Association (www .csaceliacs.org), the most grassroots effort, is the least commercial. It maintains a listing and organizes regional groups for support.

CELIAC DISEASE "LITE"

While celiac disease affects only 1 percent of the population, two common intestinal conditions affect many more people:

irritable bowel syndrome (IBS) and acid reflux (also called reflux esophagitis when esophageal inflammation is documented). Both may represent lesser forms of celiac disease, what I call celiac disease "lite."

IBS is a poorly understood condition, despite its frequent occurrence. Consisting of cramping, abdominal pain, and diarrhea or loose stools alternating with constipation, it affects between 5 and 20 percent of the population, depending on definition.[41] Think of IBS as a confused intestinal tract, following a disordered script that complicates your schedule. Repeated endoscopies and colonoscopies are typically performed. Because no visible pathology is identified in IBS sufferers, it is not uncommon for the condition to be dismissed or treated with antidepressants.

Acid reflux occurs when stomach acid is permitted to climb back up the esophagus due to a lax gastroesophageal sphincter, the circular valve meant to confine acid to the stomach. Because the esophagus is not equipped to tolerate acidic stomach contents, acid in the esophagus does the same thing that acid would do to your car's paint job: It dissolves it. Acid reflux is often experienced as common heartburn, accompanied by a bitter taste in the back of the mouth.

There are two general categories of each of these conditions: IBS and acid reflux *with* positive markers for celiac disease, and IBS and acid reflux *without* positive markers for celiac disease. People with IBS have a 4 percent likelihood of testing positive for one or more celiac markers.[42] People with acid reflux have a 10 percent chance of having positive celiac markers.[43]

Conversely, 55 percent of celiac sufferers have IBS-like symptoms and between 7 and 19 percent have acid reflux.[44,45,46] Interestingly, 75 percent of celiac sufferers obtain relief from acid reflux with wheat removal, while nonceliac people who do not eliminate wheat nearly always relapse after a course of acid-suppressing medication but continued gluten consumption.[47] Could it be the wheat?

Eliminate wheat, acid reflux improves, symptoms of IBS improve. Unfortunately, this effect has not been quantified, though investigators have speculated on how large a role gluten plays in nonceliac sufferers of IBS and acid reflux.[48] I have personally witnessed complete or partial relief from symptoms of IBS and acid reflux with gluten removal from the diet many hundreds of times, whether or not celiac markers are abnormal.

LET CELIAC DISEASE SET YOU FREE

Celiac disease is a permanent condition. Even if gluten is eliminated for many years, celiac disease or other forms of immune-mediated gluten intolerance come rushing back on reexposure.

Because susceptibility to celiac disease is, at least partly, genetically determined, it doesn't dissipate with healthy diet, exercise, weight loss, nutritional supplements, drugs, daily enemas, healing stones, or apologies to your mother-in-law. It stays with you as long as you are human and are unable to trade genes with another organism. In other words, you have celiac disease for a lifetime.

It means that even occasional casual exposure to gluten has health consequences to the celiac disease sufferer or the gluten-sensitive individual, even if immediate symptoms such as diarrhea are not provoked.

All is not lost if you have celiac disease. Food can be every bit as enjoyable without wheat, even more so. One of the essential but unappreciated phenomena accompanying wheat and gluten elimination, celiac or otherwise: You appreciate food more. You eat foods because you require sustenance and you enjoy their taste and texture. You are not driven by hidden uncontrollable impulses of the sort triggered by wheat.

Don't think of celiac disease as a burden. Think of it as *liberation*.

Losing Weight Was Just a Great Side Effect!

Dale has had a litany of health ailments. She was diagnosed with Hodgkin's disease more than two decades ago, and though she conquered that, she was plagued with sessile serrated polyosis syndrome, a condition where polyps covered almost two-thirds of her colon. In the years of checking up on her post-Hodgkin's heart health, doctors discovered she'd developed atherosclerosis.

With all these ailments, she turned to alternative health practices, and eventually found my wheat-free plan and decided to give it a try. "I felt like I began healing immediately and rapidly," said Dale. And a few months into following this style of eating, Dale returned for a follow-up colonoscopy, where the gastroenterologist told her most of the polyps were gone. He told Dale it was a first—apparently polyps never just "disappear" on their own.

"My doctors have been continually astonished at my progress and very pleased. I can't say what component of my self-treatment got rid of the polyps," said Dale. "I don't really know if eliminating wheat was part of it, but I have to tell you the day of the colonoscopy was one of the best days of my life! Who ever says that?!"

In addition to a clean colonoscopy, the Hodgkin's-induced arthritis in her ankle also mysteriously cleared up after she went wheat-free. Then she radically improved her lipid profile.

On top of that, she lost fifty pounds in just one year. "It began coming off immediately, steadily, effortlessly," she said. "At first I lost the twenty pounds I have repeatedly lost and regained my entire adult life. Then I began to see numbers on the scale that I hadn't seen since college." Dale's body fat percentage dropped from 35 to 18, and her pants size went from a 14 or 16 to a size 2. Dale said prior to the wheat belly diet, the lowest size she'd ever worn was a 10 or 12.

"I'm surprised at how much more familiar my body seems to me now than the one with all the extra weight I was carrying around for the past forty years!" she said. "I'm delighted that at the age of fifty-eight I'm in not only in the best shape of my life, but in far better shape than I ever thought possible—stronger, more flexible, more energetic."

The best part about it all? Dale said there was nothing hard about going wheat-free, much less losing the weight. In fact, she wasn't even attempting to lose weight; the original motivation to eliminate wheat was for the sole purpose of helping her health. "Losing weight was just an extremely gratifying side effect!"

CHAPTER 7

DIABETES NATION: WHEAT AND INSULIN RESISTANCE

I'VE KICKED IT IN THE JAW, beaten it, and called it names. Let's now look this thing called diabetes square in the eye.

PRESIDENT OF THE SOUP BONE CLUB

When I was a kid growing up in Lake Hiawatha, New Jersey, my mother used to point to one person or another and declare him or her the "president of the soup bone club." That's the title she gave local people who thought they were big shots in our little town of 5,000. One time, for instance, the husband of a friend of hers droned on about how he could fix all the ills of the country if only he were elected president—though he was unemployed, was missing two front teeth, and had been arrested twice for drunk driving over the past two years. Thus, my mother's gracious appointment of the man as the president of the soup bone club.

Wheat, too, is the leader of an unenviable group, the worst carbohydrate in the bunch, the one most likely to lead us down the path of diabetes. Wheat is president of its own little soup bone club, chief among carbohydrates. Drunk, foul-mouthed, and unbathed, still wearing last week's T-shirt, it gets elevated to special "fiber-rich," "complex carbohydrate," and "healthy whole grain" status by all the agencies that dispense dietary advice.

Because of wheat's incredible capacity to send blood sugar levels straight up, initiate the glucose-insulin roller coaster ride that drives appetite, generate addictive brain-active exorphins, and grow visceral fat, it is the one essential food to eliminate in a serious effort to prevent, reduce, or eliminate diabetes. You could eliminate walnuts or pecans, but you will have no impact on diabetic risk. You could eliminate spinach or cucumbers and have no effect on diabetic risk. You could banish all pork or beef from your table and still have no effect.

But you could remove wheat and an entire domino effect of changes develop: less triggering of blood sugar rises, no exorphins to drive the impulse to consume more, no initiation of the glucose-insulin cycle of appetite. And if there's no glucose-insulin cycle, there's little to drive appetite except genuine physiologic need for sustenance, not overindulgence. If appetite shrinks, calorie intake is reduced, visceral fat disappears, insulin resistance improves, blood sugars fall. Diabetics can become nondiabetics, prediabetics can become nonprediabetics. All the phenomena associated with poor glucose metabolism recede, including high blood pressure, inflammatory phenomena, glycation, small LDL particles, triglycerides.

In short, remove wheat and thereby reverse a *constellation* of phenomena that would otherwise result in diabetes and all its associated health consequences, three or four medications if not seven, and years shaved off your life.

Think about that for a moment: The personal and societal costs of developing diabetes are substantial. On average, one person with diabetes incurs $180,000 to $250,000 in direct and indirect health care costs if diagnosed at age fifty[1] and dies eight years earlier than someone without diabetes.[2] That's as much as a quarter of a million dollars and half the time spent watching your children grow up that you sacrifice to this disease, a disease caused in large part by food—in particular, a specific list of foods. President of this soup bone club: wheat.

The clinical data documenting the effects of wheat elimination on diabetes are somewhat blurred by lumping wheat into the larger category of carbohydrates. Typically, health-conscious people who follow conventional dietary advice to reduce fat and eat more "healthy whole grains" consume approximately 75 percent of their carbohydrate calories from wheat products. That's more than enough hobnobbing with the soup bone club to take you down the road to the increased medical costs, health complications, and shortened life span of diabetes. But it also means that, if you knock off the top dog, the pack disperses.

PASSING WATER THAT TASTES LIKE HONEY

Wheat and diabetes are closely interwoven. In many ways, the history of wheat is also the history of diabetes. Where there's wheat, there's diabetes. Where there's diabetes, there's wheat. It's a relationship as cozy as McDonald's and hamburgers. But it wasn't until the modern age that diabetes became not just a disease of the idle rich but of every level of society. Diabetes has become Everyman's Disease.

Diabetes was virtually unknown in the Neolithic Age, when Natufians first began to harvest wild einkorn wheat. It was certainly unknown in the Paleolithic Age, the millions of years preceding the agricultural ambitions of Neolithic Natufians. The archaeological record and observations of modern hunter-gatherer societies suggest that humans almost never developed diabetes nor died of diabetic complications before grains were present in the diet.[3,4] The adoption of grains into the human diet was followed by archaeological evidence of increased infections, bone diseases such as osteoporosis, increased infant mortality, and reduction in life span, as well as diabetes.[5]

For example, the 1534 bc Egyptian "Eber's papyrus," discovered in the Necropolis of Thebes and harking back to the period when Egyptians incorporated ancient wheat into their diet, describes the excessive urine production of diabetes. Adult diabetes (type 2) was described by the Indian physician Sushruta in the fifth century bc, who called it *madhumeha*, or "honey-like urine," due to its sweet taste (yes, he diagnosed diabetes by tasting urine) and the way the urine of diabetics attracted ants and flies. Sushruta also presciently ascribed diabetes to obesity and inactivity and advised treatment with exercise.

The Greek physician Aretaeus called this mysterious condition diabetes, meaning "passing water like a siphon." Many centuries later, another urine-tasting diagnostician, Dr. Thomas Willis, added "mellitus," meaning "tasting like honey." Yes, passing water like a siphon that tastes like honey. You'll never look at your diabetic aunt the same way again.

Starting in the 1920s, diabetes treatment took a huge leap forward with the administration of insulin, which proved lifesaving for diabetic children. Child diabetics experience damage to the insulin-producing beta cells of the pancreas, impairing its ability to make insulin. Unchecked, blood glucose climbs to dangerous levels, acting as a diuretic (causing urinary water loss). Metabolism is impaired, since glucose is unable to enter the body's cells due to lack of insulin. Unless insulin is administered, a condition called diabetic ketoacidosis develops, followed by coma and death. The discovery of insulin earned Canadian physician Sir Frederick Banting the Nobel Prize in 1923, spawning an era in which all diabetics, children and adults, were administered insulin.

While the discovery of insulin was truly lifesaving for children, it sent the understanding of adult diabetes off course for many decades. After insulin was discovered, the distinction between type 1 and type 2 diabetes remained blurred. It was therefore a surprise in the fifties when it was discovered that adult type 2 diabetics don't lack insulin until advanced phases of the disease. In fact, most adult type 2 diabetics have high quantities of insulin (several times greater than normal). Only in the eighties was the concept of insulin resistance discovered, explaining why abnormally high levels of insulin were present in adult diabetics.[6]

Unfortunately, the discovery of insulin resistance failed to enlighten the medical world when the eighties' notion of reducing fat and saturated fat in the diet led to a nationwide open season on carbohydrates. In particular, it led to the idea that "healthy whole grains" would salvage the health of Americans believed to be threatened by overconsumption of fats. It inadvertently led to a thirty-year experiment in what can happen to people who reduce fats but replace lost fat calories with "healthy whole grains" such as wheat.

The result: weight gain, obesity, bulging abdomens of visceral fat, prediabetes and diabetes on a scale never before witnessed, affecting males and females alike, rich and poor, herbivores and carnivores, reaching across all races and ages, all "passing water like a siphon that tastes like honey."

WHOLE GRAIN NATION

Adult diabetes through the ages was mostly the domain of the privileged who didn't have to hunt for their food, farm the land, or prepare their own meals. Think Henry VIII, gouty and obese, sporting a fifty-four-inch waistline, gorging nightly on banquets topped off with marzipan, loaves of bread, sweet puddings, and ale. Only during the last half of the nineteenth century and into the twentieth century, when sucrose (table sugar) consumption increased across all societal levels, common laborer on up, did diabetes become more widespread.[7]

The transition of the nineteenth into the twentieth century therefore witnessed an increase in diabetes, which then stabilized for many years. For most of the twentieth century, the incidence of adult diabetes in the United States remained relatively constant—until the mid-eighties.

Then things took an abrupt turn for the worse.

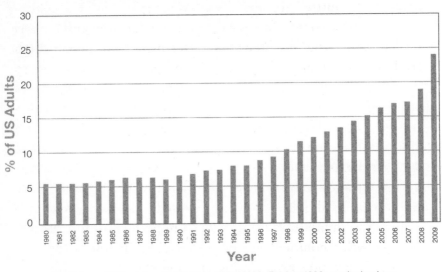

Percentage of US adults with diabetes, 1980–2009. The late 1980s marked a sharp upward trend, with the most dramatic spikes in 2009 and 2010 (not shown). Source: Centers for Disease Control and Prevention

Today diabetes is epidemic, as common as tabloid gossip. In 2009, twenty-four million Americans were diabetic, a number that represents explosive growth compared to just a few years earlier. The number of Americans with diabetes is growing faster than any other disease condition with the exception of obesity (if you call obesity a disease). If you're not diabetic yourself, then you likely have friends who are diabetic, coworkers who are diabetic, neighbors who are diabetic. Given the exceptionally high incidence in the elderly, your parents are (or were) likely to be diabetic.

And diabetes is just the tip of the iceberg. For every diabetic, there are three or four people with prediabetes (encompassing the conditions impaired fasting glucose, impaired glucose tolerance, and metabolic syndrome) waiting in the wings. Depending on whose definition you use, an incredible 22 to 39 percent of all US adults have prediabetes.[8] The combined total of people with diabetes and prediabetes in 2008 was eighty-one million, or one in three adults over eighteen years of age.[9] That's more than the total number of people, adults and children, diabetic and nondiabetic, living in the entire United States in 1900.

If you also count the people who don't yet meet full criteria for prediabetes but just show high after-meal blood sugars, high triglycerides, small LDL particles, and poor responsiveness to insulin (insulin resistance)—phenomena that can still lead to heart disease, cataracts, kidney disease, and eventually diabetes—you would find few people in the modern age who are *not* in this group, children included.

This disease is not just about being fat and having to take medications; it leads to serious complications, such as kidney failure (40 percent of all kidney failure is caused by diabetes) and limb amputation (more limb amputations are performed for diabetes than any other nontraumatic disease). We're talking *real* serious.

It's a frightening modern phenomenon, the widespread democratization of a formerly uncommon disease. The widely broadcast advice to put a stop to it? Exercise more, snack less . . . and eat more "healthy whole grains."

PANCREATIC ASSAULT AND BATTERY

The explosion of diabetes and prediabetes has been paralleled by an increase in people who are overweight and obese.

Actually, it would be more accurate to say that the explosion of diabetes and prediabetes has been in large part *caused* by the explosion in overweight and obesity, since weight gain leads to impaired insulin sensitivity and greater likelihood that excess visceral fat accumulates, the fundamental conditions required to create diabetes.[10] The fatter Americans become, the greater the number that develop prediabetes and diabetes. In 2009, 26.7 percent of American adults, or seventy-five million people, met criteria for obesity—i.e., a body mass index (BMI) of 30 or greater—with an even greater number falling into the overweight (BMI 25 to 29.9) category.[11] No state has yet met, nor is any approaching, the 15 percent goal for obesity set by the US Surgeon General's *Call to Action to Prevent and Decrease Overweight and Obesity*. (As a result, the Surgeon General's office has repeatedly emphasized that Americans need to increase their level of physical activity, eat more reduced-fat foods, and, yes, increase consumption of whole grains.)

Weight gain is predictably accompanied by diabetes and prediabetes, though the precise weight point at which they develop can vary from individual to individual, a genetic component of risk. One 5-foot-5 woman might develop diabetes at a weight of 240 pounds, while another 5-foot-5 woman might show diabetes at 140 pounds. Such variation is determined genetically.

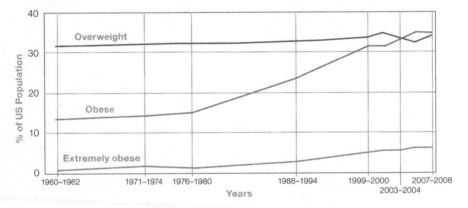

Trends in obesity and overweight in Americans, 1960–2008. Overweight is defined as BMI of 25–30; obese BMI ≥ 30; extremely obese BMI ≥ 35. While the percentage of overweight Americans has remained flat, that of obese Americans has ballooned, and the extremely obese have also increased at an alarming rate. Source: Centers for Disease Control and Prevention

The economic costs of such trends are staggering. Gaining weight is exceptionally costly, both in terms of health care costs and the personal toll on health.[12] Some estimates show that, over the next twenty years, an incredible 16 to 18 percent of all health care costs will be consumed by health issues arising from excessive weight: not genetic misfortune, birth defects, psychiatric illness, burns, or post-traumatic stress disorder from the horrors of war—no, just getting fat. The cost of Americans becoming obese dwarfs the sum spent on cancer. More money will be spent on health consequences of obesity than education.

Yet another factor parallels the trends in diabetes, prediabetes, and weight gain. You guessed it: wheat consumption. Whether it's for convenience, taste, or in the name of "health," Americans have become helpless wheataholics, with per capita annual consumption of wheat products (white and wheat bread, durum pasta) having increased by twenty-six pounds since 1970.[13] If national wheat consumption is averaged across all Americans—babies, children, teenagers, adults, the elderly—the average American consumes 133 pounds of wheat per year. (Note that 133 pounds of wheat flour is equal to approximately 200 loaves of bread, or a bit more than half a loaf of bread per day.) Of course, this means that many adults eat far more than that amount, since no baby or young child included in the averaging process eats 133 pounds of wheat per year.

That said, babies eat wheat, children eat wheat, teenagers eat wheat, adults eat wheat, the elderly eat wheat. Each group has its own preferred forms—baby food and animal crackers, cookies and peanut butter sandwiches, pizza and Oreos, whole wheat pasta and whole grain bread, dry toast and Ritz crackers—but, in the end, it's all the same. In parallel with increased consumption, we also have the silent replacement of wheat from four-foot-tall *Triticum aestivum* with high-yield dwarf strains and new gluten structures not previously consumed by humans.

Physiologically, the relationship of wheat to diabetes makes perfect sense. Products made with wheat dominate our diet and push blood sugar higher than virtually all other foods. This sends measures such as HbA1c (reflecting the average preceding sixty to ninety days' blood glucose) higher. The cycle of glucose-insulin reaching high levels several times every day provokes growth of visceral fat. Visceral fat—wheat belly—is closely aligned with resistance to insulin that, in turn, leads to even higher levels of glucose and insulin.[14]

The early phase of growing visceral fat and diabetes is accompanied by a 50 percent *increase* in pancreatic beta cells responsible for producing insulin, a physiologic adaptation to meet the enormous demands of a body that is resistant to insulin. But beta cell adaptation has limits.

High blood sugars, such as those occurring after a nice cranberry muffin consumed on the car ride to work, provoke the phenomenon of "glucotoxicity," actual damage to pancreatic insulin–producing beta cells that results from high blood sugars.[15] The higher the blood sugar, the more damage to beta cells. The effect is progressive and starts at a glucose level of 100 mg/dl, a value many doctors call normal. After two slices of whole wheat bread with low-fat turkey breast, a typical blood glucose would be 140 to 180 mg/dl in a nondiabetic adult, more than sufficient to do away with a few precious beta cells—which are never replaced.

Your poor, vulnerable pancreatic beta cells are also damaged by the process of lipotoxicity, loss of beta cells due to increased triglycerides and fatty acids, such as those developing from repeated carbohydrate ingestion. Recall that a diet weighted toward carbohydrates results in increased VLDL particles and triglycerides that persist in both the after-meal and between-meal periods, conditions that further exacerbate lipotoxic attrition of pancreatic beta cells.

Pancreatic injury is further worsened by inflammatory phenomena, such as oxidative injury, leptin, various interleukins, and tumor necrosis factor, all resulting from the visceral fat hotbed of inflammation, all characteristic of prediabetic and diabetic states.[16]

Over time and repeated sucker punches from glucotoxicity, lipotoxicity, and inflammatory destruction, beta cells wither and die, gradually reducing the number of beta cells to less than 50 percent of the normal starting number.[17] That's when diabetes is irreversibly established.

In short, carbohydrates, especially those such as wheat products that increase blood sugar and insulin most dramatically, initiate a series of metabolic phenomena that ultimately lead to irreversible loss of the pancreas's ability to manufacture insulin: diabetes.

FIGHTING CARBOHYDRATES WITH CARBOHYDRATES?

A Paleolithic or Neolithic human breakfast might consist of wild fish, reptiles, birds or other game (not always cooked), leaves, roots, berries, or insects. Today it will more likely be a bowl of breakfast cereal consisting of wheat flour, cornstarch, oats, high-fructose corn syrup, and sucrose. It won't be called "wheat flour, cornstarch, oats, high-fructose corn syrup, and sucrose," of course, but something more catchy such as Crunchy Health Clusters or Fruity Munchy Squares. Or it might be waffles and pancakes with maple syrup. Or a toasted English muffin spread with preserves or a pumpernickel bagel with low-fat cream cheese. For most Americans, extreme carbohydrate indulgence starts early and continues throughout the day.

We shouldn't be one bit shocked that, as our physical lives have become less demanding—when's the last time you skinned an animal, butchered it, chopped wood to last the winter, or washed your loincloth in the river by hand? —and rapidly metabolized foods of convenience and indulgence proliferate, diseases of excess will result.

Nobody becomes diabetic by gorging on too much wild boar they've hunted, or wild garlic and wild berries they've gathered . . . or too many veggie omelets, too much salmon, or too much kale, pepper slices, and cucumber dip. But plenty of people develop diabetes because of too many muffins, bagels, breakfast cereals, pancakes, waffles, pretzels, crackers, cakes, cupcakes, croissants, donuts, and pies.

As we've discussed, foods that increase blood sugar the most also cause diabetes. The sequence is simple: Carbohydrates trigger insulin release from the pancreas, causing growth of visceral fat; visceral fat causes insulin resistance and inflammation. High blood sugars, triglycerides, and fatty acids damage the pancreas. After years of overwork, the pancreas succumbs to the thrashing it has taken from glucotoxicity, lipotoxicity, and inflammation, essentially "burning out," leaving a deficiency of insulin and an increase in blood glucose—diabetes.

Treatments for diabetes reflect this progression. Medications such as pioglitazone (Actos) to reduce insulin resistance are prescribed in the early phase of diabetes. The drug metformin, also prescribed in the early phase, reduces glucose production by the liver. Once the pancreas is exhausted from years of glucotoxic, lipotoxic, and inflammatory pummeling, it is no longer able to make insulin, and insulin injections are prescribed.

Part of the prevailing standard of care to prevent and treat diabetes, a disease caused in large part by carbohydrate consumption . . . is to advise increased consumption of carbohydrates.

Years ago, I used the ADA diet in diabetic patients. Following the carbohydrate intake advice of the ADA, I watched patients gain weight, experience deteriorating blood glucose control and increased need for medication, and develop diabetic complications such as kidney disease and neuropathy. Just as Ignaz Semmelweis caused the incidence of childbed fever in his practice to nearly vanish just by washing his hands, *ignoring* ADA diet advice and cutting carbohydrate intake leads to improved blood sugar control, reduced HbA1c, dramatic weight loss, and improvement in all the metabolic messiness of diabetes such as high blood pressure and triglycerides.

The ADA advises diabetics to cut fat, reduce saturated fat, and include 45 to 60 grams of carbohydrate—preferably "healthy whole grains"—in each meal, or 135 to 180 grams of carbohydrates per day, not including snacks. It is, in essence, a fat-phobic, carbohydrate-centered diet, with 55 to 65 percent of calories from carbohydrates. If I were to sum up the views of the ADA toward diet, it would be: Go ahead and eat sugar and foods that increase blood sugar, just be sure to adjust your medication to compensate.

But while "fighting fire with fire" may work with pest control and passive-aggressive neighbors, you can't charge your way out of credit card debt and you can't carbohydrate-stuff your way out of diabetes.

The ADA exerts heavy influence in crafting national attitudes toward nutrition. When someone is diagnosed with diabetes, they are sent to a diabetes educator or nurse who counsels them in the ADA diet principles. If a patient enters the hospital and has diabetes, the doctor orders an "ADA diet." Such dietary "guidelines" can, in effect, be enacted into health "law." I've seen smart diabetes nurses and educators who, coming to understand that carbohydrates cause diabetes, buck ADA advice and counsel patients to curtail carbohydrate consumption. Because such advice flies in the face of ADA guidelines, the medical establishment demonstrates its incredulity by firing these rogue employees. Never underestimate the convictions of the conventional, particularly in medicine.

The list of ADA-recommended foods includes:

- whole grain breads, such as whole wheat or rye
- whole grain, high-fiber cereal
- cooked cereal such as oatmeal, grits, hominy, or cream of wheat
- rice, pasta, tortillas
- cooked beans and peas, such as pinto beans or black-eyed peas
- potatoes, green peas, corn, lima beans, sweet potatoes, winter squash
- low-fat crackers and snack chips, pretzels, and fat-free popcorn

In short, eat wheat, wheat, corn, rice, and wheat.

Goodbye to Wheat, Goodbye to Diabetes

Maureen, a sixty-three-year-old mother of three grown children and grandmother to five, came to my office for an opinion regarding her heart disease prevention program. She'd undergone two heart catheterizations and received three stents in the past two years, despite taking a cholesterol-reducing statin drug.

Maureen's laboratory evaluation included lipoprotein analysis that, in addition to low HDL cholesterol of 39 mg/dl and high triglycerides of 233 mg/dl, uncovered an excess of small LDL particles; 85 percent of all Maureen's LDL particles were classified as small—a severe abnormality.

Maureen had also been diagnosed with diabetes two years earlier, first identified during one of the hospitalizations. She had received counseling on the restrictions of both the heart "healthy" diet of the American Heart Association and the American Diabetes Association diet. Her first introduction to diabetes medication was metformin. However, after a few months she required the addition of one, then another, medication (this most recent drug a twice-a-day injection) to keep her blood sugars in the desired range. Recently, Maureen's doctor had started talking about the possibility of insulin injections.

Ask any diabetic about the effects of this diet approach, and they will tell you that any of these foods increase blood sugar up to the 200 to 300 mg/dl range or higher. According to ADA advice, this is just fine . . . but be sure to track your blood sugars and speak to your doctor about adjustments in insulin or medication.

Does the ADA diet contribute to a diabetes cure? There's the gratuitious marketing claim of "working toward the cure." But *real* talk about a cure?

In their defense, I don't believe that most of the people behind the ADA are evil; many, in fact, are devoted to helping fund the effort to discover the cure for childhood diabetes. But I believe

Because the small LDL pattern, along with low HDL and high tri-glycerides, are closely linked to diabetes, I counseled Maureen on how to apply diet to correct the entire spectrum of abnormalities. The cornerstone of the diet: wheat elimination. Because of the severity of her small LDL pattern and diabetes, I also asked her to further restrict other carbohydrates, especially cornstarch and sugars, as well as oats, beans, rice, and potatoes. (This severe a restriction is not necessary in most people.)

Within the first three months of starting her diet, Maureen lost 28 pounds off her starting weight of 247. This early weight loss allowed her to stop the twice-daily injection. Three more months and 16 more pounds gone, and Maureen cut her medication down to the initial metformin.

After a year, Maureen had lost a total of 51 pounds, tipping the scale below 200 for the first time in 20 years. Because Maureen's blood glucose values were consistently below 100 mg/dl, I then asked her to stop the metformin. She maintained the diet, followed by continued gradual weight loss. She maintained blood glucose values comfortably in the nondiabetic range.

One year, 51 pounds lost, and Maureen said goodbye to diabetes. Provided she doesn't return to her old ways, including plenty of "healthy whole grains," she is essentially *cured*.

they got sidetracked by the low-fat dietary blunder that set the entire United States off course.

To this day, the notion of treating diabetes by increasing consumption of the foods that caused the disease in the first place, then managing the blood sugar mess with medications, persists.

We have the advantage, of course, of 20/20 hindsight, able to view the effects of this enormous dietary faux pas, like a bad B-movie video on the VCR. Let's rewind the entire grainy, shakily filmed show: Remove carbohydrates, especially those from "healthy whole grains," and an entire constellation of modern conditions reverse themselves.

DÉJÀ VU ALL OVER AGAIN

Fifth-century bc Indian physician Sushruta prescribed exercise for his obese patients with diabetes at a time when his colleagues looked to omens from nature or the position of the stars to diagnose the afflictions of their patients. Nineteenth-century French physician Apollinaire Bouchardat observed that sugar in the urine of his patients diminished during the four-month-long siege of Paris by the Prussian army in 1870 when food, especially bread, was in short supply; after the siege was over, he mimicked the effect by advising patients to reduce consumption of breads and other starches and to fast intermittently to treat diabetes, despite the practice of other physicians who advised *increased* consumption of starches.

Into the twentieth century, the authoritative *Principles and Practice of Medicine*, authored by Dr. William Osler, iconic medical educator and among the four founders of the Johns Hopkins Hospital, advised a diet for diabetics of 2 percent carbohydrate. In Dr. Frederick Banting's original 1922 publication describing his initial experiences injecting pancreatic extract into diabetic children, he notes that the hospital diet used to help control urinary glucose was a strict limitation of carbohydrates to 10 grams per day.[18]

It may be impossible to divine a cure based on primitive methods such as watching whether flies gather around urine, methods conducted without modern tools such as blood glucose testing and hemoglobin A1c. Had such testing methods been available, I believe that improved diabetic results would indeed have been in evidence. The modern cut-your-fat, eat-more-healthy-whole-grains era caused us to forget the lessons learned by astute observers such as Osler and Banting. Like many lessons, the notion of carbohydrate restriction to treat diabetes is a lesson that will need to be relearned.

I do see a glimmer of light at the end of the tunnel. The concept that diabetes should be regarded as a disease of *carbohydrate intolerance* is beginning to gain ground in the medical community. Diabetes as a by-product of carbohydrate intolerance is actively being advocated by vocal physicians and researchers such as Dr. Eric Westman of Duke University; Dr. Mary Vernon, former medical director of the University of Kansas Weight Control Program and past president of the American Society of Bariatric Physicians; and prolific researcher Dr. Jeff Volek of the University of Connecticut. Drs. Westman and Vernon report, for instance, that they typically need to reduce the insulin dose by 50 percent the *first day* a patient engages in reducing carbohydrates to avoid excessively low blood sugars.[19] Dr. Volek and his team have repeatedly demonstrated, in both humans and animals, that sharp reduction in carbohydrates reverses insulin resistance, postprandial distortions, and visceral fat.[20,21]

Several studies conducted over the past decade have demonstrated that reduction in carbohydrates leads to weight loss and improved blood sugars in people with diabetes.[22,23,24] In one of these studies, in which carbohydrates were reduced to 30 grams per day, 11.2 pounds of weight loss on average resulted and HbA1c (reflecting average blood glucose over the preceding 60 to 90 days) was reduced from 7.4 to 6.6 percent over a year.[25] A Temple University study of obese diabetics showed that reduction of carbohydrates to 21 grams per day led to an average of 3.6 pounds of weight loss over 2 weeks, along with reduction in HbA1c from 7.3 to 6.8 percent and 75 percent improvement in insulin responses.[26]

Dr. Westman has been successfully validating what many of us learn in clinical practice: Virtual *elimination* of carbohydrates, including the "dominant" carbohydrate of "healthy" diets, wheat, not only improves blood sugar control, but can *erase* the need for insulin and diabetes medications in adult (type 2) diabetics—otherwise known as a cure.

In one of Dr. Westman's recent studies, 84 obese diabetics followed a strict low-carbohydrate diet—no wheat, cornstarch, sugars, potatoes, rice, or fruit, reducing carbohydrate intake to

Wheat and Childhood (Type 1) Diabetes

Prior to the discovery of insulin, childhood, or type 1, diabetes was fatal within a few months of onset. Dr. Frederick Banting's discovery of insulin was truly a breakthrough of historic significance. But why do children develop diabetes in the first place?

Antibodies to insulin, beta cells, and other "self" proteins result in autoimmune destruction of the pancreas. Children with diabetes also develop antibodies to other organs of the body. One study revealed that 24 percent of children with diabetes had increased levels of "autoantibodies," i.e., antibodies against "self" proteins, compared to 6 percent in children without diabetes.[27]

The incidence of so-called adult (type 2) diabetes is increasing in children due to overweight, obesity, and inactivity, the very same reasons it is skyrocketing in adults. However, the incidence of type 1 diabetes is also increasing. The National Institutes of Health and the Centers for Disease Control and Prevention cosponsored the SEARCH for Diabetes in Youth study, which demonstrated that, from 1978 to 2004, the incidence of newly diagnosed type 1 diabetes increased by 2.7 percent per year. The fastest rate of increase is being seen in children under the age of four.[28] Disease registries from the interval between 1990 and 1999 in Europe, Asia, and South America show a similar increase.[29]

Why would type 1 diabetes be on the increase? Our children are likely being exposed to something. Something sets off a broad abnormal immune response in these children. Some authorities have proposed that a viral infection ignites the process, while others have pointed their finger at factors that unmask expression of autoimmune responses in the genetically susceptible.

Could it be wheat?

The changes in the genetics of wheat since 1960, such as that of high-yielding dwarf strains, could conceivably account for the recent

20 grams per day (similar to Drs. Osler and Banting's early-twentieth-century practices). After six months, waistlines (representative of visceral fat) were reduced by over 5 inches, triglycerides dropped by 70 mg/dl, weight dropped 24.5 pounds, and HbA1c was reduced from 8.8 to 7.3 percent. And 95 percent of participants

increased incidence of type 1 diabetes. Its appearance coincides with the increase in celiac disease and other diseases.

One clear-cut connection stands out: Children with celiac disease are ten times more likely to develop type 1 diabetes; children with type 1 diabetes are ten to twenty times more likely to have antibodies to wheat and/or have celiac disease.[30,31] The two conditions share fates with much higher likelihood than chance alone would explain.

The cozy relationship of type 1 diabetes and celiac disease also increases over time. While some diabetic children show evidence for celiac disease when diabetes is first diagnosed, more will show celiac signs over the ensuing years.[32]

A tantalizing question: Can avoidance of wheat starting at birth avert the development of type 1 diabetes? After all, studies in mice genetically susceptible to type 1 diabetes show that elimination of wheat gluten reduces the development of diabetes from 64 percent to 15 percent[33] and prevents intestinal damage characteristic of celiac disease.[34] The same study has not been performed in human infants or children, so this crucial question therefore remains unanswered.

Though I disagree with many of the policies of the American Diabetes Association, on this point we agree: Children diagnosed with type 1 diabetes should be tested for celiac disease. I would add that they should be retested every few years to determine whether celiac disease develops later in childhood, even adulthood. Although no official agency advises it, I don't believe it would be a stretch to suggest that parents of children with diabetes should strongly consider wheat gluten elimination, along with other gluten sources.

Should families with type 1 diabetes in one or more family members avoid wheat from the start of life to avoid triggering the autoimmune effect that leads to this lifetime disease called type 1 diabetes? Nobody knows, but it's a question that truly needs answering. The increasing incidence of the condition is going to make the issue more urgent in the coming years.

were able to reduce diabetes medications, while 25 percent were able to *eliminate* medications, including insulin, altogether.[35]

In other words, on Dr. Westman's protocol using *nutrition*—not drugs—25 percent of participants were no longer diabetic, or at least had blood sugar control improved sufficiently to manage with diet only. The remainder, while still diabetic, enjoyed better blood glucose control and reduced need for insulin and other medications.

The studies to date have achieved proof of concept: Reduction of carbohydrates improves blood sugar behavior, reducing the diabetic tendency. If taken to extremes, it is possible to *eliminate* diabetes medications in as little as six months. In some instances, I believe it is safe to call that a cure, provided excess carbohydrates don't make their way back into the diet. Let me say that again: If sufficient pancreatic beta cells remain and have not yet been utterly decimated by long-standing glucotoxicity, lipotoxicity, and inflammation, it is entirely possible for some, if not most, prediabetics and diabetics to be cured of their condition, something that virtually never happens with conventional low-fat diets such as that advocated by the American Diabetes Association.

It also suggests that *prevention* of diabetes, rather than *reversal* of diabetes, can be achieved with less intensive dietary efforts. After all, some carbohydrate sources, such as blueberries, raspberries, peaches, and sweet potatoes, provide important nutrients and don't increase blood glucose to the same extent that more "obnoxious" carbohydrates can. (You know who I'm talking about.)

So what if we follow a program not quite so strict as the Westman "cure diabetes" study, but just eliminated the most ubiquitous, diet-dominating, blood sugar–increasing food of all? In my experience, you will drop blood sugar and HbA1c, lose visceral fat (wheat belly), and free yourself from the risk of participating in this nationwide epidemic of obesity, prediabetes, and diabetes. It would scale back diabetes to pre-1985 levels, restore 1950s dress and pants sizes, even allow you to again sit comfortably on the airline flight next to other normal-weight people.

"IF IT DOESN'T FIT, YOU MUST ACQUIT"

The wheat-as-guilty-culprit in causing obesity and diabetes reminds me of the O.J. Simpson murder trial: evidence found at the scene of the crime, suspicious behavior by the accused, bloody glove linking murderer to victim, motive, opportunity . . . but absolved through clever legal sleight of hand.

Wheat looks every bit the guilty party in causing diabetes: It increases blood sugar more than nearly all other foods, providing ample opportunity for glucotoxicity, lipotoxicity, and inflammation; it promotes visceral fat accumulation; there is a fits-like-a-glove correlation with weight gain and obesity trends over the past thirty years—yet it has been absolved of all crimes by the "Dream Team" of the USDA, the American Diabetes Association, the American Dietetic Association, etc., all of whom agree that wheat should be consumed in generous quantities. I don't believe that even Johnnie Cochran could have done any better.

Can you say "mistrial"?

In the court of human health, however, you have the opportunity to redress the wrongs by convicting the guilty party and banishing wheat from your life.

CHAPTER 8

DROPPING ACID: WHEAT AS THE GREAT pH DISRUPTER

THE HUMAN BODY is a tightly controlled pH vessel. Veer up or down from the normal pH of 7.4 by just 0.5 and you're . . . dead.

The acid-base status of the body is finely tuned and maintained more tightly than the Fed regulates the discount rate. Severe bacterial infections, for instance, can be deadly because the infection yields acid by-products that overwhelm the body's capacity to neutralize the acid burden. Kidney disease likewise leads to health complications because of the kidney's impaired ability to rid the body of acid by-products.

In daily life, the pH of the body is locked at 7.4, thanks to the elaborate control systems in place. By-products of metabolism, such as lactic acid, are acids. Acids drive pH down, triggering a panic mode response from the body to compensate. The body responds by drawing from any alkaline store available, from bicarbonate in the bloodstream to alkaline calcium salts such as calcium carbonate and calcium phosphate in bones. Because maintaining a normal pH is so crucial, the body will sacrifice bone health to keep pH stable. In the great triage system that is your body, your bones will be turned into mush before pH is allowed to veer off course. When a happy net alkaline balance is struck, bones will be happy, joints will be happy.

While pH extremes in either direction are dangerous, the body is happier with a slight alkaline bias. This is subtle and not reflected in blood pH, but evident by such methods as measuring acid and alkaline products in the urine.

Acids that stress the body's pH can also come through diet. There are obvious dietary sources of acid such as carbonated sodas that contain carbonic acid. Some sodas, such as Coca-Cola, also contain phosphoric acid. The extreme acid loads of carbonated sodas stretch your body's acid-neutralizing capacity to its limits. The constant draw on calcium from bones, for instance, is associated with fivefold increased fractures in high school girls who consume the most carbonated colas.[1]

But certain foods can be not-so-obvious sources of acids in this tightly controlled pH environment. Regardless of source, the body must "buffer" the acid challenge. The composition of the diet can determine whether the net effect is an acid challenge or an alkaline challenge.

Proteins from animal products are meant to be the main acid-generating challenge in the human diet. Meats such as chicken, pork roast, and Arby's roast beef sandwiches are therefore a major source of acid in the average American diet. Acids yielded by meats, such as uric acid and sulfuric acid (the same as in your car's battery and acid rain), need to be buffered by the body. The fermented product of bovine mammary glands (cheese!) is another highly acidic group of foods, particularly reduced-fat, high-protein cheeses. Any food derived from animal sources, in short, generates an acid challenge, whether fresh, fermented, rare, well done, with or without special sauce.[2]

However, animal products may not be as harmful to pH balance as it first appears. Recent research suggests that protein-rich meats have other effects that partially negate the acid load. Animal protein exerts a bone-strengthening effect through stimulation of the hormone insulin-like growth factor (IGF-1), which triggers bone growth and mineralization. ("Insulin-like" refers to its similarity in structure to insulin, not similarity in effect.) The net effect of proteins from animal sources, despite their acid-generating properties, is that of increasing bone health. Children, adolescents, and the elderly, for instance, who increase protein intake from meat show increased bone calcium content and improved measures of bone strength.[3]

Vegetables and fruits, on the other hand, are the dominant alkaline foods in the diet. Virtually everything in your produce department will drive pH toward the alkaline direction. From kale to kohlrabi, generous consumption of vegetables and fruits serve to neutralize the acidic burden from animal products.

BONE BREAKER

Hunter-gatherer diets of meats, vegetables, and fruits, along with relatively neutral nuts and roots, yield a net alkaline effect.[4] Of course, the struggle for the hunter-gatherer wasn't pH regulation, but dodging the arrows of an invading conqueror or the ravages of gangrene. So perhaps acid-base regulation did not play a major role in the health and longevity of primitive people who rarely survived beyond their thirty-fifth birthday. Nonetheless, the nutritional habits of our ancestors set the biochemical stage for modern human adaptation to diet.

Around 10,000 years ago, the formerly alkaline human diet pH balance shifted to the acid side with the introduction of grains, especially the most dominant of grains, wheat. The modern human diet of plentiful "healthy whole grains" but lacking in vegetables and fruit is highly acid-charged, inducing a condition called acidosis. Over years, acidosis takes its toll on your bones.

Like the Federal Reserve, bones from skull to coccyx serve as a repository, not of money but of calcium salts. Calcium, identical to that in rocks and mollusk shells, keeps bones rigid and strong. Calcium salts in bone are in dynamic balance with blood and tissues and provide a ready source of alkalinizing material to counter an acid challenge. But, like money, the supply is not infinite.

While we spend our first eighteen or so years growing and building bone, we spend the rest of our lives tearing it back down, a process regulated by body pH. The chronic mild metabolic acidosis engendered by our diet worsens as we age, starting in our teens and continuing through the eighth decade.[5,6] The acidic pH pulls calcium carbonate and calcium phosphate from bone to maintain the body pH of 7.4. The acidic environment also stimulates bone-resorbing cells within bones, known as osteoclasts, to work harder and faster to dissolve bone tissue to release the precious calcium.

The problem comes when you habitually ingest acids in the diet, then draw on calcium stores over and over and over again to neutralize these acids. Though bones have a lot of stored calcium, the supply is not inexhaustible. Bones will eventually become demineralized—i.e., depleted of calcium. That's when osteopenia (mild demineralization) and osteoporosis (severe demineralization), frailty, and fractures develop.[7] (Frailty and osteoporosis usually go hand in hand, since bone density and muscle mass parallel each other.) Incidentally, taking calcium supplements is no more effective at reversing bone loss than randomly tossing some bags of cement and bricks into your backyard is at building a new patio.

An excessively acidified diet will eventually show itself as bone fractures. An impressive analysis of the worldwide incidence of hip fracture demonstrated a striking relationship: The higher the ratio of protein intake from vegetables to the protein intake from animal products, the fewer hip fractures occur.[8] The magnitude of difference was substantial: While a vegetable-to-animal-protein intake ratio of 1:1 or less was associated with as many as 200 hip fractures per 100,000 population, a vegetable-to-animal-protein intake ratio of between 2:1 and 5:1 was associated with less than 10 hip fractures per 100,000 population—a reduction of more than 95 percent. (At the highest intakes of vegetable protein, the incidence of hip fracture practically *vanished*.)

The fractures that result from osteoporosis are not just tumbling down the stairs kinds of fractures. They can also be vertebral fractures from a simple sneeze, a hip fracture from misjudging the sidewalk curb, a forearm fracture from pushing a rolling pin.

Modern eating patterns therefore create a chronic acidosis that in turn leads us to osteoporosis, bone fragility, and fractures. At age fifty, 53.2 percent of women can expect to experience a fracture in their future, as can 20.7 percent of men.[9] Contrast this with a fifty-year-old woman's risk for breast cancer of 10 percent and risk for endometrial cancer of 2.6 percent.[10]

Until recently, osteoporosis was thought to be largely a condition peculiar to postmenopausal females who have lost the bone-preserving effects of estrogen. It is now understood that the decline in bone density begins *years* before menopause. In the 9,400-participant Canadian Multicentre Osteoporosis Study, females began to show declining bone density in the hip, vertebra, and femur at age twenty-five, with a precipitous decline resulting in accelerated loss at age forty; men show a less marked decline starting at age forty.[11] Both men and women showed another phase of accelerated bone loss at age seventy and onward. By age eighty, 97 percent of females have osteoporosis.[12]

So even youth does not ensure protection from bone loss. In fact, loss of bone strength is the rule over time, largely due to the chronic low-grade acidosis we create with diet.

WHAT DO ACID RAIN, CAR BATTERIES, AND WHEAT HAVE IN COMMON?

Unlike all other foods derived from plants, grains generate acidic by-products, the only plant products to do so. Because wheat is, by a long stretch, the foremost grain in most Americans' diet, it contributes substantially to the acid burden of a meat-containing diet.

Wheat is among the most potent sources of sulfuric acid, yielding more sulfuric acid per gram than any meat.[13] (Wheat is surpassed only by oats in quantity of sulfuric acid produced.) Sulfuric acid is dangerous stuff. Put it on your hand and it will cause a severe burn. Get it in your eyes and you can go blind. (Go take a look at the warnings prominently displayed on your car battery.) The sulfuric acid in acid rain erodes stone monuments, kills trees and plants, and disrupts the reproductive behavior of aquatic animals. The sulfuric acid produced by wheat consumption is undoubtedly dilute. But even in teensy-weensy quantities in dilute form, it is an overwhelmingly potent acid that rapidly overcomes the neutralizing effects of alkaline bases.

Grains such as wheat account for 38 percent of the average American's acid load, more than enough to tip the balance into the acid range. Even in a diet limited to 35 percent of calories from animal products, adding wheat shifts the diet from net alkaline to strongly net acid.[14]

One way to gauge acid-induced extraction of calcium from bone is to measure urinary calcium loss. A University of Toronto study examined the effect of increasing gluten consumption from bread on the level of calcium lost in the urine. Increased gluten intake increased urinary calcium loss by an incredible 63 percent, along with increased markers of bone resorption—i.e., blood markers for bone weakening that lead to bone diseases such as osteoporosis.[15]

So what happens when you consume a substantial quantity of meat products but fail to counterbalance the acid load with plentiful alkaline plant products such as spinach, cabbage, and green peppers? An acid-heavy situation results. What happens if acids from meat consumption are not counterbalanced by alkaline plants and the pH scales are tipped even more to the acidic side by grain products such as wheat? That's when it gets ugly. Diet is then shifted sharply to that of an acid-rich situation.

The result: a chronic acid burden that eats away at bone health.

WHEAT, TOUPÉ, AND A CONVERTIBLE

Remember Ötzi? He was the Tyrolean Iceman found buried and mummified in the glaciers of the Italian Alps, preserved since his death more than 5,000 years ago, circa 3300 bc. While the remains of unleavened einkorn bread were discovered in Ötzi's gastrointestinal tract, most of the digestive contents were meats and plants. Ötzi lived and died 4,700 years after humans began incorporating grains such as cold-tolerant einkorn into their diet, but wheat remained a relatively minor portion of the diet in his mountain-dwelling culture. Ötzi was primarily a hunter-gatherer most of the year. In fact, he was likely hunting with his bow and arrow when he met his violent end at the hand of another hunter-gatherer.

The meat-rich diet of hunter-gatherer humans such as Ötzi provided a substantial acid load. Ötzi's greater consumption of meat than most modern humans (35 to 55 percent of calories from animal products) therefore yielded more sulfuric and other organic acids.

Despite the relatively high consumption of animal products, the abundant nongrain plants in the diets of hunter-gatherers yielded generous amounts of alkalinizing potassium salts, such as potassium citrate and potassium acetate, that counterbalanced the acidic load. The alkalinity of primitive diets has been estimated to be six- to ninefold greater than that of modern diets due to the high plant content.[16] This resulted in alkaline urine pH as high as 7.5 to 9.0, compared to the typical modern acidic range of 4.4 to 7.0.[17]

Wheat and other grains enter the picture, however, and shift the balance back to acid, accompanied by calcium loss from bone.

Ötzi's relatively modest consumption of einkorn wheat likely meant that his diet remained net alkaline most of the year. In contrast, in our modern world of plenty, with unlimited supplies of cheap wheat-containing foods on every corner and table, the acidic load tips the scales heavily toward net acid.

If wheat and other grains are responsible for tipping the pH balance toward acid, what happens if you do nothing more than remove wheat from the modern diet and replace the lost calories with other plant foods such as vegetables, fruits, beans, and nuts? The balance shifts back into the alkaline range, mimicking the hunter-gatherer pH experience.[18]

Wheat is therefore the great disrupter. It's the floozy girlfriend of the midlife crisis male, busting apart the entire happy family. Wheat shifts a diet that had hopes of being net alkaline to net acid, causing a constant draw of calcium out of bone.

The conventional solution to the "healthy whole grain" acid diet and its osteoporosis-promoting effects are prescription drugs such as Fosamax and Boniva, agents that claim to reduce the risk for osteoporotic fractures, especially of the hip. The market for osteoporosis drugs has already topped $10 billion a year, serious money even by the jaded standards of the pharmaceutical industry.

Once again wheat enters the picture, adding its peculiar health-disrupting effects, embraced by the USDA and providing new and bountiful revenue opportunities for Big Pharma.

TWO WHEAT HIPS TO MATCH YOUR WHEAT BELLY

Ever notice how people with a wheat belly almost invariably also have arthritis of one or more joints? If you haven't, take notice of how many times someone who carts around the characteristic front loader also limps or winces with hip, knee, or back pain.

Osteoarthritis is the most common form of arthritis in the world, more common than rheumatoid arthritis, gout, or any other variety. Painful "bone-on-bone" loss of cartilage resulted in knee and hip replacements in 773,000 Americans in 2010 alone.[19]

This is no small problem. More than forty-six million people, or one in seven Americans, have been diagnosed with osteoarthritis by their physicians.[20] Many more hobble around without formal diagnosis.

Conventional thought for years was that common arthritis of the hips and knees was the simple result of excessive wear and tear, like too many miles on your tires. A 110-pound woman: knees and hips likely to last a lifetime. A 220-pound woman: knees and hips take a beating and wear out. Excess weight in any part of the body—bottom, belly, chest, legs, arms—provides a mechanical stress to joints.

It has proven to be more complicated than that. The same inflammation that issues from the visceral fat of the wheat belly and results in diabetes, heart disease, and cancer also yields inflammation of joints. Inflammation-mediating hormones, such as tumor necrosis factor-alpha, interleukins, and leptin, have been shown to inflame and erode joint tissue.[21] Leptin, in particular, has demonstrated direct joint destructive effects: The greater the degree of overweight (i.e., higher BMI), the higher the quantity of leptin within joint fluid, and the greater the severity of cartilage and joint damage.[22] The level of leptin in joints precisely mirrors the level in blood.

The risk of arthritis is therefore even greater for someone with visceral fat of the wheat belly variety, as evidenced by the threefold greater likelihood of knee and hip replacements in people with larger waist circumferences.[23] It also explains why joints that *don't* bear the added weight of obesity, such as those in the hands and fingers, also develop arthritis.

Losing weight, and thereby visceral fat, improves arthritis more than can be expected from just the decreased weight load.[24] In one study of obese participants with osteoarthritis, there was

10 percent improvement in symptoms and joint function with each 1 percent reduction in body fat.[25]

The prevalence of arthritis, the common images of people rubbing their painful hands and knees, leads you to believe that arthritis is an unavoidable accompaniment of aging, as inevitable as death, taxes, and hemorrhoids. Not true. Joints do indeed have the potential to serve us for the eight or so decades of our life . . . until we ruin them with repeated insults, such as excessive acidity and inflammatory molecules such as leptin originating from visceral fat cells.

Another phenomenon that adds to the wheat-induced pounding that joints sustain over the years: glycation. You'll recall that, more than nearly all other foods, wheat products increase blood sugar, i.e., blood glucose. The more wheat products you consume, the higher and more frequently blood glucose increases, the more glycation occurs. Glycation represents an irreversible modification of proteins in the bloodstream and in body tissues, including joints such as the knees, hips, and hands.

The cartilage in joints is uniquely susceptible to glycation, since cartilage cells are extremely long-lived and are incapable of reproducing. Once damaged, they do not recover. The very same cartilage cells residing in your knee at age twenty-five will (we hope) be there when you are eighty; therefore, these cells are susceptible to all the biochemical ups and downs of your life, including your blood sugar adventures. If cartilage proteins, such as collagen and aggrecan, become glycated, they become abnormally stiff. The damage of glycation is cumulative, making cartilage brittle and unyielding, eventually crumbling.[26] Joint inflammation, pain, and destruction results, the hallmarks of arthritis.

So high blood sugars that encourage growth of a wheat belly, coupled with inflammatory activity in visceral fat cells and glycation of cartilage, lead to destruction of bone and cartilage tissue in joints. Over years, it results in the familiar pain and swelling of the hips, knees, and hands.

Man Walks After Eliminating Wheat

Jason is a twenty-six-year-old software programmer: smart, lightning-quick to catch onto an idea. He came to my office with his young wife because he wanted help just to get "healthy."

When he told me that he had undergone repair of a complex congenital heart defect as an infant, I promptly interrupted him. "Whoa, Jason. I think you may have the wrong guy. That's not my area of expertise."

"Yes, I know. I just need your help to get healthier. They tell me I might need a heart transplant. I'm always breathless and I've had to be admitted to the hospital to treat heart failure. I'd like to see if there's anything you can do to either avoid having a heart transplant or, if I have to have it, help me be healthier afterwards."

I thought that was reasonable and gestured for Jason to get on the exam table. "Okay. I get it. Let me take a listen."

Jason got up from the chair slowly, visibly wincing, and inched his way onto the table, clearly in pain.

"What's wrong?" I asked.

Jason took his seat on the exam table and sighed. "Everything hurts. All my joints hurt. I can barely walk. At times, I can barely get out of bed."

"Have you been seen by any rheumatologists?" I asked.

"Yes. Three. None of them could figure out what was wrong, so they just prescribed anti-inflammatories and pain medicines."

"Have you considered dietary modification?" I asked him. "I've seen a lot of people get relief by eliminating all wheat from their diet."

"Wheat? You mean like bread and pasta?" Jason asked, confused.

That baguette may look innocent, but it's a lot harder on the joints than you think.

THE BELLY JOINT'S CONNECTED TO THE HIP JOINT

As with weight loss and the brain, people with celiac disease can teach us some lessons about wheat's effects on bones and joints.

"Yes, wheat: white bread, whole wheat bread, multigrain bread, bagels, muffins, pretzels, crackers, breakfast cereals, pasta, noodles, pancakes, and waffles. Even though it sounds like that's a lot of what you eat, trust me, there's plenty of things left to eat." I gave him a handout detailing how to navigate the wheat-free diet.

"Give it a try: Eliminate all wheat for just four weeks. If you feel better, you'll have your answer. If you feel nothing, then perhaps this is not the answer for you."

Jason returned to my office three months later. What struck me was that he sauntered easily into the room without a hint of joint pain.

The improvements he'd experienced had been profound and nearly immediate. "After five days, I couldn't believe it: I had no pain whatsoever. I didn't believe it could be true—it had to be a coincidence. So I had a sandwich. Within five minutes, about eighty percent of the pain came back. Now I've learned my lesson."

What impressed me further was that, when I first examined him, Jason had indeed been in mild heart failure. On this visit, he no longer showed any evidence of heart failure. Along with relief from the joint pain, he also told me that his breathing had improved to the point where he could jog short distances and even play a low-key game of basketball, things he had not done in years. We've now begun to back down on the medications he was taking for heart failure.

Obviously, I am a big believer in a wheat-free life. But when you witness life-changing experiences such as Jason's, it still gives me goose bumps to know that such a simple solution existed for health problems that had essentially crippled a young man.

Osteopenia and osteoporosis are common in people with celiac disease and can be present whether or not there are intestinal symptoms, affecting up to 70 percent of people with celiac antibodies.[27,28] Because osteoporosis is so common among celiac sufferers, some investigators have argued that anyone with osteoporosis should be screened for celiac disease. A Washington University Bone Clinic study found undiagnosed celiac disease in 3.4 percent of participants with osteoporosis, compared to 0.2 percent without osteoporosis.[29] Elimination of gluten from osteoporotic celiac participants promptly improved measures of bone density—without use of osteoporosis drugs.

The reasons for the low bone density include impaired absorption of nutrients, especially vitamin D and calcium, and increased inflammation that triggers release of bone-demineralizing cytokines, such as interleukins.[30] So eliminating wheat from the diet both reduced the inflammation and allowed for better absorption of nutrients.

The severity of bone weakening effects are highlighted by horror stories such as the woman who suffered ten fractures of the spine and extremities over twenty-one years starting at age fifty-seven, all occurring spontaneously. Eventually crippled, she was finally diagnosed with celiac disease.[31] Compared to people without celiac disease, celiac sufferers have a threefold increased risk for fractures.[32]

The thorny issue of gliadin antibody-positive indivduals without intestinal symptoms applies to osteoporosis as well. In one study, 12 percent of people with osteoporosis tested positive for the gliadin antibody but didn't show any symptoms or signs of celiac, i.e., wheat intolerance or "silent" celiac disease.[33]

Wheat can show itself through inflammatory bone conditions outside of osteoporosis and fractures. People with rheumatoid arthritis, a disabling and painful arthritis that can leave the sufferer with disfigured hand joints, knees, hips, elbows, and shoulders, can blend with wheat sensitivity. A study of participants with rheumatoid arthritis, none of whom had celiac disease, placed on a vegetarian, gluten-free diet demonstrated improved signs of arthritis in 40 percent of participants, as well as reduced gliadin antibody levels.[34] Perhaps it's a stretch to suggest that wheat gluten was the initial inciting cause of the arthritis, but it may exert inflammatory effects in an exaggerated way in joints made susceptible by other diseases such as rheumatoid arthritis.

In my experience, arthritis unaccompanied by celiac antibodies often responds to wheat elimination. Some of the most dramatic health turnarounds I've ever witnessed have been in obtaining relief from incapacitating joint pains. Because conventional celiac antibodies fail to identify most of these people, this has been difficult to quantify and verify, beyond the subjective improvement people experience. But this may hint at phenomena that hold the greatest promise in arthritis relief of all.

Does the outsize risk for osteoporosis and inflammatory joint disease in people with celiac represent an *exaggeration* of the situation in wheat-consuming people without celiac disease or antibodies to gluten? My suspicion is that yes, wheat exerts direct and indirect bone- and joint-destructive effects in any wheat-consuming human, just expressed more vigorously in celiac- or gluten antibody–positive people.

What if, rather than a total hip or knee replacement at age sixty-two, you opted for total wheat replacement instead?

The broader health effects of disrupted acid-base balance are only starting to be appreciated. Anyone who has taken a basic chemistry class understands that pH is a powerful factor in determining how chemical reactions proceed. A small shift in pH can have profound influence on the balance of a reaction. The same holds true in the human body.

"Healthy whole grains" such as wheat are the cause for much of the acid-heavy nature of the modern diet. Beyond bone health, emerging experiences suggest that crafting a diet that favors alkaline foods has the potential to reduce age-related muscle wasting, kidney stones, salt-sensitive hypertension, infertility, and kidney disease.

Remove wheat and experience reduced joint inflammation and fewer blood sugar "highs" that glycate cartilage, and shift the pH balance to alkaline. It sure beats taking Vioxx.

"I Wake Up in the Morning with No Aches and Pains!"

Anne had spent many years battling coronary heart disease. She tried all sorts of low-fat diets recommended by her doctors, had multiple failed stents and even bypass surgery . . . but still never felt well. She fought against overwhelming fatigue, joint pain, shortness of breath, pitting edema in her legs, and many other symptoms. She also had severe peripheral neuropathy—nerve damage that causes pain and loss of feeling all over the body. Doctors ruled out diabetes as a cause, and were stumped as to what had brought it on. Anne decided to take matters into her own hands, and discovered articles linking peripheral neuropathy with gluten—and by her own prescription, went wheat and gluten-free.

"I stopped eating bread on August 8, 2003," she said, adding that she never looked back. Within four days, she knew she was on the right track—her knee pain had already disappeared.

While many of her symptoms cleared out from cutting wheat, barley, and rye out of her diet, she realized she was still feeling bogged down after eating other grains, like those found in processed foods and the alternative grains used in her gluten-free foods. Still searching for her own means to improve her heart condition and overall health, she stumbled upon my website.

Soon after, Anne started following my guidelines—which trained her to stop worrying about fats and pay more attention to eliminating sugar and grains, specifically wheat, cornstarch, and sugar. In addition to her wheat-free diet, she eliminated cornstarch, high-fructose corn syrup, and sucrose, and used a glucometer to help her find the best foods to eat. When she dropped the sugars and high-carb foods, she also dropped fifteen pounds—a weight loss that has stayed with her for two years now.

In addition to keeping shortness of breath and edema at bay, and lowering her blood sugar levels, Anne discovered that her depression lifted—depression she hadn't even realized existed until it was gone and she feels a new sense of overall happiness. "I am sixty-eight years old and feel great," said Anne. "I wake up in the morning with *no* aches and pains. Life is wonderful."

CHAPTER 9

CATARACTS, WRINKLES, AND DOWAGER'S HUMPS: WHEAT AND THE AGING PROCESS

The secret of staying young is to live honestly, eat slowly, and lie about your age.

Lucille Ball

WINE AND CHEESE MAY BENEFIT from aging. But for humans, aging can lead to everything from white lies to a desire for radical plastic surgery.

What does it mean to get old?

Though many people struggle to describe the specific features of aging, we would likely all agree that, like pornography, we know it when we see it.

The rate of aging varies from individual to individual. We've all known a man or woman at, say, age sixty-five who still could pass for forty-five—maintaining youthful flexibility and mental dexterity, fewer wrinkles, straighter spine, thicker hair. Most of us have also known people who show the reverse disposition, looking older than their years. *Biological* age does not always correspond to *chronological* age.

Nonetheless, aging is inevitable. All of us age. None will escape it—though we each progress at a somewhat different rate. And, while gauging chronological age is a simple matter of looking at your birth certificate, pinpointing biological age is another thing altogether. How can you assess how well the body has maintained youthfulness or, conversely, submitted to the decay of age?

Say you meet a woman for the first time. When you ask her how old she is, she replies, "Twenty-five years old." You do a double take because she has deep wrinkles around her eyes, liver spots on the back of her hands, and a fine tremor to her hand movements. Her upper back is bowed forward (given the unflattering name of "dowager's hump"), her hair gray and thin. She looks ready for the retirement home, not like someone in the glow of youth. Yet she is insistent. She has no birth certificate or other legal evidence of age, but insists that she is twenty-five years old—she's even got her new boyfriend's initials tattooed on her wrist.

Can you prove her wrong?

Not so easy. If she were a caribou, you could measure antler wingspan. If she were a tree, you could cut her down and count the rings.

In humans, of course, there are no rings or antlers to provide an accurate, objective biological marker of age that would prove that this woman is really seventysomething and not twentysomething, tattoo or no.

No one has yet identified a visible age marker that would permit you to discern, to the year, just how old your new friend is. It's not for lack of trying. Age researchers have long sought such biological markers, measures that can be tracked, advancing a year for every chronological year of life. Crude gauges of age have been identified involving measures such as maximal oxygen uptake, the quantity of oxygen consumed during exercise at near-exhaustion levels; maximum heart rate during controlled exercise; and arterial pulse-wave velocity, the amount of time required for a pressure pulse to be transmitted along the length of an artery, a phenomenon reflecting arterial flexibility. These measures all decline over time, but none correlate perfectly to age.

Wouldn't it be even more interesting if age researchers identified a do-it-yourself gauge of biological age? You could, for instance, know at age fifty-five that, by virtue of exercise and healthy eating, you are biologically forty-five. Or that twenty years of smoking, booze, and French fries has made you biologically sixty-seven and that it's time to get your health habits in gear. While there are elaborate testing schemes that purport to provide such an aging index, there is no single simple do-it-yourself test that tells you with confidence how closely biological age corresponds to chronological age.

Age researchers have diligently sought a useful marker for age because, in order to manipulate the aging process, they require a measurable parameter to follow. Research into the slowing of the aging process cannot rely on simply *looking*. There needs to be some objective biological marker that can be tracked over time.

To be sure, there are a number of differing, some say complementary, theories of aging and opinions on which biological marker might provide the best gauge of biologic aging. Some age researchers believe that oxidative injury is the principal process that underlies aging and that an age marker must incorporate a measure of cumulative oxidative injury. Others have proposed that cellular debris accumulates from genetic misreading and leads to aging; a measure of cellular debris would therefore be required to yield biologic age. Still others believe that aging is genetically preprogrammed and inevitable, determined by a programmed sequence of diminishing hormones and other physiologic phenomena.

Most age researchers believe that no single theory explains all the varied experiences of aging, from the supple, high-energy, know-everything teenage years, all the way to the stiff, tired, forget-everything eighth decade. Nor can biologic age be accurately pinpointed by any one measure. They propose that the manifestations of human aging can be explained only by the work of more than one process.

We might gain better understanding of the aging process if we were able to observe the effects of *accelerated* aging. We need not look to any mouse experimental model to observe such rapid aging; we need only look at humans with diabetes. Diabetes yields a virtual proving ground for accelerated aging, with all the phenomena of aging approaching faster and occurring earlier in life—heart disease, stroke, high blood pressure, kidney disease, osteoporosis, arthritis, cancer. Specifically, diabetes research has linked high blood glucose of the sort that occurs after carbohydrate consumption with hastening your move to the wheelchair at the assisted living facility.

NO COUNTRY FOR OLD BREAD EATERS

Americans have lately been bombarded with a tidal wave of complex new terms, from collateralized debt obligations to exchange-traded derivative contracts, the sorts of things you'd rather leave to experts such as your investment banking friend. Here's another complex term you're going to be hearing a lot about in the coming years: AGE.

Advanced glycation end products, appropriately acronymed AGE, is the name given to the stuff that stiffens arteries (atherosclerosis), clouds the lenses of the eyes (cataracts), and mucks up the neuronal connections of the brain (dementia), all found in abundance in older people.[1] The older we get, the more AGEs can be recovered in kidneys, eyes, liver, skin, and other organs. While we can see some of the effects of AGEs, such as the wrinkles in our pretend twenty-five-year-old following Lucille Ball's advice, it does not yet provide a precise gauge of age that would make a liar out of her. Although we can see evidence of some AGE effects—saggy skin and wrinkles, the milky opacity of cataracts, the gnarled hands of arthritis—none are truly quantitative. AGEs nonetheless, at least in a qualitative way, identified via biopsy as well as some aspects apparent with a simple glance, yield an index of biological decay.

AGEs are useless debris that result in tissue decay as they accumulate. They provide no useful function: AGEs cannot be burned for energy, they provide no lubricating or communicating functions, they provide no assistance to nearby enzymes or hormones, nor can you snuggle with them on a cold winter's night. Beyond effects you can see, accumulated AGEs also mean loss of the kidneys' ability to filter blood to remove waste and retain protein, stiffening and atherosclerotic plaque accumulation in arteries, stiffness and deterioration of cartilage in joints such as the knee and hip, and loss of functional brain cells with clumps of AGE debris taking their place. Like sand in your spinach salad or cork in the cabernet, AGEs can ruin a good party.

While some AGEs enter the body directly because they are found in various foods, they are also a by-product of high blood sugar (glucose), the phenomenon that defines diabetes.

The sequence of events leading to formation of AGEs goes like this: Ingest foods that increase blood glucose. The greater availability of glucose to the body's tissues permits the glucose molecule to react with any protein, creating a combined glucose-protein molecule. Chemists talk of complex reactive products such as Amadori products and Schiff intermediates, all yielding a group of glucose-protein combinations that are collectively called AGEs. Once AGEs form, they are irreversible and cannot be undone. They also collect in chains of molecules, forming AGE polymers that are especially disruptive.[2] AGEs are notorious for accumulating right where they sit, forming clumps of useless debris resistant to any of the body's digestive or cleansing processes.

Thus, AGEs result from a domino effect set in motion anytime blood glucose increases. Anywhere that glucose goes (which is virtually everywhere in the body), AGEs will follow. The higher the blood glucose, the more AGEs will accumulate and the faster the decay of aging will proceed.

Diabetes is the real-world example that shows us what happens when blood glucose remains high, since diabetics typically have glucose values that range from 100 to 300 mg/dl all through the day as they chase their sugars with insulin or oral medications. (Normal fasting glucose is 90 mg/dl or less.) Blood glucose can range much higher at times; following a bowl of slow-cooked oatmeal, for instance, glucose can easily reach 200 to 400 mg/dl.

If such repetitive high blood sugars lead to health problems, we should see such problems expressed in an exaggerated way in diabetics . . . and indeed we do. Diabetics, for instance, are two to five times more likely to have coronary artery disease and heart attacks, 44 percent will develop atherosclerosis of the carotid arteries or other arteries outside of the heart, and 20 to 25 percent will develop impaired kidney function or kidney failure an average of eleven years following diagnosis.[3] In fact, high blood sugars sustained over several years virtually *guarantee* development of complications.

With repetitive high blood glucose levels in diabetes, you'd also expect higher blood levels of AGEs, and indeed, that is the case. Diabetics have 60 percent greater blood levels of AGEs compared to nondiabetics.[4]

AGEs that result from high blood sugars are responsible for most of the complications of diabetes, from neuropathy (damaged nerves leading to loss of sensation in the feet) to retinopathy (vision defects and blindness) to nephropathy (kidney disease and kidney failure). The higher the blood sugar and the longer blood sugars stay high, the more AGE products will accumulate and the more organ damage results.

Diabetics with poorly controlled blood sugars that stay high for too long are especially prone to diabetic complications, all due to the formation of abundant AGEs, even at a young age. (Before the value of "tightly" controlled blood sugars in type 1, or childhood, diabetes was appreciated, it was not uncommon to see kidney failure and blindness before age thirty. With improved glucose control, such complications have become far less common.) Large studies, such as the Diabetes Control and Complications Trial (DCCT)[5], have shown that strict reductions in blood glucose yield reduced risk for diabetic complications.

This is because the rate of AGE formation is dependent on the level of blood glucose: The higher the blood glucose, the more AGEs are created.

AGEs form even when blood sugar is normal, though at a much lower rate compared to when blood sugar is high. AGE formation therefore characterizes normal aging of the sort that makes a sixty-year-old person look sixty years old. But the AGEs accumulated by the diabetic whose blood sugar is poorly controlled cause *accelerated* aging. Diabetes has therefore served as a living model for age researchers to observe the age-accelerating effects of high blood glucose. Thus, the complications of diabetes, such as atherosclerosis, kidney disease, and neuropathy, are also the diseases of aging, common in people in their sixth, seventh, and eighth decades, uncommon in younger people in their second and third decades. Diabetes therefore teaches us what happens to people when glycation occurs at a faster clip and AGEs are permitted to accumulate. It ain't pretty.

The story doesn't end at greater levels of AGEs. Higher AGE blood levels spark the expression of oxidative stress and inflammatory markers.[6] The receptor for AGEs, or RAGE, is the gatekeeper to an assortment of oxidative and inflammatory responses, such as inflammatory cytokines, vascular endothelial growth factor, and

What Happens When You AGE?

Outside of the complications of diabetes, serious health conditions have been associated with excessive production of AGEs.

- Kidney disease—When AGEs are administered to an experimental animal, it develops all the hallmarks of kidney disease.[7] AGEs can also be found in human kidneys from persons suffering from kidney disease.
- Atherosclerosis—Oral administration of AGEs in both animals and humans causes constriction of arteries, the abnormal excessive tone (endothelial dysfunction) of arteries associated with the fundamental injury that lays the groundwork for atherosclerosis.[8] AGEs also modify LDL cholesterol particles, blocking their normal uptake by the liver and routing them for uptake by inflammatory cells in artery walls, the process that grows atherosclerotic plaque.[9] AGEs can be recovered from tissues and correlated with plaque severity: The higher the AGE content of various tissues, the more severe the atherosclerosis in arteries will be.[10]
- Dementia—In Alzheimer's dementia sufferers, brain AGE content is threefold greater than in normal brains, accumulating in the amyloid plaques and neurofibrillary tangles that are characteristic of the condition.[11] In line with the marked increase in AGE formation in diabetics, dementia is 500 percent more common in people with diabetes.[12]

tumor necrosis factor.[13] AGEs therefore set an army of oxidative and inflammatory responses in motion, all leading to heart disease, cancer, diabetes, and more.

AGE formation is therefore a continuum. But while AGEs form at even normal blood glucose levels (fasting glucose 90 mg/dl or less), they form faster at higher blood sugar levels. The higher the blood glucose, the more AGEs form. There really is *no* level of blood glucose at which AGE formation can be expected to cease entirely.

Being nondiabetic does *not* mean that you will be spared such fates. AGEs accumulate in nondiabetics and wreak their age-

- Cancer—While the data are only spotty, the relationship of AGEs to cancer may prove to be among the most important of all AGE-related phenomena. Evidence for abnormal AGE accumulation has been identified in cancers of the pancreas, breast, lung, colon, and prostate.[14]
- Male erectile dysfunction—If I haven't already gotten the attention of male readers, then this should do it: AGEs impair erectile capacity. AGEs are deposited in the portion of penile tissue responsible for the erectile response (corpus cavernosum), disabling the penis' ability to engorge with blood, the process that drives penile erections.[15]
- Eye health—AGEs damage eye tissue, from the lens (cataracts) to the retina (retinopathy) to the lacrimal glands (dry eyes).[16]

Many of the damaging effects of AGEs work through increased oxidative stress and inflammation, two processes underlying numerous disease processes.[17] On the other hand, recent studies have shown that reduced AGE exposure leads to reduced expression of inflammatory markers such as c-reactive protein (CRP) and tumor necrosis factor.[18]

AGE accumulation handily explains why many of the phenomena of aging develop. Control over glycation and AGE accumulation therefore provides a potential means to reduce all the consequences of AGE accumulation.

advancing effects. All it takes is a little extra blood sugar, just a few milligrams above normal, and—voilà—you've got AGEs doing their dirty work and gumming up your organs. Over time, you too can develop all the conditions seen in diabetes if you have sufficient AGE accumulation.

Along with 25.8 million diabetics, there are 79 million prediabetics in the United States today.[19] There are many more Americans who don't yet meet the ADA criteria for prediabetes, but still experience plenty of high blood sugars after consuming some amount of carbohydrate that increases blood sugar—i.e., blood sugars high enough to trigger more AGEs than normal. (If you doubt that blood sugars increase after eating, say, an apple or a slice of pizza, just pick up a simple glucose meter from your pharmacy. Test your blood sugar one hour after consuming the food of interest. More often than not, you will be shocked to see how high your blood glucose soars. Remember my two slices of whole wheat bread "experiment"? Blood glucose 167 mg/dl. That's not uncommon.)

While eggs don't increase blood sugar, nor do raw nuts, olive oil, pork chops, or salmon, carbohydrates do—all carbohydrates, from apples and oranges to jelly beans and seven-grain cereal. As we discussed earlier, from a blood sugar standpoint, wheat products are worse than nearly all other foods, skyrocketing blood sugar to levels that rival those of a full-blown diabetic—even if you're nondiabetic.

Remember, the "complex" carbohydrate contained in wheat is the unique variety of amylopectin, amylopectin A, a form distinct from amylopectin in other carbohydrates such as black beans and bananas. The amylopectin of wheat is the form most readily digested by the enzyme amylase, thus explaining the greater blood sugar–increasing property of wheat products. The more rapid and efficient digestion of wheat amylopectin means higher blood sugars over the ensuing two hours after consumption of wheat products, which in turn means greater triggering of AGE formation. If AGE formation was a contest, wheat would win nearly all the time, beating out other carbohydrate sources such as apples, oranges, sweet potatoes, ice cream, and chocolate bars.

Thus, wheat products such as your poppy seed muffin or roasted vegetable focaccia are triggers of extravagant AGE production. Put 2 and 2 together: Wheat, because of its unique blood glucose–increasing effect, makes you age faster. Via its blood sugar/AGE-increasing effects, wheat accelerates the rate at which you develop signs of skin aging, kidney dysfunction, dementia, atherosclerosis, and arthritis.

THE GREAT GLYCATION RACE

There is a widely available test that, while not capable of providing an index of biological age, provides a measure of the *rate* of biological aging due to glycation. Knowing how fast or slow you are glycating the proteins of your body helps you know whether biological aging is proceeding faster or slower than chronological age. While AGEs can be assessed via biopsy of the skin or internal organs, most people are understandably less than enthusiastic about a pair of forceps being inserted into some body cavity to snip a piece of tissue. Thankfully, a simple blood test can be used to gauge the ongoing rate of AGE formation: hemoglobin A1c, or HbA1c. HbA1c is a common blood test that, while usually used for the purpose of diabetes control, can also serve as a simple index of glycation.

Hemoglobin is the complex protein residing within red blood cells that is responsible for their ability to carry oxygen. Like all other proteins of the body, hemoglobin is subject to glycation, i.e., modification of the hemoglobin molecule by glucose. The reaction occurs readily and, like other AGE reactions, is irreversible. The higher the blood glucose, the greater the percentage of hemoglobin that becomes glycated.

Red blood cells have an expected life span of sixty to ninety days. Measuring the percentage of hemoglobin molecules in the blood that are glycated provides an index of how high blood glucose has ventured over the preceding sixty to ninety days, a useful tool for assessing the adequacy of blood sugar control in diabetics, or to diagnose diabetes.

A slender person with a normal insulin response who consumes a limited amount of carbohydrates will have approximately 4.0 to 4.8 percent of all hemoglobin glycated (i.e., an HbA1c of 4.0 to 4.8 percent), reflecting the unavoidable low-grade, normal rate of glycation. Diabetics commonly have 8, 9, even 12 percent or more glycated hemoglobin—twice or more the normal rate.

AGEs: Inside and Out

While we've focused so far on AGEs that form in the body and are largely derived from consumption of carbohydrates, there is a second source of AGEs that come directly from the diet: animal products. This can get awfully confusing, so let's start from the beginning.

AGEs originate from two general sources:

Endogenous AGEs. These are the AGEs that form within the body, as we've discussed. The main pathway to forming endogenous AGEs starts with blood glucose. Foods that increase blood glucose increase endogenous AGE formation. Foods that increase blood glucose the most trigger the greatest AGE formation. This means that all carbohydrates, all of which increase blood glucose, trigger endogenous AGE formation. Some carbohydrates increase blood glucose more than others. From an endogenous AGE viewpoint, a Snickers bar triggers AGE formation only modestly, while whole wheat bread triggers AGEs vigorously, given the greater blood glucose–increasing effect of whole wheat bread.

Interestingly, fructose, another sugar that has exploded in popularity as an ingredient in modern processed foods, increases AGE formation within the body up to several hundredfold more than glucose.[20] Occurring as high-fructose corn syrup, fructose often accompanies wheat in breads and baked products. You will be hard-pressed to find processed foods *not* containing fructose in some form, from barbecue sauce to dill pickles. Also note that table sugar, or sucrose, is 50 percent fructose, the other 50 percent being glucose. Maple syrup, honey, and agave syrup are other fructose-rich sweeteners.

Exogenous AGEs. Exogenous AGEs are found in foods that enter the body as breakfast, lunch, or dinner. In contrast to endogenous AGEs, they are not formed in the body, but are ingested preformed.

Foods vary widely in their AGE content. The foods richest in AGEs are animal products, such as meats and cheese. In particular, meats and

The majority of nondiabetic Americans are somewhere in between, most living in the range of 5.0 to 6.4 percent, above the perfect range but still below the "official" diabetes threshold of 6.5 percent.[21,22] In fact, an incredible 70 percent of American adults have an HbA1c between 5.0 percent and 6.9 percent.[23]

animal products heated to high temperature, e.g., broiling and frying, increase AGE content more than a thousandfold.[24] Also, the longer an animal product food is cooked, the richer its AGE content becomes.

An impressive demonstration of the power of exogenous AGEs to impair arterial function was demonstrated when identical diets of chicken breast, potatoes, carrots, tomatoes, and vegetable oil were consumed by two groups of diabetic volunteers. The only difference: The first group's meal was cooked for ten minutes by steaming or boiling, while the second group's meal was cooked by frying or broiling at 450°F for twenty minutes. The group given food cooked longer and at a higher temperature showed 67 percent reduced capacity for arterial relaxation, along with higher AGE and oxidative markers in the blood.[25]

Exogenous AGEs are found in meats that are also rich in saturated fat. It means that saturated fat was wrongly accused of being heart-unhealthy because it often occurred in the company of the real culprit: AGEs. Cured meats, such as bacon, sausage, pepperoni, and hot dogs, are unusually rich in AGEs. So meats are not intrinsically bad; but they can be made unhealthy through manipulations that increase AGE formation.

Beyond the diet prescription of the *Wheat Belly* philosophy, i.e., eliminate wheat while maintaining restricted intake of carbohydrates, it is wise to avoid sources of exogenous AGEs, namely cured meats, meats heated to high temperature (>350°F) for prolonged periods, and anything deep-fried. Whenever possible, avoid well-done and choose meats cooked rare or medium. (Is sashimi the perfect meat?) Cooking in water-based, rather than oil-based, liquids also helps limit AGE exposure.

All that said, AGE science is still in its infancy, with many details yet to be discovered. Given what we know about the potential long-term effects of AGEs on health and aging, however, I do not believe it is premature to start giving some thought to how to reduce your personal AGE exposure. Perhaps you'll thank me on your hundredth birthday.

HbA1c does not have to be 6.5 percent to generate adverse health consequences. HbA1c in the "normal" range is associated with increased risk for heart attacks, cancer, and 28 percent increased mortality for every 1 percent increase in HbA1c.[26,27] That trip to the all-you-can-eat pasta bar, accompanied by a couple

Hey, It's Kind of Blurry in Here

The lenses of your eyes are the wonderful, naturally engineered optical devices that are part of the ocular apparatus allowing you to view the world. The words you are now reading present images, focused by the lenses on your retina, then transposed into nervous system signals interpreted by your brain as black letter images on white background. Lenses are like diamonds: Without flaws, they are crystal clear, allowing the unimpeded passage of light. Pretty damn amazing, when you think about it.

Flawed, however, and the passage of light will be distorted.

Lenses consist of structural proteins called crystallins that, like all other proteins of the body, are subject to glycation. When proteins in the lenses become glycated and form AGEs, the AGEs cross-link and clump together. Like the little specks that can be seen in a flawed diamond, little defects accumulate in the lenses. Light scatters upon hitting the defects. Over years of AGE formation, accumulated defects cause opacity of the lenses, or cataracts.

The relationship of blood glucose, AGEs, and cataracts is well-defined. Cataracts can be produced within as little as ninety days in lab animals just by keeping blood glucose high.[28] Diabetics are especially prone to cataracts (no surprise there), with as much as fivefold increased risk compared to nondiabetics.[29]

In the United States, cataracts are common, affecting 42 percent of males and females between the ages of fifty-two and sixty-four, and increasing to 91 percent between the ages of seventy-five and eighty-five.[30] In fact, no structure in the eye escapes the damaging effects of AGEs, including the retina (macular degeneration), the vitreous (the gel-like liquid filling the eyeball), and the cornea.[31]

Any food that increases blood sugar therefore has the potential to glycate the crystallins of the lenses of your eyes. At some point, injury to the lens exceeds its limited capacity for defect resorption and crystallin renewal. That's when the car in front of you is lost in a blurry haze, unimproved by putting on your glasses or squinting.

of slices of Italian bread and finished off with a little bread pudding, sends your blood glucose up toward 150 to 250 mg/dl for three or four hours; high glucose for a sustained period glycates hemoglobin, reflected in higher HbA1c.

HbA1c—i.e., glycated hemoglobin—therefore provides a running index of glucose control. It also reflects to what degree you are glycating body proteins beyond hemoglobin. The higher your HbA1c, the more you are also glycating the proteins in the lenses of your eyes, in kidney tissue, arteries, skin, etc.[32] In effect, HbA1c provides an ongoing index of aging rate: The higher your HbA1c, the faster you are aging.

So HbA1c is much more than just a feedback tool for blood glucose control in diabetics. It also reflects the rate at which you are glycating other proteins of the body, the rate at which you are aging. Stay at 5 percent or less, and you are aging at the normal rate; over 5 percent, and time for you is moving faster than it should, taking you closer to the great nursing home in the sky.

So foods that increase blood glucose levels the most and are consumed more frequently are reflected by higher levels of HbA1c that in turn reflect a faster rate of organ damage and aging. So if you hate your boss at work and you'd like to hasten his approach to old age and infirmity, bake him a nice coffee cake.

WHEAT-FREE IS ANTI-AGING

You'll recall that foods made from wheat increase blood sugar more than nearly all other foods, including table sugar. Pitting wheat against most other foods would be like putting Mike Tyson in the ring against Truman Capote: no contest, a blood sugar KO in no time. Unless you're a premenopausal, size 2, twenty-three-year-old female long-distance runner who, by virtue of minimal visceral fat, vigorous insulin sensitivity, and the advantages of abundant estrogen, enjoys little increase in blood sugar, two slices of whole wheat bread will likely launch your blood sugar into the 150 mg/dl range or higher—more than enough to set the AGE-forming cascade in motion.

If glycation accelerates aging, can *not* glycating *slow* aging?

Such a study has been performed in an experimental mouse model, with an AGE-rich diet yielding more atherosclerosis, cataracts, kidney disease, diabetes, and shorter life spans compared to longer-lived and healthier mice consuming an AGE-poor diet.[33]

The clinical trial required for final proof of this concept in humans has not yet been performed, i.e., AGE-rich versus AGE-poor diet followed by examination of organs for the damage of aging. This is a practical stumbling block to virtually all anti-aging research. Imagine the pitch: "Sir, we will enroll you in one of two 'arms' of the study: You will either follow a high-AGE diet or a low-AGE diet. After five years, we are going to assess your biological age." Would you accept potential enrollment in the high-AGE group? And how do we assess biological age?

It seems plausible that, if glycation and AGE formation underlie many of the phenomena of aging, and if some foods trigger AGE formation more vigorously than others, a diet low in those foods should slow the aging process, or at least the facets of aging that advance through the process of glycation. A low HbA1c value signifies that less age-promoting endogenous glycation is ongoing. You will be less prone to cataracts, kidney disease, wrinkles, arthritis, atherosclerosis, and all the other expressions of glycation that plague humans, especially those of the wheat-consuming kind.

Perhaps it will even allow you to be honest about your age.

CHAPTER 10

MY PARTICLES ARE BIGGER THAN YOURS: WHEAT AND HEART DISEASE

IN BIOLOGY, SIZE is everything.

Filter-feeding shrimp, measuring just a couple of inches in length, feast on microscopic algae and plankton suspended in ocean water. Larger predatory fish and birds, in turn, consume the shrimp.

In the plant world, the tallest plants, such as 200-foot kapok trees of the tropical forest, obtain advantage with height, reaching high above the jungle canopy for sunlight required for photosynthesis, casting shadows on struggling trees and plants below.

And so it goes, all the way from carnivorous predator to herbivorous prey. This simple principle predates humans, precedes the first primate who walked the earth, and dates back over a billion years since multicellular organisms gained evolutionary advantage over single-celled organisms, clawing their way through the primordial seas. In countless situations in nature, bigger is better.

Muffins Make You Small

"Drink me."

So Alice drank the potion and found herself ten inches tall, now able to pass through the door and cavort with the Mad Hatter and Cheshire Cat.

To LDL particles, that bran muffin or ten-grain bagel you had this morning is just like Alice's "Drink me" potion: It makes them small. Starting at, say, 29 nm in diameter, bran muffins and other wheat products will cause LDL particles to shrink to 23 or 24 nm.[1]

Just as Alice was able to walk through the tiny door once she had shrunk to ten inches, so the reduced size of LDL particles allows them to begin a series of unique misadventures that normal-size LDL particles cannot enjoy.

Like humans, LDL particles present a varied range of personality types. Large LDL particles are the phlegmatic civil servant who puts in his time and collects his paycheck, all in anticipation of a comfortable state-supported retirement. Small LDLs are the frenetic, antisocial, cocaine-crazed particles that fail to obey the normal rules, causing indiscriminate damage just for laughs. In fact, if you could design an evildoing particle perfectly suited to form gruel-like atherosclerotic plaque in the walls of arteries, it would be small LDL particles.

Large LDL particles are taken up by the liver LDL receptor for disposal, following the normal physiologic route for LDL particle metabolism. Small LDL particles, in contrast, are poorly recognized by the liver LDL receptor, allowing them to linger much longer in the bloodstream. As a

The Law of Big in the ocean and plant worlds also applies within the microcosm of the human body. In the human bloodstream, low-density lipoprotein (LDL) particles, what most of the world wrongly recognizes as "LDL cholesterol," follow the same size rules as shrimp and plankton.

Large LDL particles are, as their name suggests, relatively large. Small LDL particles are—you guessed it—small. Within the human body, large LDL particles provide a survival advantage to the host human. We're talking about size differences on a nanometer (nm) level, a level of a billionth of a meter. Large LDL par-

result, small LDL particles have more time to cause atherosclerotic plaque, lasting an average of five days compared to the three days of large LDL.[2] Even if large LDL particles are produced at the same rate as small LDL, the small will substantially outnumber the large by virtue of increased longevity. Small LDL particles are also taken up by inflammatory white blood cells (macrophages) that reside in the walls of arteries, a process that rapidly grows atherosclerotic plaque.

You've heard about the benefit of antioxidants? Oxidation is part of the process of aging, leaving a wake of oxidatively modified proteins and other structures that can lead to cancer, heart disease, and diabetes. When exposed to an oxidizing environment, small LDL particles are 25 percent more likely to oxidize than large LDL particles. When oxidized, LDL particles are more likely to cause atherosclerosis.[3]

The glycation phenomenon, discussed in chapter 9, shows itself with small LDL particles as well. Compared to large particles, small LDL particles are eightfold more susceptible to endogenous glycation; glycated small LDL particles, like oxidized LDL, are more potent contributors to atherosclerotic plaque.[4] The action of carbohydrates is therefore twofold: Small LDL particles are formed when there are plentiful carbohydrates in the diet; carbohydrates also increase blood glucose that glycates small LDL. Foods that increase blood glucose the most therefore translate into both greater *quantities* of small LDL and increased *glycation* of small LDL.

So heart disease and stroke are not just about high cholesterol. They are caused by oxidation, glycation, inflammation, small LDL particles . . . yes, the processes triggered by carbohydrates, especially those made of wheat.

ticles are 25.5 nm in diameter or larger, while small LDL particles are less than 25.5 nm in diameter. (This means LDL particles, big and small, are thousands of times smaller than a red blood cell but larger than a cholesterol molecule. Around ten thousand LDL particles would fit within the period at the end of this sentence.)

For LDL particles, size of course does not make the difference between eating or being eaten. It determines whether LDL particles will accumulate in the walls of arteries, such as those of your heart (coronary arteries) or neck and brain (carotid and cerebral arteries)—or not. In short, LDL size determines to a large degree whether you will have a heart attack or stroke at age fifty-seven or whether you'll continue to pull the handle on casino slot machines at age eighty-seven.

Small LDL particles are, in fact, an exceptionally common cause of heart disease, showing up as heart attacks, angioplasty, stents, bypass, and many other manifestations of atherosclerotic coronary disease.[5] In my personal experience with thousands of patients with heart disease, nearly 90 percent express the small LDL pattern to at least a moderate, if not severe, degree.

The drug industry has found it convenient and profitable to classify this phenomenon in the much-easier-to-explain category of "high cholesterol." But cholesterol has little to do with the disease of atherosclerosis; cholesterol is a convenience of measurement, a remnant of a time when it was not possible to characterize and measure the various lipoproteins (i.e., lipid-carrying proteins) in the bloodstream that cause injury, atherosclerotic plaque accumulation, and, eventually, heart attack and stroke.

So it's not really about cholesterol. It's about the particles that cause atherosclerosis. Today you and I are able to directly quantify and characterize lipoproteins, relegating cholesterol to join frontal lobotomies in the outdated medical practice garbage dump in the sky.

One crucial group of particles, the granddaddy of them all, is very low-density lipoproteins, or VLDL. The liver packages various proteins (such as apoprotein B) and fats (mostly triglycerides) together as VLDL particles, so-called because abundant fats make the particle lower in density than water (thus accounting for the way olive oil floats above vinegar in salad dressing). VLDL particles are then released, the first lipoprotein to enter the bloodstream.

Large and small LDL particles share the same parents, namely VLDL particles. A series of changes in the bloodstream determines whether VLDL will be converted to big or small LDL particles. Interestingly, the composition of diet has a very powerful influence over the fate of VLDL particles, determining what proportion will be big LDL versus what proportion will be small LDL. You may not be able to choose the members of your own family, but you can readily influence what offspring VLDL particles will have and thereby whether or not athero-sclerosis develops.

THE BRIEF, WONDROUS LIFE OF
LDL PARTICLES

At the risk of sounding tedious, let me tell you a few things about these lipoproteins in your bloodstream. This will all make sense in just a few paragraphs. At the end of it, you will know more about this topic than 98 percent of physicians.

"Parent" lipoproteins of LDL particles, VLDL, enter the bloodstream after release from the liver, eager to spawn their LDL offspring. On release from the liver, VLDL particles are richly packed with triglycerides, the currency of energy in multiple met-abolic processes. Depending on diet, more or less VLDLs are pro-duced by the liver. VLDL particles vary in triglyceride content. In a standard cholesterol panel, excessive VLDL will be reflected by higher levels of triglycerides, a common abnormality.

VLDL is an unusually social being, the lipoprotein life of the party, interacting freely with other lipoproteins passing its way. As VLDL particles bloated with triglycerides circulate in the blood-stream, they give triglycerides to both LDL and HDL (high-density lipoproteins) in return for a cholesterol molecule. Triglyceride-enriched LDL particles are then processed through another reaction (via hepatic lipase) that removes triglycerides provided by VLDL.

So LDL particles begin large, 25.5 nm or greater in diameter, and receive triglycerides from VLDL in exchange for cholesterol. They then lose triglycerides. The result: LDL particles become both triglyceride- and cholesterol-depleted, and thereby several nanometers smaller in size.[6,7]

It doesn't take much in the way of excess triglycerides from

To Lipitor or Not: The Role of Wheat

As noted earlier, wheat consumption increases LDL cholesterol; eliminating wheat reduces LDL cholesterol, all by way of small LDL particles. But it may not look that way at first.

Here's where it gets kind of confusing.

The standard lipid panel that your doctor relies on to crudely gauge risk for heart disease uses a calculated LDL cholesterol value—*not* a measured value. All you need is a calculator to sum up LDL cholesterol from the following equation (called the Friedewald calculation):

LDL cholesterol = total cholesterol − HDL cholesterol − (triglycerides ÷ 5)

The three values on the right side of the equation—total cholesterol, HDL cholesterol, and triglycerides—are indeed measured. Only LDL cholesterol is calculated.

The problem is that this equation was developed by making several assumptions. For this equation to work and yield reliable LDL cholesterol values, for instance, HDL must be 40 mg/dl or greater, triglycerides 100 mg/dl or less. Any deviation from these values and the calculated LDL value will be thrown off.[8,9] Diabetes, in particular, throws off the accuracy of the calculation, often to an extreme degree; 50 percent

VLDL to begin the cascade toward creating small LDL. At a triglyceride level of 133 mg/dl or greater, within the "normal" cutoff of 150 mg/dl, 80 percent of people develop small LDL particles.[10] A broad survey of Americans, age 20 and older, found that 33 percent have triglyceride levels of 150 mg/dl and higher—more than sufficient to create small LDL; that number increases to 42 percent in those 60 and older.[11] In people with coronary heart disease, the proportion who have small LDL particles overshadows that of all other disorders; small LDL is, by far, the most frequent pattern expressed.[12]

That's just triglycerides and VLDL present in the usual fasting blood sample. If you factor in the increase in triglycerides that

inaccuracy is not uncommon. Genetic variants can also throw the calculation off (e.g., apo E variants).

Another problem: If LDL particles are small, calculated LDL will *underestimate* real LDL. Conversely, if LDL particles are large, calculated LDL will *overestimate* real LDL.

To make the situation even more confusing, if you shift LDL particles from undesirably small to healthier large by some change in diet—a good thing—the calculated LDL value will often appear to go *up,* while the real value is actually going *down.* While you achieved a genuinely beneficial change by reducing small LDL, your doctor tries to persuade you to take a statin drug for the *appearance* of high LDL cholesterol. (That's why I call LDL cholesterol "fictitious LDL," a criticism that has not stopped the ever-enterprising pharmaceutical industry from deriving $27 billion in annual revenues from sales of statin drugs. Maybe you benefit, maybe you don't; calculated LDL cholesterol might not tell you, even though that is the FDA-approved indication: high *calculated* LDL cholesterol.)

The only way for you and your doctor to truly know where you stand is to actually measure LDL particles in some way, such as LDL particle number (by a laboratory method called nuclear magnetic resonance, or NMR, lipoprotein analysis) or apoprotein B. (Because there is one apoprotein B molecule per one LDL particle, apoprotein B provides a virtual LDL particle count.) It's not that tough, but it requires a health practitioner willing to invest the extra bit of education to understand these issues.

typically follows a meal (the "postprandial" period), increases that typically send triglyceride levels up two- to fourfold for several hours, small LDL particles are triggered to an even greater degree.[13] This is likely a good part of the reason why nonfasting triglycerides, i.e., triglycerides measured without fasting, are proving to be an impressive predictor of heart attack, with as much as five- to seventeen-fold increased risk for heart attack with higher levels of nonfasting triglycerides.[14]

VLDL is therefore the crucial lipoprotein starting point that begins the cascade of events leading to small LDL particles. Anything that increases liver production of VLDL particles and/or increases the triglyceride content of VLDL particles will ignite the process. Any foods that increase triglycerides and VLDL during the several hours after eating—i.e., in the postprandial period—will also cascade into increased small LDL.

NUTRITIONAL ALCHEMY:
CONVERTING BREAD TO TRIGLYCERIDES

So what sets the entire process in motion, causing increased VLDL/triglycerides that, in turn, trigger the formation of small LDL particles that cause atherosclerotic plaque?

Simple: carbohydrates. Chief among the carbohydrates? Wheat, of course.

For years, this simple fact eluded nutrition scientists. After all, dietary fats, maligned and feared, are composed of triglycerides. Logically, increased intake of fatty foods, such as greasy meats and butter, should increase blood levels of triglycerides. This proved true—but only transiently and to a small degree.

More recently, it has become clear that, while increased intake of fats does indeed deliver greater quantities of triglycerides into the liver and bloodstream, it also shuts down the body's own production of triglycerides. Because the body is able to produce large quantities of triglycerides that handily overwhelm the modest amount taken in during a meal, the net effect of high fat intake is little or no change in triglyceride levels.[15]

Carbohydrates, on the other hand, contain virtually no triglycerides. Two slices of whole grain bread, an onion bagel, or sourdough pretzel contain negligible triglycerides. But carbohydrates possess the unique capacity to stimulate insulin, which in turn triggers fatty acid synthesis in the liver, a process that floods the bloodstream with triglycerides.[16] Depending on genetic susceptibility to the effect, carbohydrates can send triglycerides into the hundreds or even thousands of mg/dl range. The body is so efficient at producing triglycerides that high levels, e.g., 300 mg/dl, 500 mg/dl, even 1,000 mg/dl or more, can be sustained twenty-four hours a day, seven days a week for years—provided the flow of carbohydrates continues.

In fact, the recent discovery of the process of de novo lipogenesis, the liver alchemy that converts sugars into triglycerides, has revolutionized the way nutritionists view food and its effects on lipoproteins and metabolism. One of the crucial phenomena required to begin this metabolic cascade is high levels of insulin in the bloodstream.[17,18] High insulin levels stimulate the machinery for de novo lipogenesis in the liver, efficiently transforming carbohydrates into triglycerides, which are then packaged into VLDL particles.

Today, approximately half of all calories consumed by most Americans come from carbohydrates.[19] The early twenty-first century will go down in history as The Age of Carbohydrate Consumption. Such a dietary pattern means that de novo lipogenesis can proceed to such extreme degrees that the excess fat created infiltrates the liver. That's why so-called nonalcoholic fatty liver disease, NAFLD, and nonalcoholic steatosis, NAS, have reached such epidemic proportions that gastroenterologists have their own convenient abbreviations for them. NAFLD and NAS lead to liver cirrhosis, an irreversible disease similar to that experienced by alcoholics, thus the nonalcoholic disclaimer.[20]

Ducks and geese are also capable of packing their livers full of fat, an adaptation that allows them to fly long distances without sustenance, drawing on stored liver fat for energy during annual migration. For fowl, it's part of an evolutionary adaptation. Farmers take advantage of this fact when they produce geese and duck livers full of fat: Feed the birds carbohydrates from grains, yielding foie gras and the fatty paté you spread on whole wheat crackers. But for humans, fatty liver is a perverse, unphysiologic consequence of being told to consume more carbohydrates. Unless you're dining with Hannibal Lecter, you don't want a foie gras– like liver in your abdomen.

This makes sense: Carbohydrates are the foods that encourage fat storage, a means of preserving the bounty from times of plenty. If you were a primitive human, satiated from your meal of freshly killed boar topped off with some wild berries and fruit, you would store the excess calories in case you failed to catch another boar or other prey in the coming days or even weeks. Insulin helps store the excess energy as fat, transforming it into triglycerides that pack the liver and spill over into the bloodstream, energy stores to be drawn from when the hunt fails. But in our bountiful modern times, the flow of calories, especially those from carbohydrates such as grains, never stops, but flows endlessly. Today, *every* day is a day of plenty.

The situation is worsened when excess visceral fat accumulates. Visceral fat acts as a triglyceride repository, but one that causes a constant flow of triglycerides into and out of fat cells, triglycerides that enter the bloodstream.[21] This results in liver exposure to higher blood levels of triglycerides, which further drives VLDL production.

Diabetes provides a convenient testing ground for the effects of high-carbohydrate eating, such as a diet rich in "healthy whole grains." The majority of adult (type 2) diabetes is brought on by excessive carbohydrate consumption; high blood sugars and diabetes itself are reversed in many, if not most, cases by reduction of carbohydrates.[22]

Diabetes is associated with a characteristic "lipid triad" of low HDL, high triglycerides, and small LDL, the very same pattern created by excessive carbohydrate consumption.[23]

Dietary fats therefore make only a modest contribution to VLDL production, while carbohydrates make a much larger contribution. This is why low-fat diets rich in "healthy whole grains" have become notorious for increasing triglyceride levels, a fact often glossed over as harmless by advocates of such diets. (My personal low-fat adventure many years ago, in which I restricted intake of all fats, animal and otherwise, to less than 10 percent of calories—a very strict diet, à la Ornish and others— gave me a triglyceride level of 350 mg/dl due to the plentiful "healthy whole grains" I substituted for the reduced fats and meats.) Low-fat diets typically send triglycerides up to the 150, 200, or 300 mg/dl range. In genetically susceptible people who struggle with triglyceride metabolism, low-fat diets can cause triglycerides to skyrocket to the *thousands* of mg/dl range, sufficient to cause fatty liver NAFLD and NAS, as well as damage to the pancreas.

Low-fat diets are not benign. The high-carbohydrate, plentiful whole grain intake that unavoidably results when fat calories are reduced triggers higher blood glucose, higher insulin, greater deposition of visceral fat, and more VLDL and triglycerides, all of which cascades into greater proportions of small LDL particles.

If carbohydrates such as wheat trigger the entire domino effect of VLDL/triglycerides/small LDL particles, then reducing carbohydrates should do the opposite, particularly reducing the dominant dietary carbohydrate: wheat.

IF THY RIGHT EYE OFFEND THEE . . .

And if thy right eye offend thee, pluck it out, and cast it from thee: for it is profitable for thee that one of thy members should perish, and not that thy whole body should be cast into hell.

Matthew 5:29

Dr. Ronald Krauss and his colleagues at the University of California-Berkeley were pioneers in drawing the connection between carbohydrate intake and small LDL particles.[24] In a series of studies, they demonstrated that, as carbohydrates as a

No Need for Statins

Chuck came to me because he had heard that it was possible to reduce cholesterol without drugs.

Although it had been labeled "high cholesterol," what Chuck really had, as uncovered by lipoprotein testing, was a great excess of small LDL particles. Measured by one technique (NMR), he showed 2,440 nmol/L small LDL particles. (Little to none is desirable.) This gave Chuck the appearance of high LDL cholesterol of 190 mg/dl, along with low HDL cholesterol of 39 mg/dl and high triglycerides of 173 mg/dl.

Three months into his wheat-free experience (he replaced lost wheat calories with real foods such as raw nuts, eggs, cheese, vegetables, meats, avocados, and olive oil), Chuck's small LDL was reduced to 320 nmol/L. This was reflected on the surface by an LDL cholesterol of 123 mg/dl, an increase in HDL to 45 mg/dl, a drop in triglycerides to 45 mg/dl, and 14 pounds of weight lost from his belly.

Yes, indeed: Marked and rapid reduction of "cholesterol," no statin drug in sight.

percentage of diet increased from 20 to 65 percent and fat content decreased, there was an explosion of small LDL particles. Even people who start with *zero* small LDL particles can be forced to develop them by increasing the carbohydrate content of their diet. Conversely, people with plenty of small LDL particles will show marked reductions (approximately 25 percent) with reduction in carbohydrates and an increase in fat intake over just several weeks.

Dr. Jeff Volek and his colleagues at the University of Connecticut have also published a number of studies demonstrating the lipoprotein effects of reduced carbohydrates. In one such study, carbohydrates, including wheat flour products, sugared soft drinks, foods made of cornstarch or cornmeal, potatoes, and rice were eliminated, reducing carbohydrates to 10 percent of total calories. Subjects were instructed to consume unlimited beef, poultry, fish, eggs, cheese, nuts and seeds, and low-carbohydrate vegetables and salad dressings. Over twelve weeks, small LDL particles were reduced by 26 percent.[25]

From the standpoint of small LDL particles, it is nearly impossible to tease out the effects of wheat versus other carbohydrates, such as candy, soft drinks, and chips, since all of these foods trigger small LDL formation to varying degrees. We can safely predict, however, that foods that increase blood sugar the most also trigger insulin the most, followed by the most vigorous stimulation of de novo lipogenesis in the liver and greater visceral fat deposition, followed by increased VLDL/triglycerides and small LDL. Wheat, of course, fits that description perfectly, triggering greater spikes in blood sugar than nearly all other foods.

Accordingly, reduction or elimination of wheat yields unexpectedly vigorous reductions in small LDL, provided the lost calories are replaced with those from vegetables, proteins, and fats.

CAN "HEART HEALTHY" *CAUSE* HEART DISEASE?

Who doesn't love a Mission Impossible double agent story, where the trusted companion or lover suddenly double-crosses the secret agent, having worked for the enemy all along?

How about the nefarious side of wheat? It's a food that has been painted as your savior in the battle against heart disease, yet the most current research shows it is anything but. (Angelina Jolie made a movie about multiple layers of espionage and betrayal called *Salt*. How about a similar movie starring Russell Crowe called *Wheat*, about a middle-aged businessman who thinks he's eating healthy foods, only to find out . . . ? Okay, maybe not.)

While Wonder Bread claims to "build strong bodies 12 ways,"

the many "heart healthy" varieties of bread and other wheat products come in a range of disguises. But whether stone-ground, sprouted grain, or sourdough, organic, "fair trade," "hand-crafted," or "home-baked," it's still wheat. It is still a combination of gluten proteins, glutenins, and amylopectin, triggering wheat's unique panel of inflammatory effects, neurologically active exorphins, and excessive glucose levels.

Don't be misled by other health claims attached to a wheat product. It may be "vitamin-enriched" with synthetic B vitamins, but it's still wheat. It could be organic stone-ground, whole grain bread with added omega-3 from flax oil, but it's still wheat. It could help you have regular bowel movements and emerge from the ladies' room with a satisfied smile, but it's still wheat. It could be taken as the sacrament and blessed by the pope, but—holy or not—it's still wheat.

I think you're probably getting the idea. I hammer this point home because it exposes a common ploy used by the food industry: Add "heart healthy" ingredient(s) to a food and call it a "heart healthy" muffin, cracker, or bread. Fiber, for instance, does indeed have modest health benefits. So does the linolenic acid of flaxseed and flaxseed oil. But no "heart healthy" ingredient will erase the adverse health effects of the wheat. "Heart healthy" bread packed with fiber and omega-3 fats will still trigger high blood sugar, glycation, visceral fat deposition, small LDL particles, exorphin release, and inflammatory responses.

IF YOU CAN'T STAND THE WHEAT, GET OUT OF THE KITCHEN

Foods that increase blood glucose to a greater degree therefore trigger VLDL production by the liver. Greater VLDL availability, through interaction with LDL particles, favors formation of small

LDL particles that linger for longer periods of time in the bloodstream. High blood glucose encourages glycation of LDL particles, particularly those that are already oxidized.

LDL particle longevity, oxidation, glycation . . . it all adds up to heightened potential to trigger the formation and growth of atherosclerotic plaque in arteries. Who's the head honcho, the top dog, the master at creating VLDL, small LDL, and glycation? Wheat, of course.

There's a silver lining to this dark wheat cloud: If wheat consumption causes marked increase in small LDL and all its associated phenomena, then elimination of wheat should reverse it. Indeed, that is what happens.

Dramatic reductions in small LDL particles can be accomplished by eliminating wheat products, provided your diet is otherwise healthy and you don't replace lost wheat calories with other foods that contain sugar or readily convert to sugar on consumption.

Think of it this way: Anything that provokes an increase in blood sugar will also, in parallel, provoke small LDL particles. Anything that keeps blood sugar from increasing, such as proteins, fats, and reduction in carbohydrates such as wheat, reduces small LDL particles.

Note that the insight gained by looking at LDL particles, rather than LDL cholesterol, leads us to conclusions about diet that are in stark contrast to the conventional advice for heart health. In effect, the popular fiction of calculated LDL cholesterol has perpetuated another fiction, that of the health benefits of reducing fat and increasing consumption of "healthy whole grains." All the while, when viewed from the deeper insights gained from techniques such as lipoprotein analysis, we see that this advice achieved the *opposite* of what it intended.

The China Study: A Love Story

The China Study is a twenty-year effort conducted by Cornell University's Dr. Colin Campbell to study the eating habits and health of the Chinese people. Dr. Campbell argues that the data show that "People who ate the most animal-based foods got the most chronic disease . . . People who ate the most plant-based foods were the healthiest and tended to avoid chronic disease." The China Study findings have been held up as evidence that all animal products exert adverse health effects and that the human diet should be plant-based. To Dr. Campbell's credit, the data were made available to anyone interested in reviewing them in his 894-page book, *Diet, Life-Style, and Mortality in China* (1990).

One person with a deep fascination with health and numbers took him up on his offer and, over months of data crunching, performed an extensive reanalysis. Denise Minger, a twenty-three-year-old raw food advocate and former vegan, dove into Campbell's data, hoping to understand the raw findings, and made her analyses public in a blog she started in January 2010.

Then the fireworks began.

After months of reanalysis, Minger came to believe that Campbell's original conclusions were flawed and that many of the purported findings were due to selective interpretation of the data. But what was most astounding was what she uncovered about wheat. Let Ms. Minger tell the story in her own quite capable words.

When I first started analyzing the original China Study data, I had no intention of writing up an actual critique of Campbell's much-lauded book. I'm a data junkie. I mainly wanted to see for myself how closely Campbell's claims aligned with the data he drew from—if only to satisfy my own curiosity.

I was a vegetarian/vegan for over a decade and have nothing but respect for those who choose a plant-based diet, even though I am no longer vegan. My goal, with the China Study analysis and elsewhere, is to figure out the truth about nutrition and health without the interference of biases and dogma. I have no agenda to promote.

I propose that Campbell's hypothesis is not altogether wrong but, more accurately, incomplete. While he has skillfully identified the importance of whole, unprocessed foods in achieving and maintaining health, his focus on wedding animal products with disease has come at the expense of exploring—or even acknowledging—the presence of other diet-disease patterns that may be stronger, more relevant, and ultimately more imperative for public health and nutritional research.

Sins of Omission

Ms. Minger below refers to values called correlation coefficients, symbol r. An r of 0 means two variables share no relationship whatsoever and any apparent association is purely random, while an r of 1.00 means that two variables coincide perfectly, like white on rice. A negative r means two variables behave in opposite directions, like you and your ex-spouse. She continues:

> Perhaps more troubling than the distorted facts in the China Study are the details Campbell leaves out. Why does Campbell indict animal foods in cardiovascular disease (correlation of 0.01 for animal protein and −0.11 for fish protein), yet fail to mention that wheat flour has a

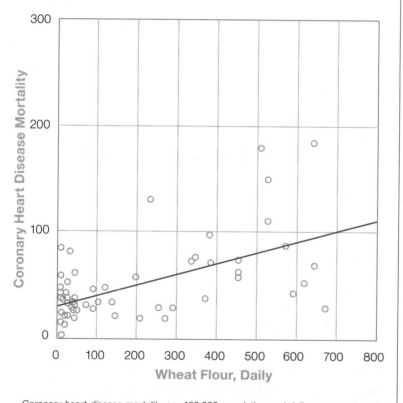

Coronary heart disease mortality per 100,000 population and daily consumption of wheat flour, grams per day. This reflects some of the earlier data from the China Study, demonstrating a linear relationship between wheat flour consumption and coronary heart disease mortality: The greater the wheat flour consumption, the more likely chance of death from heart disease. Source: Denise Minger, rawfoodsos.com

(continued on page 166)

The China Study: A Love Story (cont.)

correlation of 0.67 with heart attacks and coronary heart disease, and plant protein correlates at 0.25 with these conditions?

Why doesn't Campbell also note the astronomical correlations wheat flour has with various diseases: 0.46 with cervical cancer, 0.54 with hypertensive heart disease, 0.47 with stroke, 0.41 with diseases of the blood and blood-forming organs, and the aforementioned 0.67 with myocardial infarction and coronary heart disease? Could the "Grand Prix of epidemiology" have accidentally uncovered a link between the Western world's leading cause of death and its favorite glutenous grain? Is the "staff of life" really the staff of death?

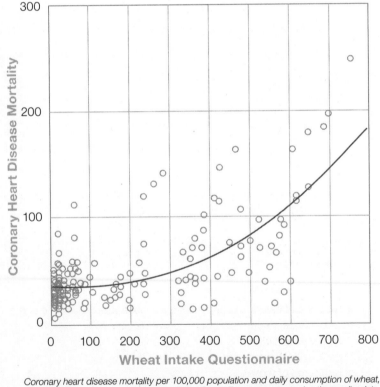

Coronary heart disease mortality per 100,000 population and daily consumption of wheat, grams per day, from later data from the China Study. Even more concerning than earlier data, these data suggest that increasing wheat intake leads to increased death from coronary heart disease, with an especially sharp increase in mortality at an intake of more than 400 grams (just under 1 pound) per day. Source: Denise Minger, rawfoodsos.com

When we pluck out the wheat variable from the 1989 China Study II questionnaire (which has more recorded data) and consider potential nonlinearity, the outcome is even creepier.

Wheat is the strongest positive predictor of body weight (in kilograms; r = 0.65, p<0.001) out of any diet variable. And it's not just

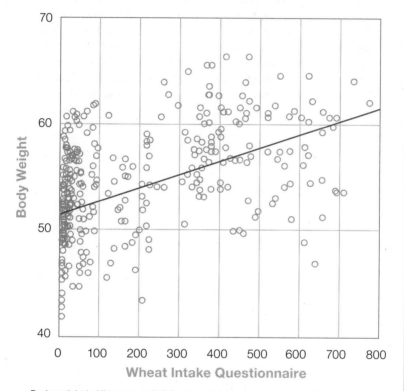

Body weight in kilograms and daily wheat intake, grams per day. The more wheat consumed, the higher the body weight. Source: Denise Minger, rawfoodsos.com

because wheat eaters are taller, either, because wheat consumption also strongly correlates with body mass index (r = 0.58, p<0.001):

What's the only thing heart disease–prone regions have in common with Westernized nations? That's right: consumption of high amounts of wheat flour.

The full impressive text of Ms. Minger's ongoing ideas can be found in her blog, Raw Food SOS, at http://rawfoodsos.com.

(continued on page 168)

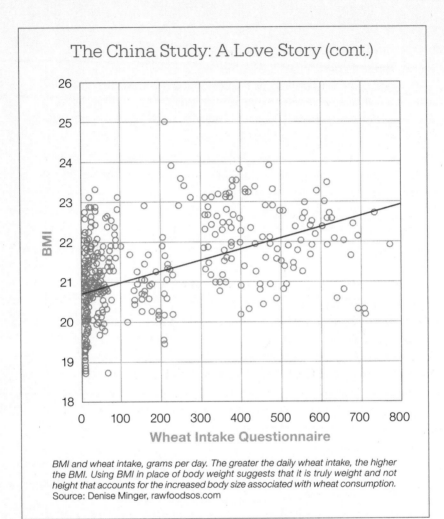

BMI and wheat intake, grams per day. The greater the daily wheat intake, the higher the BMI. Using BMI in place of body weight suggests that it is truly weight and not height that accounts for the increased body size associated with wheat consumption.
Source: Denise Minger, rawfoodsos.com

CHAPTER 11

IT'S ALL IN YOUR HEAD: WHEAT AND THE BRAIN

OKAY. SO WHEAT MESSES WITH your bowels, amps up your appetite, and makes you the brunt of beer belly jokes. But is it really that bad?

Wheat's effects reach the brain in the form of opiate-like peptides. But the polypeptide exorphins responsible for these effects come and go, dissipating over time. Exorphins cause your brain to instruct you to eat more food, increase calorie consumption, and desperately scratch at the stale crackers at the bottom of the box when there's nothing else left.

But all these effects are reversible. Stop eating wheat, the effect goes away, the brain recovers, and you're again ready to help your teenager tackle quadratic equations.

But wheat's effects on the brain don't end there. Among the most disturbing of wheat's effects are those exerted on brain tissue itself—not "just" on thoughts and behavior, but on the cerebrum, cerebellum, and other nervous system structures, with consequences ranging from incoordination to incontinence, from seizures to dementia. And, unlike addictive phenomena, these are *not* entirely reversible.

WATCH WHERE YOU STEP: WHEAT AND CEREBELLAR HEALTH

Imagine I was to blindfold you and set you loose in an unfamiliar room full of odd angles, nooks and crannies, and randomly placed objects to stumble over. Within a few steps you're likely to find yourself face-first in the shoe rack. Such are the struggles of someone with a condition known as cerebellar ataxia. But these people struggle with eyes wide open.

These are the people you often see using canes and walkers, or stumbling over a crack in the sidewalk that results in a fractured leg or hip. Something has impaired their ability to navigate the world, causing them to lose control over balance and coordination, functions centered in a region of the brain called the cerebellum.

The majority of people with cerebellar ataxia consult with a neurologist, often to have their condition deemed idiopathic, without known cause. No treatment is prescribed, nor has a treatment been developed. The neurologist simply suggests a walker, advises removing potential stumbling hazards in the home, and discusses adult diapers for the urinary incontinence that will eventually develop. Cerebellar ataxia is progressive, getting worse with each passing year until the sufferer is unable to comb his hair, brush his teeth, or go to the bathroom alone. Even the most basic self-care activities will eventually need to be performed by someone else. At this point, the end is near, as such extreme debilitation hastens complications such as pneumonia and infected bedsores.

Between 10 and 22.5 percent of people with celiac disease have nervous system involvement.[1,2] Of all forms of ataxia that are diagnosed, 20 percent have abnormal blood markers for gluten. Of people with unexplained ataxia—i.e., no other cause can be identified—abnormal blood markers for gluten are measured in 50 percent of the afflicted.[3]

Problem: The majority of people with ataxia triggered by wheat gluten have no signs or symptoms of intestinal disease, no celiac-like warnings to send the signal that gluten sensitivity is at work.

The destructive immune response responsible for the diarrhea and abdominal cramps of celiac disease can also be directed against brain tissue. While the gluten-brain connection underlying neurological impairment was suspected as long ago as 1966, it was thought to be due to the nutritional deficiencies accompanying celiac disease.[4] More recently, it has become clear that brain and nervous system involvement results from a direct immune attack on nerve cells. The antigliadin antibodies triggered by gluten can bind to Purkinje cells of the brain, cells unique to the cerebellum.[5] Brain tissue such as Purkinje cells do not have the capacity to regenerate: Once damaged, cerebellar Purkinje cells are gone . . . forever.

In addition to loss of balance and coordination, wheat-induced cerebellar ataxia can show such odd phenomena as, in the arcane language of neurology, nystagmus (lateral involuntary twitching of the eyeballs), myoclonus (involuntary muscle twitching), and chorea (chaotic involuntary jerking motions of the limbs). One study of 104 people with cerebellar ataxia also revealed impaired memory and verbal abilities, suggesting that wheat-induced destruction may involve cerebral tissue, the seat of higher thought and memory.[6]

The typical age of onset of symptoms of wheat-induced cerebellar ataxia is forty-eight to fifty-three. On MRI of the brain, 60 percent show atrophy of the cerebellum, reflecting the irreversible destruction of Purkinje cells.[7]

Only limited recovery of neurological function occurs with wheat gluten elimination due to the poor capacity of brain tissue to regenerate. Most people simply stop getting worse once the flow of gluten stops.[8]

The first hurdle in diagnosing ataxia that develops from wheat exposure is to have a physician who even considers the diagnosis in the first place. This can be the toughest hurdle of all, since much of the medical community continues to embrace the notion that wheat is good for you. Once considered, however, the diagnosis is a bit trickier than just diagnosing intestinal celiac disease, especially since some antibodies (the IgA form specifically) are not involved in wheat-induced brain disease. Add to this the little problem that a brain biopsy is objectionable to most people, and it takes a well-informed neurologist to make the diagnosis. The diagnosis may rest on a combination of suspicion and positive HLA DQ markers, along with observation of improvement or stabilization with wheat and gluten elimination.[9]

The painful reality of cerebellar ataxia is that, in the great

From a Cane to the Treadmill

When I first met Meredith, she was sobbing. She'd come to me because of a minor heart question (an EKG variant that proved benign).

"Everything hurts! My feet especially," she said. "They've treated me with all kinds of drugs. I hate them because I've had lots of side effects. The one I just started two months ago makes me so hungry that I can't stop eating. I've gained fifteen pounds!"

Meredith described how, in her work as a schoolteacher, she was barely able to stand in front of her class any longer because of the pain in her feet. More recently, she had also started to doubt her ability to walk, since she was also starting to feel unsteady and uncoordinated. Just getting dressed in the morning was taking longer and longer due to both the pain as well as the increasing clumsiness that impaired such simple activities as putting on a pair of pants. Although only fifty-six years old, she was forced to use a cane.

I asked her if her neurologist had any explanations for her disability. "None. They all say there's no good reason. I've just got to live with it. They can give me medicines to help with the pain, but it's probably going to get worse." That's when she broke down and started crying again.

I suspected there was a wheat issue just by looking at Meredith.

majority of cases, you won't know you have it until you start tripping over your own feet, drifting into walls, or wetting your pants. Once it shows itself, your cerebellum likely is already shrunken and damaged. Halting all wheat and gluten ingestion at this point is only likely to keep you out of the assisted living facility.

All of this due to the muffins and bagels you so crave.

FROM YOUR HEAD DOWN TO YOUR TOES: WHEAT AND PERIPHERAL NEUROPATHY

While cerebellar ataxia is due to wheat-triggered immune reactions on the brain, a parallel condition occurs in the nerves of the

Beyond the obvious difficulty she had walking into the room, her face was puffy and red. She described her struggles with acid reflux and the abdominal cramping and bloating diagnosed as irritable bowel syndrome. She was about sixty pounds overweight and had a modest quantity of edema (water retention) in her calves and ankles.

So I asked Meredith to venture down the wheat-free path. By this time, she was so desperate for any helpful advice that she agreed to try. I also took the gamble of scheduling her for a stress test that would require her to walk at a moderate speed up an incline on a treadmill.

Meredith returned two weeks later. I asked her if she thought she could manage the treadmill. "No problem! I stopped all wheat immediately after I talked to you. It took about a week, but the pain started to go away. Right now I have about ninety percent less pain than I had a couple of weeks ago. I'd say it's nearly gone. I've already stopped one of the medicines for the pain and I think I'll stop the other later this week." She also clearly no longer needed her cane.

She related how her acid reflux and irritable bowel symptoms had also disappeared completely. And she'd lost nine pounds in the two-week period.

Meredith tackled the treadmill without difficulty, handily managing the 3.6-miles-per-hour, 14 percent grade.

legs, pelvis, and other organs. It is called peripheral neuropathy.

A common cause of peripheral neuropathy is diabetes. High blood sugars occurring repeatedly over several years damage the nerves in the legs, causing reduced sensation (thus allowing a diabetic to step on a thumbtack without knowing it), diminished control over blood pressure and heart rate, and sluggish emptying of the stomach (diabetic gastroparesis), among other manifestations of a nervous system gone haywire.

A similar degree of nervous system chaos occurs with wheat exposure. The average age of onset of gluten-induced peripheral neuropathy is fifty-five. As with cerebellar ataxia, the majority of sufferers do not have intestinal symptoms that suggest celiac disease.[10]

Unlike cerebellar Purkinje cells' inability to regenerate, peripheral nerves have limited capacity to undergo repair once the offending wheat and gluten are removed, with the majority of people experiencing at least partial reversal of their neuropathy. In one study of thirty-five gluten-sensitive patients with peripheral neuropathy who were positive for the antigliadin antibody, the twenty-five participants on a wheat- and gluten-free diet improved over one year, while the ten control participants who did not remove wheat and gluten deteriorated.[11] Formal studies of nerve conduction were also performed, demonstrating improved nerve conduction in the wheat- and gluten-free group, and deterioration in the wheat- and gluten-consuming group.

Because the human nervous system is a complex web of nerve cells and networks, peripheral neuropathy triggered by wheat gluten exposure can show itself in a variety of ways, depending on what collection of nerves are affected. Loss of sensation to both legs along with poor leg muscle control is the most common, called sensorimotor axonal peripheral neuropathy. Less commonly, only one side of the body may be affected (asymmetrical neuropathy); or the autonomic nervous system, the part of the nervous system responsible for automatic functions such as blood pressure, heart rate, and bowel and bladder control, can be affected.[12] If the autonomic nervous system is affected, such phenomena as losing consciousness or becoming light-headed while standing up due to poor blood pressure control, inability to empty the bladder or bowels, and inappropriately rapid heart rate can result.

Peripheral neuropathy, regardless of how it is expressed, is progressive and will get worse and worse unless all wheat and gluten are removed.

WHOLE GRAIN BRAIN

I think that we can all agree: "Higher" brain functions, such as thinking, learning, and memory, should be off-limits to intruders. Our minds are deeply personal, representing the summation of everything that is you and your experiences. Who wants nosy neighbors or marketing pitchmen to gain access to the private domain of the mind? While the notion of telepathy is fascinating to think about, it's also really creepy to think that someone could read your thoughts.

For wheat, *nothing* is sacred. Not your cerebellum, not your cerebral cortex. While it can't read your mind, it sure can influence what goes on inside it.

The effect of wheat on the brain is more than just influence over mood, energy, and sleep. Actual brain *damage* is possible, as seen in cerebellar ataxia. But the cerebral cortex, the center of memory and higher thinking, the storehouse of you and your unique personality and memories, the brain's "gray matter," can also be pulled into the immune battle with wheat, resulting in encephalopathy, or brain disease.

Gluten encephalopathy shows itself as migraine headaches and stroke-like symptoms, such as loss of control over one arm or leg, difficulty speaking, or visual difficulties.[13,14] On MRI of the brain, there is characteristic evidence of damage surrounding blood vessels in cerebral tissue. Gluten encephalopathy will also show many of the same balance and coordination symptoms as those that occur with cerebellar ataxia.

In one particularly disturbing Mayo Clinic study of thirteen patients with the recent diagnosis of celiac disease, dementia was also diagnosed. Of those thirteen, frontal lobe biopsy (yes, brain biopsy) or postmortem examination of the brain failed to identify any other pathology beyond that associated with wheat gluten exposure.[15] Prior to death or biopsy, the most common symptoms were memory loss, the inability to perform simple arithmetic, confusion, and change in personality. Of the thirteen, nine died due to progressive impairment of brain function. Yes: fatal dementia from wheat.

In what percentage of dementia sufferers can their deteriorating mind and memory be blamed on wheat? This question has not yet been satisfactorily answered. However, one British research group that has actively investigated this question has, to date, diagnosed sixty-one cases of encephalopathy, including dementia, due to wheat gluten.[16]

Wheat is therefore associated with dementia and brain dysfunction, triggering an immune response that infiltrates memory and mind. The research into the relationship of wheat, gluten, and brain damage is still preliminary, with many unanswered questions remaining, but what we do know is deeply troubling. I shudder to think what we might find next.

Gluten sensitivity can also show itself as seizures. The seizures that arise in response to wheat tend to occur in young people, often teenagers. The seizures are typically of the temporal lobe variety—i.e., originating in the temporal lobe of the brain, just beneath the ears. People with temporal lobe seizures experience hallucinations of smell and taste, odd and inappropriate emotional feelings such as overwhelming fear for no cause, and repetitive behaviors such as smacking the lips or hand movements. A peculiar syndrome of temporal lobe seizures unresponsive to seizure medications and triggered by calcium deposition in a part of the temporal lobe called the hippocampus (responsible for forming new memories) has been associated with both celiac disease and gluten sensitivity (positive antigliadin antibodies and HLA markers without intestinal disease).[17]

Of celiac sufferers, from 1 to 5.5 percent can be expected to be diagnosed with seizures.[18,19] Temporal lobe seizures triggered by wheat gluten are improved after gluten elimination.[20,21] One study

Wheat Free and Free from ADHD

Ed had a unique heart problem that a cadre of doctors could not figure out how to solve. (Like many other heart patients, he was on the frustrating nutrition information roller coaster: One doctor told him to lay off alcohol, while another suggested he drink to raise his HDL levels.)

So Ed started shopping around for ideas himself. He came across my website and saw that I recommended a wheat-free diet for heart health, and also made mention of its effect on some people's thyroid problems and blood sugars. Ed had also developed thyroid problems over the years, and figured it was a long shot. But he decided to try it.

First off, he lost seven pounds in just ten days of going wheat-free. But what really caught his attention was that he began to realize that his nearly lifelong problems of ADHD and dyslexia were subsiding. "I could start reading stuff without having to read it over and over," Ed said. "I got calmer, my mind got more focused." Instead of having to read something five or six times, he could understand it after just one time. "That really surprised me," he said.

"My concentration continued to get better with each month," Ed says, adding that he really noticed a big change after four months. He said it was happening all along, but "you wake up one day and realize 'Wow, I haven't felt cloudy for a long time.'"

While going wheat free hasn't done much to help his initial heart problems, fifteen months into this wheat-free diet, Ed feels "better than ever." He admits he cheated a bit at first, and at a birthday party or other event would take a bite of cake but toss the rest. But soon enough, even that wasn't a problem. "I gradually felt better, so it was easier to go along with it," he said.

demonstrated that epileptics who experience the much more serious generalized (grand mal) seizures were twice as likely (19.6 percent compared to 10.6 percent) to have gluten sensitivity in the form of increased levels of antigliadin antibodies without celiac disease.[22]

It's a sobering thought that wheat has the capacity to reach into the human brain and cause changes in thought, behavior, and structure, occasionally to the point of provoking seizures.

IS IT WHEAT OR IS IT GLUTEN?

Gluten is the component of wheat confidently linked with triggering destructive immune phenomena, whether expressed as celiac disease, cerebellar ataxia, or dementia. However, many health effects of wheat, including those on the brain and nervous system, have *nothing* to do with immune phenomena triggered by gluten. The addictive properties of wheat, for instance, expressed as overwhelming temptation and obsession, obstructed by opiate-blocking drugs, are not directly due to gluten, but to exorphins, the breakdown product of gluten. While the component of wheat responsible for behavioral distortions in people with schizophrenia and children with autism and ADHD has not been identified, it is likely that these phenomena are also due to wheat exorphins and not a gluten-triggered immune response. Unlike gluten sensitivity, which can usually be diagnosed with the antibody tests, there is at present no marker that can be measured to assess exorphin effects.

Nongluten effects can *add* to gluten effects. The psychological influence of wheat exorphins on appetite and impulse, or the glucose-insulin effects, and perhaps other effects of wheat that have yet to be described, can occur independently or in combination with immune effects. Someone suffering with undiagnosed intestinal celiac disease can have odd cravings for the food that damages their small intestine, but also show diabetic blood sugars with wheat consumption, along with wide mood swings. Someone else without celiac disease can accumulate visceral fat and show neurological impairment from wheat. Others may become helplessly tired, overweight, and diabetic, yet suffer neither intestinal nor nervous system immune effects of wheat gluten. The tangle of health consequences of wheat consumption is truly impressive.

The tremendously varying way the neurological effects of wheat can be experienced complicates making the "diagnosis." Potential immune effects can be gauged with antibody blood tests. But nonimmune effects are not revealed by any blood test and are therefore more difficult to identify and quantify.

The world of the "wheat brain" has just started giving way to the light of day. The brighter the light shines, the uglier the situation gets.

CHAPTER 12

BAGEL FACE: WHEAT'S DESTRUCTIVE EFFECT ON THE SKIN

IF WHEAT AND its effects can grasp hold of organs such as the brain, intestines, arteries, and bones, can it also affect the largest organ of the body, the skin?

Indeed it can. And it can display its peculiar effects in more ways than Krispy Kreme has donuts.

Despite its outwardly quiet facade, skin is an active organ, a hotbed of physiologic activity, a waterproof barrier fending off the attacks of billions of foreign organisms, regulating body temperature through sweat, enduring bumps and scrapes every day, regenerating itself to repel the constant barrage. Skin is the physical barrier separating you from the rest of the world. Each person's skin provides a home to ten trillion bacteria, most of which assume residence in quiet symbiosis with their mammalian host.

Any dermatologist can tell you that skin is the outward reflection of internal body processes. A simple blush demonstrates this fact: the acute and intense facial vasodilatation (capillary dilation) that results when you realize the guy you flipped off in traffic was your boss. But the skin reflects more than our emotional states. It can also display evidence of internal physical processes.

Wheat can exert age-advancing skin effects, such as wrinkles and lost elasticity, through the formation of advanced glycation end products. But wheat has plenty more to say about your skin's health than just making you age faster.

Wheat expresses itself—actually, the body's *reaction* to wheat expresses itself—through the skin. Just as digestive by-products of wheat lead to joint inflammation, increased blood sugar, and brain effects, so too can they result in reactions in the skin, effects that range from petty annoyances to life-threatening ulcers and gangrene.

Skin changes do not generally occur in isolation: If an abnormality due to wheat is expressed on the skin surface, then it usually means that the skin is not the only organ experiencing an unwanted response. Other organs may be involved, from intestines to brain—though you may not be aware of it.

YO, PIMPLE FACE

Acne: the common affliction of adolescents and young adults, responsible for more distress than prom night.

Nineteenth-century doctors called it "stone-pock," while ancient physicians often made issue of the rash-like appearance minus the itching. The condition has been attributed to everything from emotional struggles, especially those involving shame or guilt, to deviant sexual behavior. Treatments were often dreadful, including powerful laxatives and enemas, foul-smelling sulfur baths, and prolonged exposure to X-ray.

Aren't the teenage years already tough enough?

As if teenagers need any more reason to feel awkward, acne visits the twelve- to eighteen-year-old set with uncommon frequency.

It is, along with the onslaught of bewildering hormonal effects, a nearly universal phenomenon in Western cultures, affecting more than 80 percent of teenagers, up to 95 percent of sixteen- to eighteen-year-olds, sometimes to disfiguring degrees. Adults are not spared, with 50 percent of those over age twenty-five having intermittent bouts.[1]

While acne may be nearly universal in American teenagers, it is not a universal phenomenon in all cultures. Some cultures display no acne whatsoever. Cultures as wide ranging as the Kitavan Islanders of Papua New Guinea, the Aché hunter-gatherers of Paraguay, natives of the Purus Valley in Brazil, African Bantus and Zulus, Japan's Okinawans, and Canadian Inuit are curiously spared the nuisance and embarrassment of acne.

Are these cultures spared the heartbreak of acne because of unique genetic immunity?

Evidence suggests that it is not a genetic issue, but one of diet. Cultures that rely only on foods provided by their unique location and climate allow us to observe the effects of foods added or subtracted to the diet. Acne-free populations such as the Kitavans of New Guinea exist on a hunter-gatherer diet of vegetables, fruits, tubers, coconuts, and fish. The Paraguayan Aché hunter-gatherers follow a similar diet, along with adding land animals and cultivated manioc, peanuts, rice, and maize, and are also spared completely from acne.[2] Japanese Okinawans, probably the most long-lived group on planet earth, until the 1980s consumed a diet rich in an incredible array of vegetables, sweet potatoes, soy, pork, and fish; acne was virtually unknown among them.[3] The traditional Inuit diet, consisting of seal, fish, caribou, and whatever seaweed, berries, and roots that are found, likewise leaves Inuits acne-free. The diets of African Bantus and Zulus differ according to season and terrain, but are rich in indigenous wild plants such as guava, mangoes, and tomatoes, in addition to the fish and wild game they catch; once again, no acne.[4]

In other words, cultures without acne consume little to no wheat, sugar, or dairy products. As Western influence introduced processed starches such as wheat and sugars into groups such as the Okinawans, Inuits, and Zulus, acne promptly followed.[5-7] In other words, acne-free cultures had no special genetic protection from acne, but simply followed a diet that lacked the foods that provoke the condition. Introduce wheat, sugar, and dairy products, and Clearasil sales skyrocket.

Ironically, it was "common knowledge" in the early twentieth century that acne was caused or worsened by eating starchy foods such as pancakes and biscuits. This notion fell out of favor in the eighties after a single wrongheaded study that compared the effects of a chocolate bar versus a "placebo" candy bar. The study concluded that there was no difference in acne observed among the sixty-five participants regardless of which bar they consumed— except that the placebo bar was virtually the same as the chocolate bar in calories, sugar, and fat content, just minus the cocoa.[8] (Cocoa lovers have cause to rejoice: Cocoa does *not* cause acne. Enjoy your 85 percent cocoa dark chocolate.) This didn't stop the dermatologic community, however, from pooh-poohing the relationship of acne and diet for many years, largely based on this single study that was cited repeatedly.

In fact, modern dermatology largely claims ignorance on just why so many modern teenagers and adults experience this chronic, sometimes disfiguring, condition. Though discussions center around infection with *Propionibacterium acnes*, inflammation, and excessive sebum production, treatments are aimed at suppressing acne eruption, not in identifying causes. So dermatologists are quick to prescribe topical antibacterial creams and ointments, oral antibiotics, and anti-inflammatory drugs.

More recently, studies have once again pointed at carbohydrates as the trigger of acne formation, working their acne-promoting effects via increased levels of insulin.

The means by which insulin triggers acne formation is beginning to yield to the light of day. Insulin stimulates the release of a hormone called insulin-like growth factor-I, or IGF-I, within the skin. IGF-1, in turn, stimulates tissue growth in hair follicles and in the dermis, the layer of skin just beneath the surface.[9] Insulin and IGF-1 also stimulate the production of sebum, the oily protective film produced by the sebaceous glands.[10] Overproduction of sebum, along with skin tissue growth, leads to the characteristic upward-growing reddened pimple.

Indirect evidence for insulin's role in causing acne also comes from other experiences. Women with polycystic ovarian syndrome (PCOS), who demonstrate exaggerated insulin responses and higher blood sugars, are strikingly prone to acne.[11] Medications that reduce insulin and glucose in women with PCOS, such as the drug metformin, reduce acne.[12] While oral diabetes medications are usually not administered to children, it has been observed that young people who take oral diabetes medications that reduce blood sugar and insulin do experience less acne.[13]

Insulin levels are highest after carbohydrates are consumed; the higher the glycemic index of the consumed carbohydrate, the more insulin is released by the pancreas. Of course, wheat, with its uncommonly high glycemic index, triggers higher blood sugar than nearly all other foods, thereby triggering insulin more than nearly all other foods. It should come as no surprise that wheat, especially in the form of sugary donuts and cookies—i.e., high–glycemic index wheat with high–glycemic index sucrose—causes acne. But it's also true of your multigrain bread cleverly disguised as healthy.

Also in line with insulin's ability to provoke acne formation is the role of dairy. While most health authorities obsess over the fat content of dairy and recommend low-fat or skim products, acne is not caused by the fat. The unique proteins in bovine products are the culprit that trigger insulin out of proportion to the sugar content, a unique insulinotropic property that explains the 20 percent increase in severe acne in teenagers consuming milk.[14,15]

Overweight and obese teenagers generally get that way not through overconsumption of spinach or green peppers, nor of salmon or tilapia, but of carbohydrate foods such as breakfast cereals. Overweight and obese teenagers accordingly should have more acne than slender teenagers, and that is indeed the case: The heavier the child, the more likely he or she is to have acne.[16] (It does not mean that slender kids can't have acne, but that statistical likelihood of acne increases with body weight.)

As we would expect from this line of reasoning, nutritional efforts that reduce insulin and blood sugar should reduce acne. A recent study compared a high–glycemic index diet to a low–glycemic index diet consumed by college students over twelve weeks. The low-GI diet yielded 23.5 percent less acne lesions, compared to a 12 percent reduction in the control group.[17] Participants who cut their carbohydrate intake the most enjoyed nearly a 50 percent reduction in the number of acne lesions.

In short, foods that increase blood sugar and insulin trigger the formation of acne. Wheat increases blood sugar, and thereby insulin, more than nearly all other foods. The whole grain bread you feed your teenager in the name of health actually worsens the problem. Though not life-threatening in and of itself, acne can nonetheless lead the sufferer to resort to all manner of treatments, some potentially toxic such as isotretinoin, which impairs night vision, can modify thoughts and behavior, and causes grotesque congenital malformations in developing fetuses.

Alternatively, elimination of wheat reduces acne. By also eliminating dairy and other processed carbohydrates such as chips, tacos, and tortillas, you'll largely disable the insulin machinery that triggers acne formation. If there's such a thing in this world, you might even have a grateful teenager on your hands.

WANNA SEE MY RASH?

Dermatitis herpetiformis (DH), described as skin inflammation in the form of herpes, is yet another way that an immune reaction to wheat gluten can show itself outside of the intestinal tract. It is an itchy, herpes-like (meaning similar-looking bumps; it has nothing to do with the herpes virus) rash that persists and can eventually leave discolored patches and scars. The most commonly affected areas are the elbows, knees, buttocks, scalp, and back, usually involving both sides of the body symmetrically. However, DH can also appear in less common ways, such as sores in the mouth, on the penis or vagina, or odd bruising over the palms.[18] A skin biopsy is often required to identify the characteristic inflammatory response.

Curiously, most DH sufferers do not experience intestinal symptoms of celiac disease, but most still show intestinal inflammation and destruction characteristic of celiac. People with DH are therefore subject to all the potential complications shared by people with typical celiac disease if they continue to consume wheat gluten, including intestinal lymphoma, autoimmune inflammatory diseases, and diabetes.[19]

Obviously, the treatment for DH is strict elimination of wheat and other gluten sources. The rash can improve within days in some people, while in others it dissipates gradually over months. Particularly bothersome cases, or DH that recurs because of continued wheat gluten consumption (sadly, very common), can be treated with the drug dapsone, which is taken orally. Also used to treat leprosy, this is a potentially toxic drug marked by side effects such as headache, weakness, liver damage, and occasionally seizures and coma.

Okay, so we consume wheat and develop itchy, annoying, disfiguring rashes as a result. We then apply a potentially toxic drug to allow us to continue to consume wheat, but expose ourselves to very high risk for intestinal cancers and autoimmune diseases. Does this really make sense?

After acne, DH is the most common skin manifestation of a reaction to wheat gluten. But an incredible range of conditions beyond DH are also triggered by wheat gluten, some associated with increased levels of celiac antibodies, others not.[20] Most of these conditions can also be caused by other factors, such as drugs, viruses, or cancer. Wheat gluten, like drugs, viruses, and cancer, therefore shares the potential to cause any of these rashes.

Wheat gluten–related rashes and other skin manifestations include:

- **Oral ulcers**—Red inflamed tongue (glossitis), angular cheilitis (painful sores on the corner of the mouth), and mouth burning are common forms of oral rashes associated with wheat gluten.
- **Cutaneous vasculitis**—Raised, bruise-like skin lesions that have inflamed blood vessels identified by biopsy.
- **Acanthosis nigricans**—Black, velvety skin that usually grows on the back of the neck, but also on the armpits, elbows, and knees. Acanthosis nigricans is frighteningly common in children and adults prone to diabetes.[21]
- **Erythema nodosum**—Shiny red, hot, and painful one- to two-inch lesions that typically appear on the shins, but can occur just about anywhere else. Erythema nodosum represents inflammation of the fatty layer of the skin. They leave a brown, depressed scar on healing.
- **Psoriasis**—A reddened, scaly rash, usually over the elbows, knees, and scalp, and occasionally the entire body. Improvement on a wheat- and gluten-free diet may require several months.
- **Vitiligo**—Common painless patches of nonpigmented (white) skin. Once established, vitiligo responds inconsistently to wheat gluten elimination.
- **Behçet's disease**—These ulcers of the mouth and genitalia generally afflict teenagers and young adults. Behçet's can also show itself in myriad other ways, such as psychosis due to brain involvement, incapacitating fatigue, and arthritis.
- **Dermatomyositis**—A red, swollen rash that occurs in combination with muscle weakness and blood vessel inflammation.

- **Icthyosiform dermatoses**—An odd, scaly rash ("ichthyo-siform" means fish-like) that usually involves the mouth and tongue.
- **Pyoderma gangrenosum**—Horrific, disfiguring ulcers involving the face and limbs that are deeply scarring and can become chronic. Treatments include immune-suppressing agents such as steroids and cyclosporine. The condition can lead to gangrene, limb amputation, and death.

All of these conditions have been associated with wheat gluten exposure, and their improvement or cure observed with removal. For the majority of these conditions, the proportion due to wheat gluten versus other causes is not known, since wheat gluten is often not considered as a potential cause. In fact, most commonly a cause is not sought and treatment is instituted blindly in the form of steroid creams and other drugs.

Believe it or not, as frightening as the above list appears, it is only partial. There are quite a few more skin conditions associated with wheat gluten that are not listed here.

You can see that skin conditions triggered by wheat gluten range from simple nuisance to disfiguring disease. Outside of the relatively common mouth ulcers and acanthosis nigricans, most of these skin manifestations of wheat gluten exposure are uncommon. But in the aggregate, they add up to an impressive list of socially disruptive, emotionally difficult, and physically disfiguring conditions.

Are you getting the impression that humans and wheat gluten may be incompatible?

WHO NEEDS NAIR?

Compared to the great apes and other primates, modern *Homo sapiens* are relatively hairless. So we prize what little hair we have.

Seven-Year Itch

Kurt came to me because he was told he had high cholesterol. What his doctor labeled "high cholesterol" proved to be an excess of small LDL particles, low HDL cholesterol, and high triglycerides. Naturally, with this combined pattern, I advised Kurt to eliminate wheat forthwith.

He did so, losing eighteen pounds over three months, all from his belly. But the funny thing was what the diet change did to his rash.

Kurt told me that he'd had a reddish-brown rash over his right shoulder, spreading down to his elbow and upper back, that had plagued him for more than seven years. He'd consulted with three dermatologists, resulting in three biopsies, none of which led to a firm diagnosis. All three agreed, however, that Kurt "needed" a steroid cream to deal with the rash. Kurt followed their advice, since the rash was at times very itchy and the creams did provide at least temporary relief.

But four weeks into his new wheat-free diet, Kurt showed me his right arm and shoulder: completely rash-free.

Seven years, three biopsies, three misdiagnoses—and the solution was as simple as (eliminating) apple pie.

My dad used to urge me to eat hot chili peppers because "it will grow hair on your chest." What if Dad's advice was to avoid wheat instead because it made me *lose* the hair on top of my head? More so than cultivating a man-like "heavage," losing my hair would have captured my attention. Hot chili peppers really don't trigger hair growth on the chest or elsewhere, but wheat can indeed trigger hair loss.

Hair can be a very intimate thing for many people, a personal signature of appearance and personality. For some people, losing hair can be as devastating as losing an eye or a foot.

Hair loss is sometimes unavoidable, due to the effects of toxic drugs or dangerous diseases. People undergoing cancer chemotherapy, for instance, temporarily lose their hair, since the agents employed are designed to kill actively reproducing cancer cells, but inadvertently also kill active noncancerous cells, such as those in hair follicles. The inflammatory disease systemic lupus erythematosus, which commonly leads to kidney disease and arthritis, can also be accompanied by hair loss due to autoimmune inflammation of hair follicles.

Hair loss can occur in more ordinary situations, as well. Middle-aged men can lose their hair, followed soon after by an impulse to drive convertible sports cars.

Add wheat consumption to the list of causes of hair loss. "Alopecia areata" refers to hair loss that occurs in patches, usually from the scalp, but occasionally other parts of the body. Alopecia can even involve the entire body, leaving the sufferer completely hairless from head to toe and everything in between.

Wheat consumption causes alopecia areata due to a celiac-like inflammation of the skin. The inflamed hair follicle results in reduced hold on each individual hair, which causes shedding.[22] Within the tender spots of hair loss are increased levels of inflammatory mediators, such as tumor necrosis factor, interleukins, and interferons.[23]

When caused by wheat, alopecia can persist for as long as wheat consumption continues. Like completing a course of chemotherapy for cancer, elimination of wheat and all gluten sources usually results in prompt resumption of hair growth, no surgical hair plugs or topical creams required.

KISS MY SORE GOODBYE

In my experience, acne, mouth sores, a rash on the face or backside, hair loss, or nearly any other abnormality of the skin should prompt consideration of a reaction to wheat gluten. It may have less to do with hygiene, your parent's genes, or sharing towels with friends than with the turkey sandwich on whole wheat that was yesterday's lunch.

How many other foods have been associated with such a protean array of skin diseases? Sure, peanuts and shellfish can cause

The Case of the Bald Baker

I had a heck of a time persuading Gordon to drop the wheat.

I met Gordon because he had coronary disease. Among the causes: abundant small LDL particles. I asked him to completely remove the wheat from his diet in order to reduce or eliminate the small LDL particles and thereby obtain better control over his heart health.

Problem: Gordon owned a bakery. Bread, rolls, and muffins were part of his life every day, seven days a week. It was only natural that he would eat his products with most meals. For two years, I urged Gordon to drop the wheat—to no avail.

One day Gordon came to the office wearing a ski cap. He told me how he had started to lose clumps of hair, leaving divot-like bald patches scattered over his scalp. His primary care doctor diagnosed alopecia, but couldn't divine a cause. Likewise, a dermatologist was at a loss to explain Gordon's dilemma. The hair loss was very upsetting to him, resulting in his asking his primary care doctor for an antidepressant and concealing the embarrassing situation with a cap.

Wheat, of course, was my first thought. It fit Gordon's overall health picture: small LDL particles, wheat belly body configuration, high blood pressure, prediabetic blood sugars, vague stomach complaints, and now hair loss. I made yet another pitch for Gordon to once and for all remove the wheat from his diet. After the emotional trauma of losing most of his hair and now having to conceal his patchy scalp, he finally agreed. It meant bringing food to his bakery and not eating his own products, something he had some difficulty in explaining to his employees. Nonetheless, he stuck to it.

Within three weeks, Gordon reported that hair had begun to sprout up in the bald patches. Over the next two months, vigorous growth resumed. Along with his proud pate, he also lost twelve pounds and two inches from his waist. The intermittent abdominal distress was gone, as was his prediabetic blood sugar. Six months later, reassessment of his small LDL particles demonstrated 67 percent reduction.

Inconvenient? Perhaps. But it sure beats a toupee.

hives. But what other food can be blamed for such an incredible range of skin diseases, from a common rash all the way to gangrene, disfigurement, and death? I certainly don't know of any other than wheat.

PART THREE

SAY GOODBYE
TO WHEAT

CHAPTER 13

GOODBYE, WHEAT: CREATE A HEALTHY, DELICIOUS, WHEAT-FREE LIFE

HERE'S WHERE WE get down to the real, practical nitty-gritty: Like trying to rid your bathing suit of sand, it can be tough to remove this ubiquitous food from our eating habits, this thing that seems to cling to every nook, crack, and cranny of American diets.

My patients often panic when they realize how much of a transformation they will need to make in the contents of their cupboards and refrigerators, in their well-worn habits of shopping, cooking, and eating. "There's nothing left to eat! I'll starve!" Many also recognize that more than two hours without a wheat product triggers insatiable cravings and the anxiety of withdrawal. When Bob and Jillian patiently hold the hands of *Biggest Loser* contestants sobbing over the agony of losing only three pounds this week, you have an idea of what wheat elimination can be like for some people.

Trust me, it's worth it. If you've gotten this far, I assume that you are at least contemplating a divorce from this unfaithful and abusive partner. My advice: Show no mercy. Don't dwell on the good times from twenty years ago, when angel food cake and cinnamon rolls provided consolation after you were fired from your job, or the beautiful seven-layer cake you had at your wedding. Think of the health beatings you've taken, the emotional kicks in the stomach you've endured, the times he begged you to take him back because he has really changed.

Forget it. It won't happen. There is no rehabilitation, only elimination. Spare yourself the divorce court theatrics: Declare yourself free of wheat, don't ask for alimony or child support, don't look back or reminisce about the good times. Just *run*.

BRACE YOURSELF FOR HEALTH

Forget everything you've learned about "healthy whole grains." For years we've been told they should dominate our diet. This line of thinking says that a diet filled with "healthy whole grains" will make you vibrant, popular, good-looking, sexy, and successful. You will also enjoy healthy cholesterol levels and regular bowel movements. Stint on whole grains and you will be unhealthy, malnourished, succumb to heart disease or cancer. You'll be thrown out of your country club, barred from your bowling league, and ostracized from society.

Instead, remember that the need for "healthy whole grains" is pure fiction. Grains such as wheat are no more a necessary part of the human diet than personal injury attorneys are to your backyard pool party.

Let me describe a typical person with wheat deficiency: slender, flat tummy, low triglycerides, high HDL ("good") cholesterol, normal blood sugar, normal blood pressure, high energy, good sleep, normal bowel function.

In other words, the sign that you have the "wheat deficiency syndrome" is that you're normal, slender, and healthy.

Contrary to popular wisdom, including that of your friendly neighborhood dietitian, there is no deficiency that develops from elimination of wheat—provided the lost calories are replaced with the right foods.

If the gap left by wheat is filled with vegetables, nuts, meats, eggs, avocados, olives, cheese—i.e., *real* food—then not only won't you develop a dietary deficiency, you will enjoy better health, more energy, better sleep, weight loss, and reversal of all the abnormal phenomena we've discussed. If you fill the gap left by excising wheat products with corn chips, energy bars, and fruit drinks, then, yes, you will simply have replaced one undesirable group of foods with another undesirable group; you've achieved little. And you may indeed become deficient in several important nutrients, as well as continue in the unique American shared experience of getting fat and becoming diabetic.

So removing wheat is the first step. Finding suitable replacements to fill the smaller—remember, wheat-free people naturally and unconsciously consume 350 to 400 fewer calories per day—calorie gap is the second step.

In its simplest form, a diet in which you eliminate wheat but allow all other foods to expand proportionally to fill the gap, while not perfect, is still a far cry better than the same diet that includes wheat. In other words, remove wheat and just eat a little more of the foods remaining in your diet: Eat a larger portion of baked chicken, green beans, scrambled eggs, Cobb salad, etc. You may still realize many of the benefits discussed here. However, I'd be guilty of oversimplifying if I suggested that all it takes is removing wheat. If *ideal* health is your goal, then it does indeed matter what foods you choose to fill the gap left by eliminating wheat.

Should you choose to go further than just removing wheat, you must replace lost wheat calories with *real* food. I distinguish real food from highly processed, herbicided, genetically modified, ready-to-eat, high-fructose corn syrup–filled, just-add-water food products, the ones packaged with cartoon characters, sports figures, and other clever marketing ploys.

This is a battle that needs to be fought on all fronts, since there are incredible societal pressures to not eat real food. Turn on the TV and you won't see ads for cucumbers, artisanal cheeses, or locally raised cage-free eggs. You *will* be inundated with ads for potato chips, frozen dinners, soft drinks, and the rest of the cheap-ingredient, high-markup world of processed foods.

A great deal of money is spent pushing the products you need to avoid. Kellogg's, known to the public for its breakfast cereals ($6.5 billion in breakfast cereal sales in 2010), is also behind Yoplait yogurt, Häagen-Dazs ice cream, Lärabar health bars, Keebler Graham Crackers, Famous Amos chocolate chip cookies, Cheez-It crackers, as well as Cheerios and Apple Jacks. These foods fill supermarket aisles, are highlighted at aisle end caps, are strategically placed at eye level on the shelves, and dominate daytime and nighttime TV. They comprise the bulk of ads in many magazines. And Kellogg's is just one food company among many. Big Food also pays for much of the "research" conducted by dietitians and nutrition scientists, they endow faculty positions at universities and colleges, and they influence the content of media. In short, they are everywhere.

And they are extremely effective. The great majority of Americans have fallen for their marketing hook, line, and sinker. It's made even more difficult to ignore when the American Heart Association and other health organizations endorse their products. (The American Heart Association's heart-check mark stamp of approval, for instance, has been bestowed on more than 800 foods, including Honey Nut Cheerios and, until recently, Cocoa Puffs.)

And here you are trying to ignore them, tune them out, and march to your own drummer. It's not easy.

One thing is clear: *There is no nutritional deficiency that develops when you stop consuming wheat and other processed foods.* Furthermore, you will simultaneously experience reduced exposure to sucrose, high-fructose corn syrup, artificial food colorings and flavors, cornstarch, and the list of unpronounceables on the product label. Again, there is *no genuine nutritional deficiency* from any of this. But this hasn't stopped the food industry and its friends at the USDA, the American Heart Association, the American Dietetic Association, and the American Diabetes Association from suggesting that these foods are somehow necessary for health and that doing without them might be unhealthy. Nonsense. Absolute, unadulterated, 180-proof, whole grain nonsense.

Some people, for instance, are concerned that they will not consume sufficient fiber if they eliminate wheat. Ironically, if you replace wheat calories with those from vegetables and raw nuts, fiber intake goes *up*. If two slices of whole wheat bread containing 138 calories are replaced by a calorically equivalent handful of raw nuts such as almonds or walnuts (approximately 24 nuts), you will match or exceed the 3.9 grams of fiber from the bread. Likewise, a calorie-equivalent salad of mixed greens, carrots, and peppers will match or exceed the amount of fiber in the bread. This is, after all, how primitive hunter-gatherer cultures—the cultures that first taught us about the importance of dietary fiber—obtained their fiber: through plentiful consumption of plant foods, not bran cereals or other processed fiber sources. Fiber intake is therefore not a concern if wheat elimination is paired with increased consumption of healthy foods.

The dietary community assumes that you live on taco chips and jelly beans, and you therefore require foods "fortified" with various vitamins. However, all those assumptions fall apart if you don't exist on what you can obtain from a bag at the local convenience store but consume real foods instead. B vitamins, such as B_6, B_{12}, folic acid, and thiamine, are added to baked, processed wheat products; dietitians therefore warn us that forgoing these products will yield vitamin B deficiencies. Also untrue. B vitamins are present in more than ample quantities in meats, vegetables, and nuts. While bread and other wheat products are required by law to have added folic acid, you'll exceed the folic acid content of wheat products several times over just by eating a handful of sunflower seeds or asparagus. A quarter cup of spinach or four asparagus spears, for instance, matches the quantity of folic acid in most breakfast cereals. (Also, the *folates* of natural sources may be superior to the *folic acid* in fortified processed foods.) Nuts and green vegetables are, in general, exceptionally rich sources of folate and represent the way that humans were meant to obtain it. (Pregnant or lactating females are the exception and may still benefit from folic acid or folate supplementation to meet their increased needs in order to prevent neural tube defects.) Likewise, vitamin B_6 and thiamine are obtained in much greater amounts from 4 ounces of chicken or pork, an avocado, or ¼ cup of ground flaxseed than from an equivalent weight of wheat products.

In addition, eliminating wheat from your diet actually enhances B vitamin absorption. It is not uncommon, for instance, for vitamin B_{12} and folate, along with levels of iron, zinc, and magnesium, to increase with removal of wheat, since gastrointestinal health improves and, along with it, nutrient absorption.

Eliminating wheat may be inconvenient, but it is certainly not unhealthy.

SCHEDULE YOUR RADICAL WHEAT-ECTOMY

Thankfully, eliminating all wheat from your diet is not as bad as setting up mirrors and scalpels to remove your own appendix without anesthesia. For some people, it's a simple matter of passing up the bagel shop or turning down the sweet rolls. For others, it can be a distinctly unpleasant experience on par with a root canal or living with your in-laws for a month.

In my experience, the most effective and, ultimately, the easiest way to eliminate wheat is to do it abruptly and completely. The insulin-glucose roller coaster caused by wheat, along with brain-addictive exorphin effects, makes it difficult for some people to gradually reduce wheat, so abrupt cessation may be preferable. Abrupt and complete elimination of wheat will, in the susceptible, trigger the withdrawal phenomenon. But getting through the withdrawal that accompanies abrupt cessation may be easier than the gnawing fluctuations of cravings that usually accompany just cutting back—not much different from an alcoholic trying to go dry. Nonetheless, some people are more comfortable with gradual reduction rather than abrupt elimination (see my plan for that on page 206). Either way, the end result is the same.

By now, I'm confident you're attuned to the fact that wheat is not just about bread. Wheat is ubiquitous—it's in everything.

Many people, on first setting out to identify foods containing wheat, find it in nearly all the processed foods they have been eating, including the most improbable places such as canned "cream" soups and "healthy" frozen dinners. Wheat is there for two reasons: One, it tastes good. Two, it stimulates appetite. The latter reason is not for *your* benefit, of course, but for the benefit of food manufacturers. To food manufacturers, wheat is like nicotine in cigarettes: the best insurance they have to encourage continued consumption. (Incidentally, other common ingredients in processed foods that increase consumption, though not as potent as wheat's effect, include high-fructose corn syrup, sucrose, cornstarch, and salt. These are also worth avoiding.)

Removing wheat does, without question, require some forethought. Foods made with wheat have the inarguable advantage of convenience: Sandwiches and wraps, for example, are easily carried, stored, and eaten out of hand. Avoiding wheat means taking your own food to work and using a fork or spoon to eat it. It may mean you need to shop more often and—heaven forbid—cook. Greater dependence on vegetables and fresh fruit can also mean going to the store, farmers' market, or greengrocer a couple of times a week.

However, the inconvenience factor is far from insurmountable. It might mean a few minutes of advance preparation, such as cutting and wrapping a hunk of cheese and putting it in a baggie to bring along to work, along with several handfuls of raw almonds and vegetable soup in a container. It might mean setting aside some of your spinach salad from dinner to eat the following morning for breakfast. (Yes: dinner for breakfast, a useful strategy to be discussed later.)

People who habitually consume wheat products become crabby, foggy, and tired after just a couple of hours of not having a wheat product, often desperately searching for any crumb or morsel to relieve the pain, a phenomenon I've watched with dry amusement from my comfortable wheat-free vantage point. But once you've eliminated wheat from your diet, appetite is no longer driven by the glucose-insulin roller coaster of satiety and hunger, and you won't need to get your next "fix" of brain-active exorphins. After a 7:00 a.m. breakfast of two scrambled eggs with vegetables, peppers, and olive oil, for instance, you likely won't be hungry until noon or 1:00 p.m. Compare this to the 90- to 120-minute cycle of insatiable hunger most people experience after a 7:00 a.m. bowl of high-fiber breakfast cereal, necessitating a 9 o'clock snack and another 11 o'clock snack or early lunch. You can see how easy it becomes to cut the 350 to 400 calories per day from your overall consumption that results naturally and unconsciously from wheat elimination. You will also avoid the afternoon slump that many people experience at about 2:00 or 3:00 p.m., the sleepy, sluggish fog that follows a lunch of a sandwich on whole wheat bread, the mental shutdown that occurs because of the glucose high followed by the low. A lunch, for instance, of tuna (without bread) mixed with mayonnaise or olive oil–based dressing, along with zucchini slices and a handful (or several handfuls) of walnuts will not trigger the glucose-insulin high-low at all, just a seamless normal blood sugar that has no sleep- or fog-provoking effect.

Fasting: Easier Than You Think

Fasting can be one of the most powerful tools for regaining health: weight loss, reduction in blood pressure, improved insulin responses, longevity, as well as improvement in numerous health conditions.[1] Though fasting is often regarded as a religious practice (e.g., Ramadan in Islam; Nativity fast, Lent, and Assumption fast in the Greek Orthodox Christian church), it is among the most underappreciated strategies for health.

For the average person eating a typical American diet that includes wheat, however, fasting can be a painful ordeal that requires monumental willpower. People who regularly consume wheat products are rarely able to fast successfully for more than a few hours, usually giving up in a frenzy of eating everything in sight.

Interestingly, elimination of wheat makes fasting far easier, nearly effortless.

Fasting means no food, just water (vigorous hydration is also key for safe fasting), for a period of anywhere from eighteen hours to several days. People who are wheat-free can fast for eighteen, twenty-four, thirty-six, seventy-two, or more hours with little or no discomfort. The ability to fast, of course, mimics the natural situation of a hunter-gatherer, who may go without food for days or even weeks when the hunt fails or some other natural obstacle to food availability develops.

The ability to fast comfortably is *natural;* the inability to go for more than a few hours before crazily seeking calories is *unnatural.*

Most people find it hard to believe that wheat elimination can in the long run make their lives easier, not tougher. Wheat-free people are freed from the desperate cyclic scramble for food every two hours and are comfortable going for extended periods without food. When they finally sit down to eat, they are contented with less. Life . . . simplified.

Many people are, in effect, enslaved by wheat and the schedules and habits dictated to them by its availability. A radical wheatectomy therefore amounts to more than just removing one component of the diet. It removes a potent stimulant of appetite from your life, one that rules behavior and impulse frequently and relentlessly. Removing wheat will set you free.

WHEATAHOLICS AND THE WHEAT
WITHDRAWAL SYNDROME

Approximately 30 percent of people who remove wheat products abruptly from their diet will experience a withdrawal effect. Unlike opiate or alcohol withdrawal, wheat withdrawal does not result in seizures or hallucinations, blackouts, or other dangerous phenomena.

The closest parallel to wheat withdrawal is the nicotine withdrawal that results from quitting cigarettes; for some people, the experience is nearly as intense. Like nicotine withdrawal, wheat withdrawal can cause fatigue, mental fogginess, and irritability. It can also be accompanied by a vague dysphoria, a feeling of low mood and sadness. Wheat withdrawal often has the unique effect of diminished capacity to exercise that usually lasts from two to five days. Wheat withdrawal tends to be short-lived; while ex-smokers are usually still climbing the walls after three to four weeks, most ex–wheat eaters feel better after one week. (The longest I've ever seen wheat withdrawal symptoms persist is four weeks, but that was unusual.)

The people who suffer through withdrawal are usually the same people who experienced incredible cravings for wheat products on their former diet. These are the people who habitually eat pretzels, crackers, and bread every day as a result of the powerful eating impulse triggered by wheat. Cravings recur in approximately two-hour cycles, reflecting the glucose-insulin fluctuations that result from wheat products. Missing a snack or meal causes these people distress: shakiness, nervousness, headache, fatigue, and intense cravings, all of which can persist for the duration of the withdrawal period.

What causes wheat withdrawal? It is likely that years of high-carbohydrate eating makes the metabolism reliant on a constant supply of readily absorbed sugars such as those in wheat. Removing sugar sources forces the body to adapt to mobilizing and burning fatty acids instead of more readily accessed sugars, a process that requires several days to kick in. However, this step is a necessary part of converting from fat *deposition* to fat *mobilization* and shrinking the visceral fat of the wheat belly. Wheat withdrawal shares physiologic effects with carbohydrate-restricted diets. (Atkins diet aficionados call it induction flu, the tired, achy feeling that develops with the no-carbohydrate induction phase of the program.) Depriving the brain of wheat gluten–derived exorphins also adds to the withdrawal effect, the phenomenon that is likely responsible for the wheat cravings and dysphoria.

There are two ways to soften the blow. One is to taper wheat gradually over a week, an approach that works for only some people. However, be warned: Some people are so addicted to wheat that they find even this tapering process to be overwhelming because of the repetitive reawakening of addictive phenomena with each bite of bagel or bun. For people with strong wheat addiction, going cold turkey (shall we call it cold noodle?) may be the only way to break the cycle. It's similar to alcoholism. If your friend drinks two fifths of bourbon a day and you urge him to cut back to two glasses a day, he would indeed be healthier and live longer—but it would be virtually impossible for him to do it.

Second, if you believe that you are among those who will experience withdrawal, choosing the right time to transition off wheat is important. Select a period of time when you don't need to be at your best—e.g., a week off from work or a long weekend. The mental fog and sluggishness experienced by some people can be significant, making prolonged concentration and work performance difficult. (You should certainly not expect any sympathy from your boss or coworkers, who will probably scoff at your explanation and say things like "Tom's afraid of the bagels!")

While wheat withdrawal can be annoying, and even cause you to snap at loved ones and coworkers, it is harmless. I have never seen any genuine adverse effects, nor have any ever been reported, beyond those described above. Passing up the toast and muffins is difficult for some, charged with lots of emotional overtones, with chronic cravings that can revisit you for months and years—but it is good for your health, not harmful.

Fortunately, not everyone experiences the full withdrawal syndrome. Some don't experience it at all, wondering what all the fuss is about. Some people can just quit smoking cold turkey and never look back. Same with wheat.

THE FOUR-WEEK TAPER PROGRAM

What if the prospect of wheat elimination just seems too overwhelming—too frightening, too much of a change in habits? Others try and are unable to deal with the degree of fatigue, mental "fog," and emotional disruption. If you find yourself unable to eliminate wheat from your life for one of the above reasons, then consider this gradual taper program.

Most people include wheat products in their diet for breakfast, lunch, dinner, and snacks. One way to gradually taper wheat is to follow a stepwise approach and choose one meal at a time and make it wheat-free. Much as people who struggle with alcohol follow a 12-step program to conquer their addiction, so can you use a step-by-step approach to undo the effects of this peculiar grain.

Week One: Snap Out of Wheat Snacks

Think about your snacking habits. Do you often reach for pretzels to feed the midday munchies? Granola bars, cookies, wheat crackers, cereal bars—all of these snack stalwarts are made with wheat. So for the first week, tackle these smaller meals first by replacing them with raw nuts, cheese, sliced veggies, or one of the *Lose the Wheat Belly, Lose the Weight!* wheat-free recipes like a slice of cheesecake, a piece of apple walnut "bread," or ginger spice cookies. This way you're making a difference, but not going right after a major meal.

Week Two: Dish Out Dinner

Now that you've adjusted to wheat-free snacking, go after a main meal that's probably easiest to break free of wheat: dinner. Sure, some people may be used to a nightly feast of pasta, rolls, pizza, and bread. But dinner is also a natural fit for lean meats, quality cheeses, and a plate full of delicious vegetables topped with flavorful oils, herbs, and spices.

Dinner is also the best meal to start with when it comes to battling withdrawal, since you'll already be home if you have any symptoms. If this disrupts your sleep or you find yourself waking up in the middle of the night with insatiable wheat cravings, consider doing something to enhance your sleep. For instance, consider taking melatonin, the over-the-counter sleep hormone, one hour before bedtime. Doses of 0.5 mg to 6 mg work well; individualize your dose to your desired level of sleep, i.e., if 1 mg fails to do the job, increase to 2 or 3 mg, etc. The over-the-counter antihistamine diphenhydramine (brand name Benadryl), 25 to 50 mg, can also be used either by itself or in combination with melatonin. The only side effects I see with melatonin are vivid, colorful dreams (the kind you had as a child) and a mild sleep "hangover" with diphenhydramine.

Week Three: Leave It Out of Lunch

Next, tackle lunch while still keeping snacks and dinner wheat-free. Replace the sandwich with a container of tuna mixed with mayonnaise, chopped onions, dill, and garlic powder. Again, salads, lean meat, and lettuce "wraps" all can fill the void. Avoid carbohydrates of any sort at lunch, wheat-containing or not, to avoid the afternoon "slump" many people get at about 3:00-4:00 p.m. Do this for a week while maintaining your wheat-free dinner.

Week Four: Ban It from Breakfast

Last, tackle the toughest meal of all: breakfast. Breakfast for many people has become a wheat-fest of breakfast cereal, waffles, or bagels that generate a powerful emotional attachment. It's also the meal that is most likely to trigger the most annoying withdrawal phenomena. But it's also the most crucial meal, the make-it-or-break-it step that will finally set you free. Replace your wheat-containing breakfast with an Egg and Pesto Breakfast Wrap,

olives, feta cheese, and olive oil, or two banana-blueberry muffins or a berry-coconut smoothie from the *Lose the Wheat, Lose the Weight!* recipes. Withdrawal will still be triggered, but it should be at a much more manageable level.

Remember: The *Lose the Wheat, Lose the Weight!* program I advocate is *not* calorie restricted, nor is it about feeling hungry and deprived. Eat as much as you want, but choose from a list of foods that do not include wheat products. Because you've removed a powerful appetite stimulant from your diet—wheat—calorie consumption drops, the urge to snack is reduced, nighttime binging is slashed, and weight drops, all while you are not bothering to count calories, fat grams, or deprive yourself.

NO GOING BACK

Yet another odd phenomenon: Once you have followed a wheat-free diet for a few months, you may find that reintroduction of wheat provokes undesirable effects ranging from joint aches to asthma to gastrointestinal distress. They can occur whether or not withdrawal happened in the first place. The most common reexposure "syndrome" consists of gas, bloating, cramps, and diarrhea that lasts for six to forty-eight hours. In fact, the gastrointestinal effects of reexposure to wheat in many ways resemble that of acute food poisoning, not unlike ingesting bad chicken or fecally contaminated sausage.

The next most common reexposure phenomenon is joint aches, a dull arthritis-like pain that usually affects multiple joints such as elbows, shoulders, and knees, and that can last up to several days. Others experience acute worsening of asthma sufficient to require inhalers for several days. Behavioral or mood effects are also common, ranging from low mood and fatigue to anxiety and rage (usually in males).

It's not clear why this happens, since no research has been

I Gained Thirty Pounds from One Cookie!

No, it's not a *National Enquirer* headline alongside "New York woman adopts alien!" For people who have walked away from wheat, it might actually be true.

In those susceptible to the addictive effects of wheat, all it takes is one cookie, cracker, or pretzel in a moment of indulgence. A bruschetta at the office party or a handful of pretzels at happy hour opens up the floodgates of impulse. Once you start, you can't stop: more cookies, more crackers, followed by shredded wheat for breakfast, sandwiches for lunch, more crackers for snacks, pasta and rolls for dinner, etc. Like any addict, you rationalize your behavior: "It can't really be all that bad. This recipe is from a magazine article on healthy eating." Or: "I'll be bad today, but I'll stop tomorrow." Before you know it, all the weight you lost is regained within weeks. I've seen people regain thirty, forty, even seventy pounds before they put a stop to it.

Sadly, those who suffered most severely from wheat withdrawal on removal are the same people who are prone to this effect. Unrestrained consumption can result even after the most minimal "harmless" indulgence. People who are not prone to this effect may be skeptical, but I've witnessed it in hundreds of patients. People who are susceptible to this effect know quite well what it means.

Short of taking opiate-blocking drugs such as naltrexone, there is no healthy and easy way to bypass this unpleasant but necessary stage. People prone to this phenomenon simply need to be vigilant and not let the little wheat devil standing on their shoulder whisper, "Go on! It's just one little cookie."

devoted to exploring it. My suspicion is that low-grade inflammation was likely present in various organs during wheat-consuming days. It heals after wheat removal and reignites with reexposure to wheat. I suspect that the behavioral and mood effects are due to exorphins, similar to what the schizophrenic patients experienced in the Philadelphia experiments.

The best way to avoid reexposure effects: Avoid wheat once you've eliminated it from your diet.

WHAT ABOUT OTHER CARBOHYDRATES?

After you've removed wheat from your diet, what's left?

Remove wheat and you've removed the most flagrant problem source in the diet of people who follow otherwise healthy diets. Wheat is really the worst of the worst in carbohydrates. But other carbohydrates can be problem sources as well, though on a lesser scale compared to wheat.

I believe that we've all survived a forty-year period of excessive carbohydrate consumption. Reveling in all the new processed food products that hit supermarket shelves from the seventies onward, we indulged in carbohydrate-rich breakfast foods, lunch, dinner, and snacks. As a result, for decades we've been exposed to wide fluctuations of blood sugar and glycation, increasingly severe resistance to insulin, growth of visceral fat, and inflammatory responses, all of which leads us to have tired, beaten pancreases that are unable to keep up with the demand to produce insulin. Continued carbohydrate challenges forced on flagging pancreatic function leads us down the path of prediabetes and diabetes, hypertension, lipid abnormalities (low HDL, high triglycerides, small LDL particles), arthritis, heart disease, stroke, and all the other consequences of excessive carbohydrate consumption.

For this reason, I believe that, in addition to wheat elimination, an overall reduction in carbohydrates is also beneficial. It helps further unwind all the carbohydrate-indulgent phenomena that we've cultivated all these years.

If you wish to roll back the appetite-stimulating, insulin-distorting, and small LDL–triggering effects of foods beyond wheat, or if substantial weight loss is among your health goals, then you should consider reducing or eliminating the following foods in addition to eliminating wheat.

- **Cornstarch and cornmeal**—Cornmeal products such as tacos, tortillas, corn chips, and corn breads, breakfast cereals, and sauces and gravies thickened with cornstarch.

- **Snack foods**—Potato chips, rice cakes, popcorn. These foods, like foods made of cornstarch, send blood sugar straight up to the stratosphere.
- **Desserts**—Pies, cakes, cupcakes, ice cream, sherbet, and other sugary desserts all pack too much sugar.
- **Rice**—White or brown; wild rice. Modest servings are relatively benign, but large servings (more than ½ cup) generate adverse blood sugar effects.
- **Potatoes**—White, red, sweet potatoes, and yams cause effects similar to those generated by rice.
- **Legumes**—Black beans, butter beans, kidney beans, lima beans; chickpeas; lentils. Like potatoes and rice, there is potential for blood sugar effects, especially if serving size exceeds ½ cup.
- **Gluten-free foods**—Because the cornstarch, rice starch, potato starch, and tapioca starch used in place of wheat gluten causes extravagant rises in blood sugar, they should be avoided.
- **Fruit juices, soft drinks**—Even if they are "natural," fruit juices are not that good for you. While they contain healthy components such as flavonoids and vitamin C, the sugar load is simply too great for the benefit. Small servings of two to four ounces are generally fine, but more will trigger blood sugar consequences. Soft drinks, especially carbonated, are incredibly unhealthy mostly due to added sugars, high-fructose corn syrup, colorings, and the extreme acid challenge from the carbonic acid carbonation.
- **Dried fruit**—Dried cranberries, raisins, figs, dates, apricots.
- **Other grains**—Nonwheat grains such as quinoa, sorghum, buckwheat, millet, and possibly oats lack the immune system and exorphin consequences of wheat. However, they post substantial carbohydrate challenges, sufficient to generate high blood sugars. I believe these grains are safer than wheat, but small servings (less than ½ cup) are key to minimize the blood sugar impact.

In terms of mitigating wheat's adverse effects, there is no need to restrict fats. But some fats and fatty foods really should not be part of anyone's diet. These include hydrogenated (trans) fats in processed foods, fried oils that contain excessive by-products of oxidation and AGE formation, and cured meats such as sausages, bacon, hot dogs, salami, etc. (sodium nitrite and AGEs).

THE GOOD NEWS

So what *can* you eat?

There are several basic principles that can serve you well in your wheat-free campaign.

Eat vegetables. You already knew that. While I am no fan of conventional wisdom, on this point conventional wisdom is absolutely correct: Vegetables, in all their wondrous variety, are the best foods on planet earth. Rich in nutrients such as flavonoids and fiber, they should form the centerpiece of everyone's diet. Prior to the agricultural revolution, humans hunted and gathered their food. The gathered part of the equation refers to plants such as wild onions, garlic mustard, mushrooms, dandelions, purslane, and countless others. Anyone who says, "I don't like vegetables" is guilty of not having tried them all, the same people who think that the world of vegetables ends at creamed corn and canned green beans. You can't "not like it" if you haven't tried it. The incredible range of tastes, textures, and versatility of vegetables means there are choices for everyone, from eggplant sliced and baked with olive oil and meaty portobello mushrooms; to a Caprese salad of sliced tomatoes, mozzarella, fresh basil, and olive oil; to daikon radish and pickled ginger alongside fish. Extend your vegetable variety beyond your usual habits. Explore mushrooms such as shiitake and porcini. Adorn cooked dishes with alliums such as scallions, garlic, leeks, shallots, and chives. Vegetables shouldn't just be for dinner; think about vegetables for any time of day, including breakfast.

Eat *some* fruit. Notice that I did not say, "Eat fruits and vegetables." That's because the two don't belong together, despite the phrase sliding out of the mouths of dietitians and others echoing conventional thinking. While vegetables should be consumed ad libitum, fruit should be consumed in limited quantities. (See the sidebar below to find the best choices.)

(continued on page 216)

The *Lose the Wheat, Lose the Weight!* Fruit Scale

Fruits are rich in healthy nutrients like flavonoids, antioxidants, vitamin C, potassium, and fiber. However, fruit also comes with a lot of sugar. Some fruit has as much sugar as a candy bar. Dietitians tell us this is okay since it's natural sugar. Wrong! Modern fruit has been cultivated, fertilized, hybridized, crossbred, gassed, and herbicided for size, beauty, and, yes, sugar content—*too much* sugar content.

The modern apple or banana has been bred to make the typical eleven-year-old happy: plenty of sugar. One medium-size banana, for instance, contains 27 grams total carbohydrates, 24 grams "net" carbohydrates (total carbohydrates minus fiber content), according to the USDA Food and Nutrient Database.

Unless you are willing and/or able to grow your own wild strawberries and plantains, however, most of us still need to pick and choose among the fruits that we are able to purchase at the supermarket or greengrocer. It helps to be selective, choosing the most nutritious, meaning richest in health-promoting flavonoids/antioxidants, while also selecting ones that have the lowest sugar content.

Portion control is crucial with fruit; for most fruit, staying at ½ cup per serving will keep your sugar intake below the radar. Here's a quick guide to fruit from the best on down to the not-so-good:

Berries
Berries top the list with the greatest in healthy flavonoids, in particular the especially health-promoting class of flavonoids, the anthocyanins, the class of flavonoids that confer the purple, reddish, or blue color to berries. Ounce for ounce, berries pack the greatest nutrient content with the

(continued)

The *Lose the Wheat,*
Lose the Weight! Fruit Scale—*cont.*

least sugar. A ½–cup serving of most berries usually provide no more than 6 to 10 grams carbohydrate. Wonderful berries include:

- Açaí
- Bearberries
- Bilberries
- Blackberries
- Blueberries
- Cherries
- Chokeberries
- Cranberries
- Goji berries
- Gooseberries
- Huckleberries
- Kiwifruit ("kiwi")
- Pomegranates (not really a berry but berry-like in its nutritional composition)
- Raspberries
- Strawberries
- Wolfberries

Citrus

Rich in vitamin C and citrus flavonoids such as narigenin and hesperetin, citrus fruits provide unique health effects. Unfortunately, modern agriculture provides us sugar-rich varieties. While there are hundreds of varieties of citrus around the world (since citrus is so readily hybridizable), in the United States our selection is more limited to the options listed below. The key with citrus, as it is with many other fruits and non-wheat carbohydrates, is serving size: Keep it small, e.g., no more than ½ cup at a time, which provides 6 to 11 grams net carbs (kumquats are the lowest; tangerines and clementines the highest).

- Clementines
- Grapefruit
- Kumquats
- Lemons
- Limes
- Oranges
- Pomelo
- Tangerines

Common Fruit

I list these popular fruits under the label "common" only because they have become the staples of what most Americans regard as fruit nowadays. These are all wonderful fruits but tend to dominate the fruit bowl. As with citrus, enjoy your peaches, pears, and apples but be careful of portion size to limit sugar exposure. A ½-cup serving of these fruits yields between 7 and 9 grams carbohydrates, a quantity within the tolerance of most people without provoking excessive blood sugar and other phenomena.

The exceptions are grapes, which provide up to 13 grams net carbo-hydrates, and plums with 21 grams net carbohydrates. Also, note that a ½-cup serving is usually less than a whole piece of fruit; a 3-inch diam-eter apple, for instance, provides 21 grams net carbs, a quantity suffi-cient to challenge your tolerance.

- Apples
- Apricots
- Nectarines
- Peaches
- Pears

Melons

Melons, like cucumbers and gourds, grow on vines. Ounce for ounce, they have carbohydrate content similar to other fruit, generally 6 to 7 grams per ½-cup serving. The problem with melons are that they are generally consumed in far greater quantities, e.g., half of a honeydew melon, which contains a whopping 53 grams net carbohydrates, or a 1-inch thick wedge of watermelon, with 43 grams net carbohydrates. So, again, it's important to get that ½ cup out and measure what you're going to eat.

- Cantaloupe
- Casaba
- Crenshaw
- Honeydew
- Musk melon
- Watermelon

And the Type to Stay Away From . . . Tropical Fruit

Tropical fruits, more than most other fruits, provide potential for overex-posure to sugars. Bananas enjoy an undeserved place as most popular fruit in the world. They are, no doubt, delicious and portable, but pack too much sugar. Mangoes and bananas are the worst culprits. With tropical fruit, even a ½-cup serving may challenge your sugar tolerance. A ½-cup serving of banana, for instance, contains 15 grams net carbs, but a whole medium-size banana contains 24 grams net carbs. Pineapple and mango are next in line, each with 12.5 grams net carbs per ½ cup. Tropical fruit are therefore best consumed in the smallest quantities—for example, ¼ cup or ½ of a banana at a time.

Eat raw nuts. Raw almonds, walnuts, pecans, pistachios, hazelnuts, Brazil nuts, and cashews are wonderful. And you can eat as much as you want. They're filling and full of fiber, monounsaturated oils, and protein. They reduce blood pressure, reduce LDL cholesterol (including small LDL particles), and consuming them several times a week can add two years to your life.[2]

You can't overdo nuts, provided they're raw. (Raw means not roasted in hydrogenated cottonseed or soybean oils, not "honey roasted," not beer nuts or any of the other endless variations in processed nuts, variations that transform healthy raw nuts into something that causes weight gain, high blood pressure, and increases LDL cholesterol.) This is not the "No more than fourteen nuts at a time" or one-hundred-calorie pack recommendation issued by dietitians fearful of fat intake. Many people are unaware that you can eat or even buy raw nuts. They're widely available in the bulk section of grocery stores, in three-pound bags in "big box" stores such as Sam's Club and Costco, and at health food stores. Peanuts, of course, are not nuts, but legumes; they cannot be consumed raw. Peanuts should be boiled or dry roasted and the label should not include ingredients such as hydrogenated soybean oil, wheat flour, maltodextrin, cornstarch, sucrose—nothing but peanuts.

Use oils generously. Curtailing oil is entirely unnecessary, part of the nutritional dietary blunders of the past forty years. Use healthy oils liberally, such as extra-virgin olive oil, coconut oil, avocado oil, and cocoa butter, and avoid polyunsaturated oils such as sunflower, safflower, corn, and vegetable oils (which trigger oxidation and inflammation). Try to minimize heating and cook at lower temperatures; never fry, since deep-frying is the extreme of oxidation that triggers, among other things, AGE formation.

Eat meats and eggs. The fat phobia of the past forty years turned us off from foods such as eggs, sirloin, and pork because of their saturated fat content—but saturated fat was never the problem. Carbohydrates *in combination* with saturated fat, however, cause measures of LDL particles to skyrocket. The problem was carbohydrates more than saturated fat. In fact, new studies have exonerated saturated fat as an underlying contributor to heart attack and stroke risk.[3] There's also the issue of exogenous AGEs that accompany animal products; AGEs are unhealthy components of meats that are among the potentially unhealthy components of animal products, but not the saturated fat. Reduced exposure to exogenous AGEs in animal products is a matter of trying to cook at lower temperatures for shorter time periods whenever possible.

Try to buy meats from grass-fed livestock (which have greater omega-3 fatty acid composition and are less likely to be antibiotic- and growth hormone–ridden), and preferentially those raised under humane conditions and not in the Auschwitz-equivalent of a factory farm. Don't fry your meats (high temperatures oxidize oils and create AGEs) and avoid cured meats entirely. You should also eat eggs. Not "one egg per week" or some such non-physiologic restriction. Eat what your body tells you to eat, since appetite signals, once rid of unnatural appetite stimulants such as wheat flour, will let you know what you require.

Eat dairy products. Enjoy cheese, another wonderfully diverse food. Recall that fat is *not* the issue, so enjoy familiar full-fat cheeses such as Swiss or Cheddar, or exotic cheeses such as Stilton, Crottin de Chavignol, Edam, or Comté. Cheese serves as a wonderful snack or the centerpiece of a meal.

Other dairy products such as cottage cheese, yogurt, milk, and butter should be consumed in limited quantities of no more than one or two servings per day. I believe that adults should limit dairy products outside of cheese due to the insulinotropic effect of dairy proteins, the tendency that dairy protein has to increase pancreatic release of insulin.[4] (The fermentation process required to make cheese reduces the content of amino acids responsible for this effect.) Dairy products should also be in the least processed form. For instance, choose full-fat, unflavored, unsweetened yogurt over sugar-containing, high-fructose corn syrup–sweetened yogurt.

The *Lose the Wheat, Lose the Weight!* Nutritional Approach for Optimal Health

Most adults are a metabolic mess created, in large part, by excessive carbohydrate consumption. Eliminating the worst carbohydrate source of all, wheat, fixes much of the problem. However, there are other carbohydrate problem sources that, if full control over metabolic distortions and weight is desired, should also be minimized or eliminated. Here's a summary.

Consume in unlimited quantities

Vegetables (except potatoes and corn)—including mushrooms, herbs, squash

Raw nuts and seeds—almonds, walnuts, pecans, hazelnuts, Brazil nuts, pistachios, cashews, macadamias; peanuts (boiled or dry roasted); sunflower seeds, pumpkin seeds, sesame seeds; nut meals

Oils—extra-virgin olive, avocado, walnut, coconut, cocoa butter, flaxseed, macadamia, sesame

Meats and eggs—preferably free-range and organic chicken, turkey, beef, pork; buffalo; ostrich; wild game; fish; shellfish; eggs (including yolks)

Cheese

Non-sugary condiments—mustards, horseradish, tapenades, salsa, mayonnaise, vinegars (white, red wine, apple cider, balsamic), Worcestershire sauce, soy sauce, chili or pepper sauces

Others: flaxseed (ground), avocados, olives, coconut, spices, cocoa (unsweetened) or cacao

Consume in limited quantities

Non-cheese dairy—milk, cottage cheese, yogurt, butter

Most people with lactose intolerance are able to consume at least some cheese, provided it is real cheese that has been subjected to a fermentation process. (You can recognize real cheese by the words "culture" or "live culture" in the list of ingredients, meaning a live organism was added to ferment the milk.) Fermentation reduces lactose content in the final cheese product.

Fruit—Berries are the best: blueberries, raspberries, blackberries, straw-berries, cranberries, and cherries. Be careful of the most sugary fruits, including pineapple, papaya, mango, and banana. Avoid dried fruit, especially figs and dates, due to the excessive sugar content.

Whole corn (not to be confused with cornmeal or cornstarch, which should be avoided)

Fruit juices

Nonwheat, nongluten grains—quinoa, millet, sorghum, teff, amaranth, buckwheat, rice (brown and white), oats, wild rice

Legumes—black beans, kidney beans, butter beans, Spanish beans, lima beans; lentils; chickpeas; potatoes (white and red), yams, sweet potatoes

Soy products—tofu, tempeh, miso, natto; edamame, soybeans

Consume rarely or never

Wheat products—wheat-based breads, pasta, noodles, cookies, cakes, pies, cupcakes, breakfast cereals, pancakes, waffles, pita, couscous; rye, bulgur, triticale, kamut, barley

Unhealthy oils—fried, hydrogenated, polyunsaturated (especially corn, sunflower, safflower, grapeseed, cottonseed, soybean)

Gluten-free foods—specifically those made with cornstarch, rice starch, potato starch, or tapioca starch

Dried fruit—figs, dates, prunes, raisins, cranberries

Fried foods

Sugary snacks—candies, ice cream, sherbet, fruit roll-ups, craisins, energy bars

Sugary fructose-rich sweeteners—agave syrup or nectar, honey, maple syrup, high-fructose corn syrup, sucrose

Sugary condiments—jellies, jams, preserves, ketchup (if contains sucrose or high-fructose corn syrup), chutney

People who are lactose intolerant also have the option of choosing dairy products that include added lactase enzyme or taking the enzyme in pill form.

The subject of soy products can be surprisingly emotionally charged. I believe this is primarily because of the proliferation of soy, like wheat, in various forms in processed foods, along with the fact that soy has been the focus of much genetic modification. Because it is now virtually impossible to tell what foods have soy that has been genetically modified, I advise patients to consume soy in modest quantities and preferably in fermented form, e.g., tofu, tempeh, miso, and natto, since fermentation degrades the lectins and phytates in soy that can potentially exert adverse intestinal effects. Soymilk can be a useful milk substitute for those with lactose intolerance, but I believe that, for the above reasons, it is best consumed in limited quantities. Similar cautions apply to whole soybeans and edamame.

Odds and ends. Olives (green, kalamata, stuffed, in vinegar, in olive oil), avocados, pickled vegetables (asparagus, peppers, radish, tomatoes), and raw seeds (pumpkin, sunflower, sesame) are among the nutritional odds and ends that provide variety. It's important to extend your food choices outside of familiar habits, since part of the success of diet is variety in order to provide plentiful vitamins, minerals, fibers, and phytonutrients. (Conversely, part of the cause of failure of many modern commercial diets is their lack of variety. The modern habit of concentrating calorie sources in one food group—wheat, for instance—means many nutrients will be lacking, thus the need for fortification.)

Condiments are to food as clever personalities are to conversation: They can run you through the full range of emotions and twists in reason, and make you laugh. Keep a supply of horseradish, wasabi, and mustards (Dijon, brown, Chinese, Creole, chipotle, wasabi, horseradish, and the unique varieties of regional mustards), and vow to never use ketchup again (especially any made with high-fructose corn syrup). Tapenades (spreads made of a paste of olives, capers, artichokes, portobello mushrooms, and roasted garlic) can be purchased ready-made to spare you the effort and are wonderful spreads for eggplant, eggs, or fish. You probably already know that salsas are available in wide variety or can be readily made in minutes using a food processor.

Seasonings should not begin and end at salt and pepper. Herbs and spices not only are a great source of variety but also add to the nutritional profile of a meal. Fresh or dried basil, oregano, cinnamon, cumin, nutmeg, and dozens of other herbs and spices are available in any well-stocked grocery store.

Grains and legumes. What role do nonwheat grains play in the wheat-free approach to weight loss and health? What about quinoa and buckwheat, for instance? Well, here's the good news (especially for you starch lovers out there): You don't have to banish ALL grains from your life. But you still have to watch out for how much of them you eat.

Because the majority of Americans have been exposed to years of low-fat, high-carbohydrate eating, thanks to the misguided advice of official agencies, we need to undo incredibly common prediabetic and diabetic phenomena by *limiting overall carbohydrate exposure.* The everyday phenomena of high triglycerides, low HDL cholesterol, abundant small LDL particles, high blood sugar, high blood pressure, and, yes, wheat bellies are powerfully and rapidly reversed by taking the first and most important step: eliminating wheat. If elimination of wheat is followed by limiting exposure to other carbohydrates, then the effect is amplified. So more bang for your buck, so to speak.

That said, nonwheat grains aren't as dangerous because they lack the two essential ingredients that make wheat the incredibly destructive grain that it is: (1) amylopectin A, and (2) gliadin that converts to opiate-receptor-binding exorphins. Recall that these two ingredients underlie wheat's unique ability to stimulate appetite. Non-wheat grains like quinoa and buckwheat lack these two appetite-stimulating factors. O if you still yearn for grain like foods, you can still have these.

But they are not entirely benign. Because nonwheat grains are still primarily carbohydrates, they can trigger undesirable effects like a surge in blood sugar and a rise in triglycerides.

So the key is to enjoy them in *small quantities.* A ½ cup of wild rice with dinner should be fine for most people, and frankly it's more than a decent serving. More than that could trigger unwanted metabolic responses in some people.

Some people, such as those with established diabetes or pre-diabetes, and substantial abnormalities like very high triglycerides (e.g., 200 mg/dl or greater) or excessive small LDL particles (more than 30 percent of total LDL) on a lipoprotein panel, would get even more benefits from avoiding the following in addition to wheat, or at least having them in even smaller quantities

But for the rest of us, I generally recommend these foods be limited to two ½-cup servings each day (so, say, ½ cup at breakfast and ½ cup at dinner).

These foods include:

- Amaranth
- Beans—red, kidney, lima, black, pinto, fava, peas, chickpeas, lentils
- Buckwheat
- Corn (i.e., corn on the cob, whole kernels)
- Millet
- Rices—wild, brown, white
- Quinoa
- Sorghum

Whenever possible, choose the forms containing more fiber—e.g., wild or brown rice over white. The difference is small and certainly makes little difference in blood sugar effects. But the somewhat greater nutritional value (e.g., B vitamins, fiber) do contribute a small benefit. Also, choose the whole form over the processed or dried form: whole cooked brown rice over dried rice starch, whole corn over cornstarch, whole beans over bean starch or flour.

In the world of grains, one grain stands apart, since it consists entirely of protein, fiber, and oils: flaxseed. Because it is essentially free of carbohydrates that increase blood sugar, ground flaxseed is the one grain that fits nicely into this approach (the unground grain is indigestible). Use ground flaxseed as a hot cereal (heated, for instance, with milk, unsweetened almond milk, coconut milk or coconut water, or soymilk, with added walnuts or blueberries) or add it to foods such as cottage cheese or chilis. You can also use it to make a breading for chicken and fish.

Beverages. It may seem austere, but water should be your first choice. One hundred percent fruit juices can be enjoyed in small quantities, but fruit drinks and soft drinks are very bad ideas. Teas and coffee, the extracts of plant products, are fine to enjoy, with or without milk, cream, coconut milk, or full-fat soymilk. If an argument can be made for alcoholic beverages, the one genuine standout in health is red wine, a source of flavonoids, anthocyanins, and now-popular resveratrol. Beer, on the other hand, is a wheat-brewed beverage in most instances and is the one clear-cut alcoholic drink to avoid or minimize. Beers also tend to be high in carbohydrates, especially the heavier ales and dark beers. If you have positive celiac markers, you should not consume any wheat- or gluten-containing beer at all.

Some people just need to have the comfortable taste and feel of foods that are made of wheat, but don't want to provoke the health headaches. In the sample menu plan that starts on p. 226, I include a number of possibilities for wheat-free substitutes, such as wheat-free pizza and wheat-free bread and muffins. (Select recipes can be found in Chapter 15.)

Vegetarians will, admittedly, have a bit of a tougher job, particularly strict vegetarians and vegans who avoid eggs, dairy, and fish. But it can be done. Strict vegetarians need to rely more heavily on nuts, nut meals, seeds, nut and seed butters, and oils; avocados and olives; and may have a bit more leeway with carbohydrate-containing beans, lentils, chickpeas, wild rice, chia seed, sweet potatoes, and yams. If nongenetically modified soy products can be obtained, then tofu, tempeh, and natto can provide another rich source of protein.

GETTING STARTED: A WEEK OF
A WHEAT-FREE LIFE

Because wheat figures prominently in the world of "comfort foods" and the universe of processed convenience foods, and generally occupies a proud place at breakfast, lunch, and dinner, some people have a hard time envisioning what their life might look like without it. Going without wheat can be downright frightening.

Breakfast, in particular, stumps many people. After all, if we eliminate wheat, we've cut out breakfast cereals, toast, English muffins, bagels, pancakes, waffles, donuts, and muffins—what's left? Plenty. But they won't necessarily be familiar breakfast foods. If you regard breakfast as just another meal, no different from lunch or dinner, the possibilities become endless.

Ground flaxseed and ground nut meals (almonds, hazelnuts, pecans, walnuts) make great hot cereals for breakfast, heated with milk, coconut milk or water, unsweetened almond milk, or soymilk, and topped with walnuts, raw sunflower seeds, and blueberries or other berries. Eggs make a return to breakfast in all their glory: fried, over-easy, hard-boiled, soft-boiled, scrambled. Add basil pesto, olive tapenade, chopped vegetables, mushrooms, goat cheese, olive oil, chopped meats (but not cured bacon, sausage, or salami) to your scrambled eggs for an endless variety of dishes. Instead of a bowl of breakfast cereal with orange juice, have a Caprese salad of sliced tomatoes and sliced mozzarella, topped off with fresh basil leaves and extra-virgin olive oil. Or save some of the salad from the previous evening's dinner for breakfast the next day. When in a hurry, grab a hunk of cheese, a fresh avocado, a plastic bag filled with pecans, and a handful of raspberries. Or try a strategy I call "dinner for breakfast," transplanting foods you ordinarily think of as lunch or dinner foods into breakfast fare. While it may appear a little odd to uninformed observers, this simple strategy is an exceptionally effective way to maintain a healthy first meal of the day.

Here is a sample of what a week-long wheat-free diet approach looks like. Note that once wheat is eliminated and an otherwise thoughtful approach to diet is followed—i.e., eating a selection of foods not dominated by the processed food industry but rich in *real* food—there is no need to count calories or adhere to formulas that dictate optimal percentages of calories from fat or proteins. These issues, very simply, take care of themselves (unless you have a medical condition that requires specific restrictions, such as gout, kidney stones, or kidney disease). So with the wheat belly diet, you will not find advice such as drink low-fat or fat-free milk, or limit yourself to four ounces of meat, since restrictions such as these are simply unnecessary when metabolism reverts back to normal—and it nearly always will once the metabolism-distorting effects of wheat are absent.

The only common diet variable in this approach is carbohydrate content. Because of the excessive carbohydrate sensitivity most adults have acquired through years of excessive carbohydrate consumption, I find that most do best maintaining daily carbohydrate intake to approximately 50 to 100 grams per day. An even stricter carbohydrate restriction is occasionally necessary if you are trying to undo prediabetes or diabetes (e.g., less than 30 grams per day), while people who exercise for prolonged periods (e.g., marathon runners, triathletes, long-distance bikers) will need increase carbohydrate intake during exercise.

Note that serving sizes specified are therefore just suggestions, not restrictions. All dishes accompanied by a recipe in Chapter 15 are in boldface and starred with an asterisk (*). Additional recipes are also included in Chapter 15. Also note that anyone with celiac disease or other antibody-positive form of wheat and gluten intolerance will need to go the extra step of examining all ingredients used in this menu and in the recipes by looking for the "gluten-free" assurance on the package. All ingredients called for are widely available as gluten-free.

DAY 1

Breakfast

Hot coconut flaxseed cereal*

Lunch

Large tomato stuffed with tuna or crabmeat mixed with
chopped onions or scallions, mayonnaise

Selection of mixed olives, cheeses, pickled vegetables

Dinner

Vegetable pizza*

Mixed green salad (or mixed red- and green-leafed lettuce)
with radicchio, chopped cucumber, sliced radishes, **worry-
free ranch dressing***

Carrot cake*

DAY 2

Breakfast

Eggs scrambled with 2 tablespoons of extra-virgin olive oil,
sun-dried tomatoes, basil pesto, and feta cheese

Handful of raw almonds, walnuts, pecans, or pistachios

Lunch

Baked portobello mushroom stuffed with crabmeat and goat
cheese

Dinner

Baked wild salmon or seared tuna steaks with **wasabi sauce***

Spinach salad with walnuts or pine nuts, chopped red onion,
Gorgonzola cheese, **vinaigrette dressing***

Ginger spice cookies*

DAY 3

Breakfast

Hummus with sliced green peppers, celery, jicama, radishes

Apple walnut "bread"* spread with cream cheese, natural peanut butter, almond butter, cashew butter, or sunflower seed butter

Lunch

Greek salad with black or kalamata olives, chopped cucumber, tomato wedges, cubed feta cheese; extra-virgin olive oil with fresh lemon juice or **vinaigrette dressing***

Dinner

Baked chicken or **three-cheese eggplant bake***

Zucchini "pasta" with baby bella mushrooms*

Dark chocolate tofu mousse*

DAY 4

Breakfast

Classic cheesecake with wheatless crust* (Yes, cheesecake for breakfast. How much better does it get than that?)

Handful of raw almonds, walnuts, pecans, or pistachios

Lunch

Turkey avocado wraps* (using flax wraps*)

Granola*

Dinner

Pecan-encrusted chicken with tapenade*

Wild rice

Asparagus with roasted garlic olive oil*

Chocolate peanut butter fudge*

DAY 5

Breakfast

Caprese salad (sliced tomato, sliced mozzarella, basil leaves, extra-virgin olive oil)

Apple walnut "bread"* spread with cream, natural peanut butter, almond butter, cashew butter, or sunflower seed butter

Lunch

Tuna avocado salad*
Ginger spice cookies*

Dinner

Shirataki noodle stir-fry*
Berry coconut smoothie*

DAY 6

Breakfast

Egg and pesto breakfast wrap*
Handful of raw almonds, walnuts, pecans, or pistachios

Lunch

Mixed vegetable soup with added flaxseed or olive oil

Dinner

Parmesan-breaded pork chops with balsamic-roasted vegetables*
Apple walnut "bread"* with cream cheese or pumpkin butter

DAY 7

Breakfast

Granola*

Apple walnut "bread"* spread with natural peanut butter, almond butter, cashew butter, or sunflower seed butter

Lunch

Spinach and mushroom salad* with **worry-free ranch dressing***

Dinner

Flax burrito: **Flaxseed wraps*** with black beans; ground beef, chicken, pork, turkey, or tofu; green peppers; jalapeño peppers; Cheddar cheese; salsa
Mexican tortilla soup*
Jicama dipped in guacamole
Classic cheesecake with wheatless crust*

The seven-day menu is a bit heavy with recipes just to illustrate some of the variety possible in adapting standard recipes into those that are healthy and don't rely on wheat. You can just as well use simple dishes that require little advanced planning or preparation, e.g., scrambled eggs and a handful of blueberries and pecans for breakfast, baked fish with a simple green salad for dinner.

Preparing meals without wheat is really far easier than you may think. With little more effort than it takes to iron a shirt, you can prepare several meals a day that center around real food, provide the variety necessary for true health, and be free of wheat.

BETWEEN MEALS

On the *Lose the Wheat, Lose the Weight!* diet plan, you will quickly break yourself of the habit of "grazing," i.e., eating many smaller meals or frequent between-meal snacks. This absurd notion will soon become a remnant of your previous wheat-consumed lifestyle since your appetite will no longer be dictated by the 90- to 120-minute-long glucose-insulin roller coaster ride of hunger.

Nonetheless, it's still nice to have an occasional snack. In a wheat-free regimen, healthy snack choices include:

Raw nuts—Again, choose raw over dry roasted, smoke-house, honey roasted, or glazed varieties. (Recall that peanuts, a legume and not a nut, should be dry roasted, not raw.)

Cheese—Cheese doesn't end at Cheddar. A plate of cheeses, raw nuts, and olives can serve as a more substantial snack. Cheese will keep at least a few hours without refrigeration and therefore makes a great portable snack. The world of cheese is as diverse as the world of wine, with wonderfully varied tastes, smells, and textures, allowing pairing of varieties with other foods.

Dark chocolates—You want cacao with just enough sugar to make it palatable. The majority of chocolates sold are chocolate-flavored sugar. The best choices contain 85 percent or more cacao. Lindt and Ghirardelli are two widely distributed brands that make delicious 85 to 90 per-cent cacao chocolates. Some people need to get accustomed to the slightly bitter, less sweet taste of high-cacao choco-lates. Shop around for your favorite brand, as some are winey tasting, others earthy. The Lindt 90 percent is my favorite, since its very low sugar content allows me to enjoy just a bit more. Two squares will not budge most people's blood sugar; some can get away with four squares (40 grams, about 2 inches by 2 inches).

You can dip or spread your dark chocolate with natural peanut butter, almond butter, cashew butter, or sunflower seed butter for a healthy version of a peanut butter cup. You can also add cocoa powders to recipes; the healthiest are the "undutched" varieties, i.e., not treated with alkali, since this process removes many of the healthful flavonoids that reduce blood pressure, increase HDL cholesterol, and induce relaxation of arteries. Ghirardelli, Hershey, and Scharffen Berger produce undutched cocoas. Mixing cocoa powder, milk/soymilk/coconut milk, cinnamon, and nonnutritive sweeteners such as stevia, sucralose, xylitol, and erythritol makes a great hot cocoa.

Low-carb crackers—As a general rule, I believe we are best sticking to "real" foods, not imitations or synthetic modifications. However, as an occasional indulgence, there are some tasty low-carb crackers that you can use to dip into hummus, guacamole, cucumber dip (remember: we're not limiting oils or fats), or salsa. Mary's Gone Crackers is one manufacturer of nonwheat crackers (caraway, herb, black pepper, and onion) and Sticks & Twigs "pretzels" (chipotle tomato, sea salt, and curry) made with brown rice, quinoa, and flaxseed. Each cracker or pretzel has a little more than 1 gram of "net" carbs (total carbohydrates minus indigestible fiber), so eating several will usually not result in an undesirable rise in blood sugar. More manufacturers are introducing crackers whose principal ingredient is flaxseed, such as Flackers, made by Minneapolis' Doctor in the Kitchen. Alternatively, if you have a food dehydrator, dried vegetables such as zucchini and carrots make great chips for dipping.

Vegetable dips—All you need are some precut veggies such as peppers, raw green beans, radishes, sliced zucchini, or scallions, and some interesting dips, such as black bean dip, hummus, vegetable dip, wasabi dip, mustards such as Dijon or horseradish, or cream cheese–based dips, all of which are widely available premade.

Despite the fact that removing wheat and other "junk" carbohydrates from the diet can leave a big gap, there is truly an incredible range and variety of foods to choose from to fill it. You may have to venture outside of your usual shopping and cooking habits, but you will find plenty of food to keep your palate interested.

With the newly reawakened taste sense, reduced impulse eating, and reduced calorie intake that accompanies the wheat-free experience, many people also describe a heightened appreciation for food. As a result, the majority of people who choose this path actually enjoy food more than during their wheat-consuming days.

THERE'S LIFE AFTER WHEAT

On the wheat-free diet plan, you'll find that you spend more time in the produce aisle, farmers' market, or vegetable stand, as well as the butcher shop and dairy aisle. You will rarely, if ever, wander into the chip, cereal, bread, or frozen food aisles.

You may also find that you are no longer cozy with the Big Food manufacturers or their New Age acquisitions or branding. New Age name, organic this or that, "natural" looking label, and—bam! Huge multinational food corporation now looks like small, environmentally conscious group of ex-hippies trying to save the world.

Social gatherings, as many celiac sufferers will attest, can amount to extravagant wheat-fests, with wheat products in anything and everything. The most diplomatic way to pass up any dish you know is a wheat bomb is to claim that you have a wheat allergy. Most civilized people will respect your health concern, preferring your deprivation to an embarrassing case of hives that could ruin the festivities. If you have been wheat-free for more than a few weeks, turning down the bruschetta, bread crumb–stuffed mushrooms, or Chex Mix should be easier, since the abnormal exorphin-crazed impulse to stuff your mouth full of wheat products should have ceased. You'll be perfectly content with the shrimp cocktail, olives, and crudité.

Eating outside the home can be a land mine of wheat, corn-starch, sugar, high-fructose corn syrup, and other unhealthy ingredients. First, there's temptation. If the waiter brings a basket of warm, fragrant rolls to your table, you've just got to turn them away. Unless your dinner partners insist on bread, it's easiest not to have it sitting right in front of you, teasing you and eroding your resolve. Second, keep it simple. Baked salmon with a ginger sauce is likely to be a safe bet. But an elaborate, multi-ingredient French dish has more potential for unwanted ingredients. This is a situation in which it helps to ask. However, if you have an immune-mediated wheat sensitivity such as celiac disease or some other severe wheat sensitivity, then you may not even be able to trust what the waiter or waitress tells you. As any celiac sufferer will attest, virtually everyone with celiac disease has had it triggered by inadvertent gluten exposure from a "gluten-free" dish. More and more restaurants are now also advertising a gluten-free menu. However, even that is no guarantee of no problems if, for instance, cornstarch or other gluten-free ingredients are used that trigger blood sugar issues. In the end, eating out of the home presents hazards that, in my experience, can only be minimized, not eliminated. Whenever possible, eat food that you or your family prepare. That way, you can be certain of what is contained in your meal.

The reality is that, for many people, the best protection against wheat is staying free from it for some time, since reexposure can invite all manner of peculiar phenomena. While it may be hard to turn down a piece of birthday cake, if you pay for the indulgence with several hours of stomach cramps and diarrhea, it makes it hard to indulge with any frequency. (Of course, if you have celiac disease or any history of abnormal celiac markers, you should *never* indulge in any wheat- or gluten-containing food.)

Our society has indeed become a "whole grain world," with wheat products filling the shelves in every convenience store, coffee shop, restaurant, and supermarket, and entire stores devoted to them, such as bakeries and bagel and donut shops. At times you may have to search and dig through the rubble to find what you need. But, along with sleep, exercise, and remembering your wedding anniversary, eliminating wheat can be viewed as a basic necessity for long life and health. A wheat-free life can be every bit as fulfilling and adventurous as, and certainly healthier than, the alternative.

CHAPTER 14

LOOKING FOR WHEAT IN ALL THE WRONG PLACES

WHILE THE FOLLOWING lists may be daunting, sticking to wheat- and gluten-free foods can be as easy as restricting yourself to foods that don't require a label.

Foods such as cucumbers, kale, cod, salmon, olive oil, walnuts, eggs, and avocados have nothing to do with wheat or gluten. They are naturally free of such things, natural and healthy without benefit of some "gluten-free" label.

But if you venture outside of familiar natural whole foods, eat in social situations, go to restaurants, or travel, then there is potential for inadvertent wheat and gluten exposure.

For some people, this is not just a game. Someone with celiac disease, for instance, may have to endure days to weeks of abdominal cramping, diarrhea, even intestinal bleeding from an inadvertent encounter with some wheat gluten mixed into the batter used to bread chicken. Even after the nasty rash of dermatitis herpetiformis heals, it can flare with just a dash of wheat-containing soy sauce. Or someone who experiences inflammatory neurological symptoms can experience abrupt decline in coordination because the gluten-free beer really wasn't. For many others who don't have immune- or inflammation-mediated gluten sensitivity, accidental exposure to wheat can bring on diarrhea, asthma, mental fog, joint pains or swelling, leg edema, behavioral outbursts in people with ADHD, autism, bipolar illness, and schizophrenia.

Many people therefore have to be vigilant about exposure to wheat. Those with autoimmune conditions such as celiac, dermatitis herpetiformis, and cerebellar ataxia also need to avoid other gluten-containing grains: rye, barley, spelt, triticale, kamut, and bulgur.

Wheat and gluten come in a dizzying variety of forms. Couscous, matzo, orzo, graham, and bran are all wheat. So are faro, panko, and rusk. Appearances can be misleading. For instance, the majority of breakfast cereals contain wheat flour, wheat-derived ingredients, or gluten despite names such as Corn Flakes or Rice Krispies.

Oats remain a topic of controversy, especially since oat products are often processed in the same equipment or facility as wheat products. Most celiac sufferers therefore avoid oats as well.

To qualify as gluten-free by FDA criteria, manufactured products (not restaurant-produced products) must be both free of gluten and produced in a gluten-free facility to prevent cross-contamination. (Some people are so gluten-sensitive that even the small amount you are exposed to by sharing a cutting device can bring on symptoms.) This means that, for the seriously sensitive, even an ingredient label that does not list wheat or any buzzwords for wheat such as "modified food starch" can *still* contain some measure of gluten. If in doubt, a call or e-mail to the customer service department may be necessary to inquire whether a gluten-free facility was used. Also, more manufacturers are starting to specify whether products are gluten-free or not gluten-free on their Web sites.

Note that wheat-free does *not* equate with gluten-free in food labeling. Wheat-free can mean, for instance, that barley malt or rye is used in place of wheat, but both also contain gluten. For the very gluten-sensitive, such as those with celiac, do not assume that wheat-free is necessarily gluten-free.

You already know that wheat and gluten can be found in abundance in obvious foods such as breads, pastas, and pastries. But there are some not-so-obvious foods that can contain wheat, as listed below.

Baguette
Barley
Beignet
Bran
Brioche
Bulgur
Burrito
Couscous
Crepe
Croutons
Durum
Einkorn
Emmer
Farina
Faro (several wheat varieties are often loosely called "faro" in Italy)
Focaccia
Gnocchi
Graham flour
Hydrolyzed vegetable protein
Kamut
Matzo
Modified food starch
Orzo
Panko (a bread crumb mixture used in Japanese cooking)
Ramen
Roux (wheat-based sauce or thickener)
Rusk
Rye
Seitan (nearly pure gluten used in place of meat)
Semolina
Soba (mostly buckwheat but usually also includes wheat)
Spelt
Strudel
Tart
Textured vegetable protein
Triticale
Udon
Wheat germ
Wraps

WHEAT-CONTAINING PRODUCTS

Wheat reflects the incredible inventiveness of the human species, as we've transformed this grain into an incredible multitude of shapes and forms. Beyond the many configurations that wheat can take listed above, there is an even greater variety of foods that contain some measure of wheat or gluten. These are listed below.

Please keep in mind that, due to the extraordinary number and variety of products on the market, this list cannot include every possible wheat- and gluten-containing item. The key is to remain vigilant and ask (or walk away) whenever in doubt.

Many foods listed below also come in gluten-free versions. Some gluten-free versions are both tasty and healthy, e.g., vinaigrette salad dressing without hydrolyzed vegetable protein. But bear in mind that the growing world of gluten-free breads, breakfast cereals, and flours, which are typically made with rice starch, cornstarch, potato starch, or tapioca starch, are not healthy substitutes. Nothing that generates diabetic-range blood sugar responses should be labeled "healthy," gluten-free or otherwise. They serve best as an occasional indulgence, not staples.

There is also an entire world of stealth sources of wheat and gluten that cannot be deciphered from the label. If the listed ingredients include nonspecific terms such as "starch," "emulsifiers," or "leavening agents," then the food contains gluten until proven otherwise.

There is doubt surrounding the gluten content of some foods and ingredients, such as caramel coloring. Caramel coloring is the caramelized product of heated sugars that is nearly always made from corn syrup, but some manufacturers make it from a wheat-derived source. Such uncertainties are expressed with a question mark beside the listing.

Not everybody needs to be extra-vigilant about the most minute exposure to gluten. The listings that follow are simply meant to raise your awareness of just how ubiquitous wheat and gluten are, and provide a starting place for people who really *do* need to be extremely vigilant about their gluten exposure.

Here's a list of unexpected sources of wheat and gluten:

Beverages

Ales, beers, lagers (though
there is an increasing
number of gluten-free
beers)
Bloody Mary mixes
Coffees, flavored
Herbal teas made with
wheat, barley, or malt
Malt liquor

Teas, flavored
Vodkas distilled from
wheat (Absolut, Grey
Goose, Stolichnaya)
Wine coolers (containing
barley malt)
Whiskey distilled from
wheat or barley

Breakfast Cereals

I trust you can tell that cereals such as Shredded Wheat and
Wheaties contain wheat. However, there are those that appear
wheat-free that most decidedly are not.

Bran cereals (All Bran,
Bran Buds, Raisin Bran)
Corn flakes (Corn Flakes,
Frosted Flakes, Crunchy
Corn Bran)
Granola cereals
"Healthy" cereals (Smart
Start, Special K, Grape
Nuts, Trail Mix Crunch)

Muesli, Mueslix
Oat cereals (Cheerios,
Cracklin' Oat Bran,
Honey Bunches of Oats)
Popped corn cereals (Corn
Pops)
Puffed rice cereals (Rice
Krispies)

Cheese

Because the cultures used to ferment some cheeses come in contact with bread (bread mold), they potentially present a gluten
exposure risk.

Blue cheese
Cottage cheese (not all)

Gorgonzola cheese
Roquefort

Coloring/Fillers/Texturizers/Thickeners

These hidden sources can be among the most problematic, since they are often buried deep in the ingredient list or sound like they have nothing to do with wheat or gluten. Unfortunately, there is often no way to tell from the label, nor will the manufacturer be able to tell you, since these ingredients are often produced by a supplier.

Artificial colors	Emulsifiers
Artificial flavors	Maltodextrin (?)
Caramel coloring (?)	Modified food starch
Caramel flavoring (?)	Stabilizers
Dextrimaltose	Textured vegetable protein

Energy, Protein, and Meal Replacement Bars

Clif Bars	Kashi GoLean bars
Gatorade Pre-Game Fuel Nutrition bars	Power Bars
	Slim-Fast meal bars
GNC Pro Performance bars	

Fast Food

At many fast food restaurants, the oil used to fry French fries may be the same oil used to fry bread crumb–coated chicken patties. Likewise, cooking surfaces may be shared. Foods you wouldn't ordinarily regard as wheat-containing often do contain wheat, such as scrambled eggs made with pancake batter or Taco Bell nacho chips and potato bites. Sauces, sausages, and burritos typically contain wheat or wheat-derived ingredients.

Foods that don't contain wheat or gluten are, in fact, the exception at fast food restaurants. It is therefore difficult, some say near impossible, to confidently obtain wheat- and gluten-free foods at these places. (You shouldn't be eating there anyway!) However, some chains, such as Subway, Arby's, Wendy's, and Chipotle Mexican Grill, confidently claim that many of their products are gluten-free and/or offer a gluten-free menu.

Hot Cereals

Cream of Wheat
Farina
Malt-O-Meal

Oatmeal
Oat bran

Meats

Breaded meats
Canned meats
Deli meats (luncheon
    meats, salami)
Hot dogs
Imitation bacon

Imitation crabmeat
Hamburger (if bread
    crumbs are added)
Sausage
Turkey, self-basting

Miscellaneous

This can be a real problem area, since identifiable wheat- or gluten-containing ingredients may not be listed on product labels. A call to the manufacturer may be necessary.

Envelopes (glue)
Gloss and lip balms
Play-Doh
Prescription and over-the-
    counter medications (A
    useful online resource
    can be found at www
    .glutenfreedrugs.com, a
listing maintained by a
    pharmacist.)
Nutritional supplements
    (Many manufacturers
    will specify "gluten-free"
    on the label.)
Lipstick
Stamps (glue)

Sauces, Salad Dressings, and Condiments

Gravies thickened with
    wheat flour
Ketchup
Malt syrup
Malt vinegar
Marinades

Miso
Mustards containing wheat
Salad dressings
Soy sauce
Teriyaki sauce

Seasonings

Curry powder   Seasoning mixes   Taco seasoning

Snacks and Desserts

Cookies, crackers, and pretzels are obvious wheat-containing snacks. But there are plenty of not-so-obvious items.

Cake frosting
Candy bars
Chewing gum (powdered coating)
Chex mixes
Corn chips
Dried fruit (lightly coated with flour)
Dry roasted peanuts
Fruit fillings with thickeners
Jelly beans (not including Jelly Bellies and Starburst)
Granola bars
Ice cream (cookies and cream, Oreo Cookie, cookie dough, cheesecake, chocolate malt)
Ice cream cones
Licorice
Nut bars
Pies
Potato chips (including Pringles)
Roasted nuts
Tiramisu
Tortilla chips, flavored
Trail mixes

Soups

Bisques
Broths, bouillon
Canned soups
Soup mixes
Soup stocks and bases

Soy and Vegetarian Products

Veggie burgers (Boca Burgers, Gardenburgers, Morningstar Farms)
Vegetarian "chicken" strips
Vegetarian chili
Vegetarian hot dogs and sausages
Vegetarian "scallops"
Vegetarian "steaks"

Sweeteners

Barley malt, barley extract
Dextrin and maltodextrin (?)

Malt, malt syrup, malt
flavoring

The *Lose the Wheat, Lose the Weight!* Shopping List

Once you've cleared the shelves of wheat-containing products, you will need to repopulate them with the essentials that allow you to navigate a wheat-free diet. These foods form the backbone of a healthy wheat-free lifestyle and provide the basic ingredients necessary to create the unique recipes that fit into this approach.

Some of the foods, such as flaxseed and nut meals, are best purchased and used within four weeks to minimize oxidation of the oils.

- Almond milk, unsweetened
- Cheeses: Keep a variety on hand, including Parmesan, mozzarella, and ricotta
- Cocoa powder, unsweetened and undutched (containing no "alkali" on the list of ingredients)
- Coconut flour
- Coconut milk
- Coconut, shredded and unsweetened
- Extracts: almond, coconut, vanilla
- Flaxseed, ground
- Ground nut meal: ground almonds, pecans, walnuts
- Lean meats
- Nut butters: Almond butter, peanut butter, sunflower seed butter
- Nuts: Raw almonds, pecans, walnuts, pistachios, hazelnuts, Brazil nuts; chopped walnuts or pecans for baking
- Oils: Extra-virgin olive, walnut, avocado, coconut, flaxseed
- Sea salt
- Shirataki noodles (in the refrigerated section)
- Soymilk (full-fat, unsweetened)
- Sweeteners—stevia, sucralose, xylitol, erythritol, Truvia, or Pure Via
- Tofu
- Vegetables

CHAPTER 15

HEALTHY WHEAT BELLY– SHRINKING RECIPES

ELIMINATING WHEAT FROM your diet is not insurmountably difficult, but it does require some creativity in the kitchen, as many of your standbys and family favorites will now be on the verboten list. I've come up with relatively simple, healthy recipes, including some that can serve to replace familiar wheat-containing dishes.

These recipes were created with several ground rules in place:

Wheat is replaced with healthy alternatives. This may seem obvious, but the majority of wheat-free foods on the market or gluten-free recipes do *not* yield truly healthy foods. Substituting wheat with cornstarch, brown rice starch, potato starch, or tapioca starch, for example, as is often done in gluten-free recipes, will make you fat and diabetic. In the recipes listed here, wheat flour is replaced with nut meals, ground flaxseed, and coconut flour, foods that are nutritious and do not share any of the abnormal responses triggered by wheat or other common wheat substitutes.

Unhealthy fats like hydrogenated, polyunsaturated, and oxidized oils are avoided. The fats used in these recipes tend to be richer in monounsaturates and saturates, especially olive oil and neutral lauric acid–rich coconut oil.

Low-carbohydrate exposure is maintained. Because a low-carb effort is healthier for a long list of reasons, such as losing visceral fat, suppressing inflammatory phenomena, reducing

Wheat-Free Makeovers

You might think that by going wheat free you'll never enjoy some of your favorite dishes again. Fear not. Many wheat-based classics can be switched with almost-perfect wheat-free matches, and most of the time you'll hardly notice the difference. Deprivation is not necessarily part of the equation. It simply means identifying healthy foods that can replace your former favorites—without triggering fatigue, mental "fog," increased appetite, blood sugar and inflammation, mood swings, etc., i.e., all the life- and health-disrupting consequences of wheat consumption.

Many familiar wheat-containing foods can be replaced with nonwheat substitutes prepared from recipes in *Lose the Wheat, Lose the Weight*. The recipes in the book serve as a starting place; many variations on the recipes are easily possible and are limited only by your imagination. For instance, chocolate chip cookies can be made using the basic recipe for ginger spice cookies just by substituting one cup of semisweet chocolate chips for the ginger, allspice, and nutmeg. Key lime cheesecake can be made using the classic cheesecake with wheatless crust recipe by substituting the juice of three limes and the zest from the peel of one lime for the lemon juice and lemon zest; leave out the vanilla extract.

Instead of having . . .	Enjoy this makeover . . .
Bagels	Apple walnut "bread" (page 289)
Carrot cake	Carrot cake (page 295)
Cheesecake	Classic cheesecake with wheatless crust (page 297)
Cereal	Hot coconut flaxseed cereal (page 258), granola (page 258)
Cookies	Ginger spice cookies (page 294)
Crackers	Flaxseed crackers (Flackers, Mary's Gone Crackers, Foods Alive)
Croutons	Slivered almonds, dry roasted pecans
Donuts	Banana-blueberry muffins*, pumpkin spice muffins*
Granola	Granola*
Muffins	Banana-blueberry muffins*, pumpkin spice muffins*
Pancakes	Almond flour pancakes
Pasta, noodles	Shirataki noodles (shirataki noodle stir-fry, page 272), zucchini "pasta" with baby bella mushrooms (page 270)
Pizza	Vegetable pizza (page 269)
Pretzels	Raw almonds, cashews, pecans, pistachios, walnuts; dry roasted peanuts (with no added ingredients)
Wraps	Flaxseed wraps (page 263)

expression of small LDL particles, and minimizing or reversing exceptionally common diabetic tendencies, these recipes are all low in carbohydrate content. The only recipe listed below that contains a more generous amount of carbohydrates is the granola; however, the granola recipe is easily modified to suit your needs.

Artificial sweeteners are used. The compromise I draw in order to re-create several familiar dishes sans sugar is to use the artificial or non-nutritive sweeteners that I believe are the most benign and well tolerated by the majority. Erythritol, xylitol, sucralose, and stevia are among the sweeteners that will not impact blood sugar levels, nor cause gastrointestinal distress as mannitol or sorbitol can. They are also safe, lacking the adverse potential health consequences of aspartame and saccharin. One widely available erythritol/stevia mix (which actually contains a *component* of stevia called rebiana) is Truvia, the sweetener I used in testing most of these recipes.

The quantity of sweeteners specified may also seem low and the quantity may need to be adjusted to your preference. Because most people who eliminate wheat from their diet have a reawakened sensitivity to sweetness, they find most conventional sweet foods *sickeningly* sweet. This has been addressed by reducing the dose of sweetener in the recipes. If you are just starting out on your wheat-free journey, however, and still desire sweetness, then feel free to increase the quantity of artificial sweetener over that specified.

Also note that the potency of various sweeteners, especially stevia powdered extracts, varies in sweetness, since some are combined with fillers like maltodextrin or inulin. Consult the label of the sweetener you purchase or use the following conversions to determine the sucrose equivalent of your sweetener.

1 cup sucrose =
1 cup Stevia Extract in the Raw (and other stevia extracts mixed with maltodextrin meant to match sucrose ounce for ounce. However, be aware that Maltodextrin can raise blood sugar.)

1 cup granulated Splenda

¼ cup stevia extract powder (e.g., Trader Joe's); however, more so than other sweeteners, stevia extract powders differ widely in sweetness. It is best to consult the label for sucrose equivalent of the specific brand you purchase.

⅓ cup + 1½ tablespoons (or approximately 7 tablespoons) Truvia

2 tablespoons liquid stevia extract

1⅓ cups erythritol

1 cup xylitol

My favorite sweeteners are liquid stevia and Truvia, since they lack the maltodextrin.

Lastly, these recipes were created with a busy schedule and limited time in mind and are therefore reasonably easy to prepare. Most ingredients used are widely available.

To be safe, please note that anyone with celiac disease or its nonintestinal equivalents should also choose ingredients that are gluten-free. All ingredients I've listed in the recipes were chosen to be readily available as gluten-free, but obviously, you can never control the behavior of every food manufacturer and what they put in their products. Check to be sure.

FOODS YOU NEED TO KNOW

The wheat-free lifestyle can be made immensely easier and more interesting by knowing about a handful of healthy ingredients that can take the place of wheat. Unlike gluten-free wheat alternatives that include cornstarch, rice starch, tapioca starch, and potato starch, these essential food ingredients will not generate unhealthy responses. Most of these foods can be purchased in major grocery stores. Some, like coconut flour and xanthan gum, can be found in specialty food stores, health food stores, or markets with large natural food sections.

Almond Butter

Almond butter is just like peanut butter except that it's ground from almonds. Like the natural form of peanut butter, almond butter settles and needs to be mixed, since many manufacturers have chosen to not use emulsifying agents. Dip dark chocolate into it or add it to your baked dishes, or just use it anywhere you might use peanut butter.

Almond Meal

Almond meal is simply ground almonds and is among the most versatile of wheat-free replacement ingredients, useful as a wheat substitute to make breads, muffins, and pancakes. Almond meal ground from whole almonds that includes skins provides a greater quantity of fiber compared to almond meal ground from blanched almonds (sometimes called almond "flour"). A half cup of almond meal contains a modest three grams "net" carbs (i.e., total carbs minus fiber), an impressive 12 grams protein, and 30 grams fat. (Remember: Fat is good!) When replacing wheat flour with almond meal in your recipes, use approximately one third less almond meal, e.g., 2 cups almond meal in place of 3 cups wheat flour.

Cocoa

Cocoa fits very nicely into a wheat-free lifestyle. Not only does it provide that wonderful chocolate taste, it is densely packed with flavonoids, plant-sourced nutrients that are anti-oxidative, reduce blood pressure, increase good HDL cholesterol, and thereby reduces cardiovascular risk.

Look for the undutched variety, i.e., cocoa not treated with alkali. Alkali treatment reduces bitterness but also dramatically reduces the flavonoid content and thereby the health benefits.

Look for cocoa powders without the word "alkali" listed on the ingredients. Scharffen Berger, Ghirardelli, and Trader Joe make widely available undutched cocoas.

Cocoa powder can replace higher sugar bittersweet or semi-sweet chocolate in recipes by using 1½ tablespoons of cocoa powder for every ounce of chocolate.

Cocoa Butter

Just as cocoa powder is an excellent healthy food, so is the oil extracted from cocoa beans. Cocoa butter provides a light cocoa flavor and can be used in place of butter in recipes and cooking when a mild cocoa flavor is desired. Use cocoa butter just as you would dairy butter or other oils and in equal amounts. Not readily available in markets, shop for cocoa butter online at www.kingarthurflour.com.

Coconut Flour

Coconut flour does a darned good job of mimicking the feel and texture of wheat flour, though it lacks the unique viscoelasticity of wheat gluten. Coconut flour in bread and cake recipes yields a finer texture than nut meals, a texture approaching that of pound cake. If you've not used coconut flour in your baking before, you will be pleasantly surprised at the warm, breadlike scent of the freshly baked flour. To make your recipe less dense, it can be combined with nut meals like almond meal and/or ground flaxseed. Coconut flour also works well with added xanthan or guar gum to increase the clinginess of the flour; ½ teaspoon per cup coconut flour can go a long way.

To replace wheat flour with coconut flour in your recipes, use approximately two thirds of the amount called for. For example, replace 3 cups wheat flour with 2 cups coconut flour, or 1 cup coconut flour with 1 cup almond meal. For baking wheat-free breads, a tablespoon or two of ground flaxseed can be added to the coconut/almond meal flour mix for fiber. The final volume of bread will be less, since there is no rising process.

Coconut flour is relatively low in carbohydrates, with 24 grams net carbs (i.e., total carbs minus fiber) per cup. A loaf of bread made with 2 cups of coconut flour will therefore yield 48 grams carbs in the entire loaf. If cut into twelve pieces, there will be a modest 2 grams carbs per slice.

Coconut Milk

Not to be confused with the coconut water that is naturally contained within coconuts, the milk is prepared by straining the coconut meat. It varies in thickness from brand to brand. It also settles and should therefore be mixed prior to use.

Coconut milk is useful as a replacement for milk or sour cream in recipes, adding thickness and a mild coconutty taste. Use coconut milk in the same way and in equal amounts. Don't be afraid of the saturated fat in coconut milk, as it is rich in the neutral fatty acid lauric acid that has no known adverse effects (see coconut oil below).

Coconut Oil

Coconut oil is tropical oil, much maligned by nutritionists in past due to its saturated fat content. It is a solid at room temperature, white in color with a light coconut scent.

Half the fatty acids of the saturated fat in coconut oil are lauric acid, which has little to no effect on increasing "bad" LDL cholesterol. There are smaller quantities of myristic and palmitic acids that do have the potential for increasing LDL. On the whole, however, the effect tends to be small and coconut oil can be a useful and delicious addition to your wheat-free pantry.

Because of its high smoke point (450° F), coconut oil is great for cooking and holds up well in a variety of dishes. Use coconut oil just as you would any other oil, though because it is a solid at room temperature, it will need to be melted prior to use.

Erythritol

Erythritol is a naturally occurring sugar alcohol sweetener that provides no calories. It is therefore useful as a sugar substitute. It is the main ingredient, for instance, in Truvía, along with rebiana from stevia.

Unlike the sugar alcohols mannitol and sorbitol, erythritol usually does not cause gas, cramping, and diarrhea unless consumed in very large quantities. Erythritol is approximately 70 percent as sweet as sucrose. A good way to start out is to replace sucrose ounce for ounce, cup for cup, until you gauge its sweetness in your recipes and increase as necessary.

Flaxseed

If there is a perfect grain, it's flaxseed. It's high in protein and has a negligible quantity of ("net") carbohydrate. The fat in flaxseed is rich in the fatty acid linolenic acid, which has health effects second only to the omega-3 fatty acids in fish. Flaxseed is an excellent source of fiber in a wheat-free diet, containing four grams per two tablespoons. Most of the fiber is the soluble variety that reduces LDL cholesterol. Just be sure to hydrate when adding flaxseed, since it is highly water absorbent and can cause constipation if you are inadequately hydrated.

Flaxseed can be eaten on its own as a hot cereal (with added unsweetened almond milk, strawberries, and walnuts, for instance) or added to other dishes. It can be used as "breading" for chicken, fish, or pork (add herbs like dried oregano and thyme). Add ground flaxseed to smoothies and nonwheat "bread" recipes to increase your fiber intake.

Flaxseed comes in two varieties: golden and brown. Different sources can also have different tastes. So if you purchase one that has, for instance, an off flavor, purchase your flaxseed from someplace else. While you can grind flaxseed yourself (it must be ground, else the hard fiber coating makes it indigestible), many grocery and health food stores sell preground flaxseed. Store your flaxseed in the refrigerator, since the linolenic acid can go rancid (oxidize) after a few months.

Guar Gum

Guar gum is a soluble fiber sourced from the guar bean. Along with xanthan gum, guar gum recreates the clinginess and solidity otherwise provided by wheat gluten. It is commonly used in ice cream to inhibit formation of ice crystals. It makes nonwheat flours like coconut regain some of the clinginess of wheat flour for baking breads, muffins, and pancakes.

Guar gum should be used sparingly, e.g., ½ to ¾ teaspoon for a "bread" recipe, else the result will be too gummy. As little as ¼ to ½ teaspoon per cup of nonwheat flour is sufficient for most recipes.

Pecan Meal

Pecan meal is simply ground pecans. Pecan meal, like walnut meal, is most useful as an ingredient in pie crusts and the crust of cheesecake, as well as "breading" for chicken and fish. For a cheesecake or pie crust every bit as delicious as one made of graham crackers, use 1½ cups pecan meal.

Shirataki Noodles

The oddly named shirataki noodles are made from the konjac root, sometimes called glucomannan. Shirataki noodles are essentially pure fiber and provide a negligible quantity of digestible carbohydrate; they are therefore a fabulous food for weight loss.

Shirataki noodles are a reasonable facsimile of wheat noodles in taste and texture, especially the tofu variety. You'll find shirataki noodles in a variety of shapes like spaghetti, fettucine, and angel hair. Miracle and House are two excellent brands. You'll find shirataki noodles at Asian markets and upscale grocery stores, including Whole Foods, in the refrigerator section, since they are packaged with liquid. Drain the liquid in a colander, rinse for 15 seconds, and cook in boiling water for about two minutes or according to package directions. Add the noodles to marinara sauce, stir-fry, or any other dish ordinarily prepared with wheat noodles.

Stevia

This plant-based sweetener from the stevia plant (even its leaves are sweet) has been around for years, but it recently got thrust into the mainstream non-nutritive sweetener spotlight when agri-giant Cargill got into the act. The FDA also recently provided its blessing, declaring stevia Generally Recognized As Safe (GRAS) in 2008. Stevia is as close as any non-nutritive sweetener can get to being problem-free.

The best stevia comes in liquid forms and is exceptionally concentrated. One teaspoon of liquid stevia concentrate is equivalent in sweetness to one cup of sugar. (Though this can vary from brand to brand; adjusting your recipes to desired sweetness will be necessary.) Many of the powdered stevia extract forms, e.g., Stevia in the Raw, are actually mostly maltodextrin derived from corn and thereby provide some calories and occasional gastrointestinal intolerances. Others contain lactose, or milk sugar, and should be avoided by those with lactose intolerance. Truvia, the Cargill product, consists of the stevia-derived rebiana along with erythritol. The quantity of stevia or stevia combined with maltodextrin or other ingredients to equal sucrose varies from one brand to another. Stevia in the Raw, for example, can be used on an equal volume basis to sucrose. Stevia liquid extracts vary, but typically four drops equals one teaspoon sucrose, while one teaspoon equals one cup sucrose. Consult the label of whatever brand you purchase.

Sunflower Seed Butter

Sunflower seed butter, like peanut butter, is a wonderful spread for wheat-free "breads." Dip your dark chocolate into it or use it in recipes in place of peanut butter for a slight variation in taste.

Sunflower seed butter can be purchased or ground from raw

sunflower seeds in a food processor. Watch the sugar content of purchased products, however.

Walnut Meal

Walnut meal is especially useful as piecrust or the crust for cheesecake recipes. Walnut meal has a nuttier taste than almonds and, while it can be used to make breads like almond meal, can yield a heavier, nutlike flavor.

Xanthan Gum

Xanthan gum is the gluten-free answer to increase clinginess of whatever wheat flour substitute you choose, such as almond meal or coconut flour. It confers more stiffness to breads, muffins, or other baked foods. It also adds a modest quantity of fiber, since it is essentially pure fiber. Bob's Red Mill is one brand that is widely available in grocery stores.

Use it sparingly, as too much will inhibit the natural rising that occurs during baking and alters the taste. For most "bread" recipes using almond meal, as little as ½ teaspoon per cup of nonwheat flour is sufficient. Recipes using coconut flour work well with slightly more, e.g., ¾ teaspoon per cup coconut flour.

Xylitol

Xylitol is a naturally occurring sugar alcohol sweetener that provides no calories. It is therefore useful as a sugar substitute. It has the added benefit of being good for dental health, as it reduces the number of bacteria in the mouth that lead to cavities.

Unlike the sugar alcohols mannitol and sorbitol, xylitol usually does not cause gas, cramping, and diarrhea unless consumed in very large quantities.

Zucchini

The noodle-like consistency of finely sliced zucchini (sliced using a vegetable peeler), along with its nearly neutral taste, make it a versatile replacement for pasta. With a measly two grams "net" carbs per cup, it easily fits into a low-carbohydrate lifestyle.

Choose smaller zucchini for slightly stronger flavor. Also, don't skimp on ingredients like basil, oregano, and Parmesan, since a more generous quantity is needed for full flavor compared to wheat flour pasta. (See the recipe for zucchini "pasta" with baby bella mushrooms on page 270.)

Zucchini Flour

Flour ground from dehydrated zucchini can be used to thicken recipes in place of wheat flour or cornstarch. Dehydrate zucchini in a dehydrator, then grind in a coffee grinder or food processor. Substitute in equivalent quantities.

BERRY-COCONUT SMOOTHIE

This smoothie is perfect for a breakfast on the run or as a quick snack. You will find it more filling than most smoothies thanks to the coconut milk. Berries are the only sweetener, which keeps the sugar to a minimum.

Makes 1 serving

½ cup coconut milk

½ cup low-fat plain yogurt

¼ cup blueberries, blackberries, strawberries, or other berries

½ cup unflavored or vanilla whey protein powder

1 tablespoon ground flaxseeds (can be purchased pre-ground)

½ teaspoon coconut extract

4 ice cubes

Combine the coconut milk, yogurt, berries, whey protein, flaxseed, coconut extract, and ice cubes. Blend until smooth. Serve immediately.

GRANOLA

This granola will satisfy most people's desire for a sweet, crunchy snack, though its taste and look are different from those of conventional granola. You can also have the granola as a cereal with milk, coconut milk, soymilk, or unsweetened almond milk. The oats (or quinoa) and dried fruit included in this mix can have blood sugar consequences, but the quantities are modest and therefore likely to have limited blood sugar effects in most people.

Makes 6 servings

½ cup quinoa flakes or old-fashioned rolled oats

½ cup ground flaxseeds (can be purchased pre-ground)

¼ cup raw hulled pumpkin seeds (pepitas)

1 cup chopped raw cashews

½ cup sugar-free vanilla syrup (e.g., Torani or DaVinci)

¼ cup walnut oil

1 cup chopped pecans

½ cup sliced almonds

¼ cup raisins, dried cherries, or unsweetened dried cranberries

Preheat the oven to 325°F.

Combine the quinoa or oats, ground flaxseeds, pumpkin seeds, ½ cup of the cashews, the vanilla syrup, and walnut oil in a large bowl and toss to coat. Spread the mixture in 8 x 8-inch baking pan and press to make an even layer about ½ inch thick. Bake until nearly dry and crispy, about 30 minutes. Let the mixture cool in the pan for at least 1 hour.

Meanwhile, combine the pecans, almonds, dried fruit, and remaining ½ cup cashews in a large bowl.

Break the cooled quinoa-flax mixture into little pieces. Stir into the nut-fruit bowl.

HOT COCONUT FLAXSEED CEREAL

You will be surprised how filling this simple hot breakfast cereal can be, especially if coconut milk is used.

Makes 1 to 2 servings

½ cup coconut milk, whole dairy milk, full-fat soymilk, or unsweetened almond milk

½ cup ground flaxseeds (can be purchased pre-ground)

¼ cup unsweetened coconut flakes

¼ cup chopped walnuts, walnut halves, or raw hulled sunflower seeds

Ground cinnamon

¼ cup sliced strawberries, blueberries, or other berries (optional)

Combine the milk, ground flaxseeds, coconut flakes, and walnuts or sunflower seeds in a microwaveable bowl and microwave for 1 minute. Serve topped with a sprinkle of cinnamon and a few berries if desired.

EGG AND PESTO BREAKFAST WRAP

This delicious wrap can be prepared the evening before and refrigerated overnight as a convenient and filling breakfast.

Makes 1 serving

1 Flaxseed Wrap (page 263)

1 tablespoon basil pesto or sun-dried tomato pesto

1 hard-boiled egg, peeled and sliced thinly

2 thin slices tomato

Handful of baby spinach or shredded lettuce

If the wrap is freshly made, allow it to cool for 5 minutes. Then spread the pesto in a 2-inch strip down the center of the wrap. Placed sliced egg on the pesto strip, followed by tomato slices. Top with spinach or lettuce. Roll up.

RICOTTA PANCAKES WITH STRAWBERRIES

These are delicate and light. Before beating the egg whites, wipe out the mixer bowl and beaters with a paper towel moistened with vinegar to ensure they are sparkling clean. Organic brown rice flour is found at many specialty stores or in the natural foods section of the supermarket. Store it in the freezer, well wrapped, to keep it fresh.

Makes 4 servings

8 medium strawberries, hulls removed

3 large eggs, yolks and whites separated

⅔ cup whole milk ricotta cheese

2 tablespoons milk

½ teaspoon vanilla extract

½ cup organic brown rice flour

½ teaspoon baking powder

¼ teaspoon baking soda

¼ teaspoon ground cinnamon

⅛ teaspoon salt

1 tablespoon unsalted butter, melted

Put the strawberries in a food processor and puree until smooth. Scrape into a bowl or pitcher and set aside.

In a large bowl, whisk the egg yolks, ricotta, milk, and vanilla until blended. Stir in the rice flour, baking powder, baking soda, cinnamon, and salt.

In a medium bowl, with an electric mixer at medium speed, beat the egg whites until frothy. Increase the mixer speed to high and beat just until stiff but not dry peaks form when the beaters are lifted. With a rubber spatula, fold the beaten whites into the rice flour mixture.

Brush a pancake griddle or large nonstick skillet with some of the melted butter. Heat over medium heat until hot. For each pancake, drop ¼ cup batter onto the griddle or skillet. Cook for about 3 minutes, or until the edges begin to look dry and the underside is browned, reducing the heat if necessary. Turn and cook for 1 to 2 minutes longer, until the underside is browned. Transfer to a warmed platter. Repeat, brushing the pan again with butter and cooking the remaining batter, making 12 pancakes.

Serve hot with the strawberry puree. (Could also top with a sugar-free strawberry syrup, such as those made by Torani or DaVinci.)

CRUSTLESS SPINACH AND CHEESE MINI-QUICHES

A muffin pan will work best for these quiches; they'll lift right out. Serve them for breakfast or for brunch with a salad or a thin slice of melon. If you're the only one in your household, prepare these and you'll have a few days worth of satisfying breakfasts. They keep 2 or 3 days and can be rewarmed in the microwave, loosely covered, for about 30 seconds.

Makes 4 servings

1 cup thinly sliced asparagus (¼-inch pieces)

1 tablespoon olive oil

1 small sweet onion (8 ounces), coarsely chopped

1 package (5 ounces) baby spinach

½ teaspoon salt

¼ teaspoon pepper

¼ teaspoon ground nutmeg

¼ teaspoon dried marjoram

4 large eggs

⅓ cup 1% milk

¾ cup shredded sharp white Cheddar cheese

Preheat the oven to 325°F. Coat 8 muffin pan cups and the top of the pan with olive oil cooking spray or healthy oil such as coconut oil, walnut oil, or olive oil.

In a small saucepan, bring ½ inch water to a boil. Add the asparagus and cook for 3 to 4 minutes, or until crisp-tender. Drain and cool briefly under cold running water. Set aside.

In a large skillet, warm the oil over medium heat. Add the onion and cook, stirring often, for 5 minutes, or until tender. Add half the spinach and 1 tablespoon water. Cook, stirring, until wilted. Add the remaining spinach and cook until wilted. Stir in the salt, pepper, nutmeg, and marjoram. Remove from the heat.

Meanwhile, in a large bowl, whisk the eggs and milk until well blended. Stir in the asparagus and spinach mixture. Using a ½-cup measure, scoop ½ cup into each prepared muffin cup, filling them right to the top. Sprinkle each with 1½ tablespoons cheese.

Bake for 18 to 20 minutes, or until puffed, lightly browned at the edges, and set. With a table knife, lift each quiche out of the cup onto plates, serving 2 per person. Serve warm.

TEX-MEX EGG TORTILLA

In Spain, tortillas are really pancake-style omelets filled with sliced potatoes. Here yellow summer squash (or zucchini) is subbed for potatoes. Be sure to read the labels on the salsa when shopping to insure there is no added sugar.

Makes 1 serving

2 large eggs

⅛ teaspoon salt

Pinch pepper

1 tablespoon plus 1 teaspoon olive oil

½ medium-size yellow summer squash, sliced ¼ inch thick (about ¾ cup)

⅛ of a long, medium-hot pepper, seeded and sliced (such as Hungarian wax or hot banana pepper), optional

1 scallion, thinly sliced

¼ cup shredded Monterey Jack or white Cheddar cheese

1 tablespoon coarsely chopped cilantro leaves

¼ ripe avocado, diced

3 tablespoons chunky medium salsa

In a small bowl, whisk the eggs, salt, and pepper with 1 tablespoon water.

In a heavy, medium-size skillet, warm the oil over medium heat. Add the squash and hot-pepper slices, if using, and cook, turning often, for 3 to 4 minutes, or until just tender and starting to brown. Add the scallion and cook for 1 minute more. Arrange the squash slices in a single layer in the skillet.

Pour in the egg mixture. Cook for about 3 minutes, lifting the edges to allow the uncooked egg to flow underneath, until just set. If egg starts to stick, loosen with a spatula and add a little more oil if needed. Sprinkle with the cheese and cilantro; cover and remove from the heat. Let stand for about 1 minute, or until the cheese has melted.

In a cup, mix the avocado and salsa. Transfer the egg to a plate and spoon the avocado mixture alongside. Serve hot.

FLAXSEED WRAP

Wraps made with flaxseed and egg are surprisingly tasty. Once you get the hang of it, you can whip up a wrap or two in just a few minutes. If you have two pie pans, you can make two wraps at a time and accelerate the process (though they will need to be microwaved one at a time). Flaxseed wraps can be refrigerated and will keep for a few days. Healthy variations are possible simply by using various vegetable juices (such as spinach or carrot) in place of the water called for.

Makes 1 serving

3 tablespoons ground flaxseeds (can be purchased pre-ground)

¼ teaspoon baking powder

¼ teaspoon onion powder

¼ teaspoon paprika

Pinch of fine sea salt or celery salt

1 tablespoon coconut oil, melted, plus more for greasing the pans

1 tablespoon water

1 large egg

Mix together the ground flaxseeds, baking powder, onion powder, paprika, and salt in a small bowl. Stir in the 1 tablespoon coconut oil. Beat in the egg and 1 tablespoon water until blended.

Grease a microwave-safe glass or plastic pie pan with coconut oil. Pour in the batter and spread evenly over the bottom. Microwave on high for 2 to 3 minutes until cooked. Let cool about 5 minutes.

To remove, lift up an edge with a spatula. If it sticks, use a pancake turner to gently loosen from the pan. Flip the wrap over and top with desired ingredients.

TURKEY-AVOCADO WRAPS

Here's one of hundreds of ways to use my flaxseed wraps for a tasty and filling breakfast, lunch, or dinner. As an alternative to making this with a sauce, spread a thin layer of hummus or pesto on the wrap before adding the other ingredients.

Makes 1 serving

Flaxseed Wrap (page 263), cooled if freshly made

3 or 4 deli slices roast turkey

2 thin slices Swiss cheese

¼ cup bean sprouts

½ Hass avocado, thinly sliced

Handful of baby spinach leaves or shredded lettuce

1 tablespoon mayonnaise, mustard, wasabi mayonnaise, or sugar-free salad dressing

Place the turkey and Swiss cheese in the center of the wrap. Spread the bean sprouts, avocado, and spinach or lettuce on top. Top with a dollop of mayo, mustard, or other favorite condiment. Roll up.

MEXICAN TORTILLA SOUP

There's no tortilla in this Mexican tortilla soup, just the idea of something to accompany foods that go with tortillas. I made this recipe for my family and it was one I regretted not doubling up on, as everybody asked for seconds.

Makes 4 servings

4 cups low-sodium chicken broth

¼ cup extra-virgin olive oil

1 pound boneless, skinless chicken breasts, cut into ½-inch chunks

2 to 3 garlic cloves, minced

1 large Spanish onion, finely chopped

1 red bell pepper, finely chopped

2 tomatoes, finely chopped

3 to 4 jalapeño chile peppers, seeded and finely chopped

   Fine sea salt and ground black pepper

2 Hass avocados

1 cup shredded Monterey Jack or Cheddar cheese (4 ounces)

½ cup chopped fresh cilantro

4 tablespoons sour cream

Bring the broth to a boil in a large saucepan over medium heat; keep warm.

Meanwhile, heat the oil in a large skillet over medium heat. Add the chicken and garlic and cook until the chicken is nicely browned, 5 to 6 minutes.

Add the cooked chicken, onion, bell pepper, tomatoes, and jalapeños to the stock. Return the broth to a boil. Reduce to a simmer, cover, and cook for 30 minutes. Add salt and black pepper to taste.

Halve the avocados lengthwise, remove the pits, and peel. Cut lengthwise into ¼-inch-thick slices.

Ladle the soup into shallow soup bowls. Top each bowl with sliced avocado, cheese, cilantro, and a spoonful of sour cream.

CHICKEN SOUP WITH CHUNKY VEGETABLES

You can mix and match the vegetables in this soup, if you like. Add some spinach or kale, or stir in leftover steamed vegetables, such as broccoli or cauliflower. The parsley and dill are optional, but they add a wonderful fresh, simmered-for-hours flavor.

Makes 4 servings

½ pound skinned and boned chicken breast halves, cut into ½-inch cubes

¼ teaspoon salt

1 box (32 ounces) reduced-sodium, organic chicken broth

1 cup water

2 large carrots, peeled and cut into thin rounds

2 medium celery stalks with leaves, thinly sliced

1 package (8 ounces) tofu Shiratake spaghetti noodles, drained and well-rinsed

1 cup cut asparagus (½-inch pieces)

2 scallions, thinly sliced

2 tablespoons snipped fresh dill (optional)

2 tablespoons chopped fresh flat-leaf parsley (optional)

Put the chicken and salt in large saucepan. Add the broth, water, carrots, and celery, and bring to a boil over high heat. Skim off the foam that rises to the surface.

Reduce the heat to low, cover and simmer for 10 minutes, or until the chicken and vegetables are tender. Stir in the noodles and asparagus, cover and simmer for 3 minutes longer, or until the asparagus is crisp-tender. Stir in the scallions, dill, and parsley, if using. Remove from the heat and let stand, covered, for 2 minutes before serving.

TUNA-AVOCADO SALAD

Few combinations burst with as much flavor and zest as this mixture of avocado with lime and fresh cilantro. If being prepared for later, the avocado and lime are best added just before serving. The salad can be served as is or with added salad dressing. Avocado salad dressings match particularly well.

4　cups mixed greens or baby spinach

1　carrot, shredded

4　ounces tuna (pouch or canned)

1　teaspoon chopped fresh cilantro

1　avocado, pitted, peeled, and cubed

2　lime wedges

Combine the greens and carrot in a salad bowl (or storage bowl). Add the tuna and cilantro and toss to combine. Just before serving, add the avocado and squeeze the lime wedges over the salad. Toss and serve immediately.

GRILLED CHICKEN CAESAR SALAD

Sure, pecans aren't really croutons, but why not? They have all the important elements: great crunch and great taste. But even better, they are very good for you.

Makes 4 servings

½ cup raw pecans, broken by hand

¼ cup plain Greek yogurt (unsweetened)

2 tablespoons fresh lemon juice

2 or 3 anchovy fillets, blotted dry, finely chopped

1 small garlic clove, finely grated

¼ cup olive oil, plus 2 teaspoons for the grill pan

¼ teaspoon salt

¼ teaspoon pepper

1 pound chicken tenders

1 bag (9 ounces, 8 cups) cut romaine or baby romaine

½ cup finely grated Parmesan cheese

Preheat the oven to 400°F. Put the pecans in a small baking dish and bake, stirring once, for 10 to 12 minutes, or until toasted. Remove from the oven and tip into a plate; let cool.

Meanwhile, in a medium bowl, put the yogurt. Whisk in the lemon juice, anchovies, and garlic, then gradually whisk in the ¼ cup oil until well blended. Stir in the salt and pepper.

Put the chicken tenders in a small dish and coat with 3 tablespoons of the dressing.

Generously brush a grill pan with some of the remaining 2 teaspoons olive oil and heat over medium-high heat for 2 minutes. Add the chicken, in batches, and cook, turning once and reducing heat if necessary, for 4 to 5 minutes, or until browned and no longer pink in the thickest part, reoiling the pan as needed. Transfer to a plate.

Put the romaine in a large salad bowl. Add the remaining dressing and cooled pecans and toss to coat well. Sprinkle with the Parmesan and top with the chicken. Serve right away.

VEGETABLE PIZZA

This recipe calls for making your own garlic oil. But if you have prepared garlic oil or herb-infused oil in your pantry, feel free to use that. Feel free to serve with a side salad to round out a meal.

Makes 2 servings

One 8½-inch rice flour tortilla

4 teaspoons extra-virgin olive oil or prepared garlic oil

1 garlic clove, smashed with the flat side of a chef's knife

¾ cup shredded fresh mozzarella cheese

½ cup sliced mushrooms

¼ cup thinly sliced red or yellow bell pepper

⅓ cup halved cherry tomatoes

2 tablespoons shredded fresh basil leaves

Pinch crushed red pepper flakes (optional)

Preheat the oven to 425°F. Place the tortilla on a baking sheet.

In a cup, mix the oil and garlic. Brush most of the oil over the tortilla. Sprinkle with the cheese and scatter the mushrooms and bell pepper strips evenly on top. Arrange the cherry tomatoes on the pizza. Bake for 10 minutes, or until the cheese is bubbly and the vegetables just tender.

Remove from the oven and slide onto a plate. Sprinkle with the basil leaves and drizzle with the remaining garlic oil. If desired, add the red pepper flakes. Cut in half. Serve hot.

ZUCCHINI "PASTA" WITH BABY BELLA MUSHROOMS

Using zucchini in place of conventional wheat pasta provides a different taste and texture, but is quite delicious in its own right. Because the zucchini is less assertive in taste than wheat pasta, the more interesting the sauce and toppings, the more interesting the "pasta" will be.

Makes 2 servings

1 pound zucchini

8 ounces uncured (nitrite-free) sausage, ground beef, turkey, chicken, or pork (optional)

3 to 4 tablespoons extra-virgin olive oil

8 to 10 baby bella or cremini mushrooms, sliced

2 to 3 garlic cloves, minced

2 tablespoons chopped fresh basil

Salt and ground black pepper

1 cup tomato sauce or 4 ounces pesto

¼ cup grated Parmesan cheese

Using a vegetable peeler, peel the zucchini. Cut the zucchini lengthwise into ribbons using the vegetable peeler until you reach the seed core. (Reserve the seed core and peel for another use, such as a salad.)

If using meat: Heat 1 tablespoon of the oil in a large skillet. Cook the meat, breaking it up with a spoon, until cooked through. Drain off the fat. Add 2 tablespoons of the oil to the skillet along with the mushrooms and garlic. Cook until the mushrooms soften, 2 to 3 minutes.

If not using meat: Heat 2 tablespoons of the oil in a large skillet over medium heat. Add the mushrooms and garlic and cook for 2 to 3 minutes.

In either case: Add the zucchini strands to the skillet and cook until the zucchini softens, no more than 5 minutes. Add the chopped basil and salt and pepper to taste.

Serve topped with tomato sauce or pesto and sprinkled with the Parmesan.

BRIE, PEAR, AND PROSCIUTTO SANDWICH

This luxurious sandwich is made in a snap. All you need is some ripe Brie cheese (feels soft to the touch), thinly sliced prosciutto, and a firm-ripe pear or crisp apple. If you don't feel like using prosciutto, substitute thinly sliced, flavorful smoked Virginia ham.

Makes 2 servings

2 flaxseed wraps (see page 263)

2 teaspoons grainy Dijon mustard

4 ounces Brie (half a wheel), rind cut off, cheese cut through center into 2 half-moon pieces

4 thin slices prosciutto (2 ounces total)

½ medium-size ripe pear, cored and cut lengthwise into 8 thin slices

(I didn't have this, but it would be very good with ½ cup or less baby arugula per sandwich, or it could be accompanied by an arugula salad.)

Preheat the oven to 375°F. Tear off two 12-inch sheets of foil.

Place a tortilla on a sheet of foil and spread with 1 teaspoon of the mustard. On the bottom half of the tortilla, place the Brie. Top with 2 slices of proscuitto and 4 slices of pear. Fold the tortilla over (don't worry if it breaks), and wrap in the foil, sealing the edges. Repeat with the other tortilla.

Place directly on the oven rack and bake for 15 minutes, or until heated and the cheese has melted. Cut in half crosswise with kitchen scissors and serve hot.

SHIRATAKI NOODLE STIR-FRY

Shirataki noodles are a versatile pasta or noodle replacement, nonwheat of course, made from the konjac root. They exert virtually no effect on blood sugar, since shirataki noodles are low-carbohydrate (3 grams or less per 8-ounce package). Some shirataki noodles have added tofu and have a less chewy, more wheat pasta–like texture. To me they taste uncannily like the ramen noodles of my youth. Like tofu, shirataki noodles will absorb the tastes and smells of the foods they accompany, having little to no taste of their own.

While this recipe is a simple Asian-type use of the noodles, shirataki noodles can also be readily adapted to Italian or other dishes, used in place of conventional wheat pasta. (One manufacturer also makes the noodles in fettuccine, penne rigate, and angel hair styles.)

Makes 2 servings

3 tablespoons toasted sesame oil

½ pound boneless chicken breast, pork loin, or firm tofu, cut into ¾-inch cubes

2 to 3 garlic cloves, minced

¼ pound fresh shiitake mushrooms, stems discarded, caps sliced

2 to 3 tablespoons soy sauce (wheat-free)

½ pound fresh or frozen broccoli, cut into small florets

4 ounces sliced bamboo shoots

1 tablespoon grated fresh ginger

2 teaspoons sesame seeds

½ teaspoon red pepper flakes

2 packages (8 ounces each) shirataki noodles

Heat 2 tablespoons of the sesame oil in a wok or large skillet over medium heat. Add the meat or tofu, garlic, shiitake mushrooms, and soy sauce and cook until the meat is fully cooked or the tofu is lightly browned on all sides. (Add a touch of water if the pan becomes too dry.)

Add the broccoli, bamboo shoots, ginger, sesame seeds, pepper flakes, and remaining 1 tablespoon sesame oil to the wok and stir over medium heat until the broccoli is crisp-tender, 4 to 5 minutes.

While the broccoli cooks, bring 4 cups water to a boil in a large saucepan. Rinse the shirataki noodles in a colander under cold running water for about 15 seconds and drain. Pour the noodles into the boiling water and cook for 3 minutes. Drain the noodles and transfer to the wok with the vegetables. Cook and stir over medium-high heat for 2 minutes to heat through.

CRAB CAKES

These "breaded" wheat-free crab cakes are incredibly easy to prepare. If served with tartar sauce or other compatible sauce and spinach or green leafy lettuce, this dish can easily serve as a main course.

Makes 4 servings

2 tablespoons extra-virgin olive oil

½ red bell pepper, finely diced

¼ yellow onion, finely chopped

2 tablespoons finely minced fresh green chile pepper or to taste

¼ cup ground walnuts

1 large egg

1½ teaspoons curry powder

½ teaspoon ground cumin

Fine sea salt

1 six-ounce can crabmeat, drained and flaked

¼ cup ground flaxseeds (can be purchased pre-ground)

1 teaspoon onion powder

½ teaspoon garlic powder

Baby spinach or mixed salad greens

Tartar sauce (optional)

Preheat the oven to 325°F. Line a baking sheet with foil.

Heat the oil in a large skillet over medium heat. Add the bell pepper, onion, and chile pepper and cook until tender, 4 to 5 minutes. Set aside to cool slightly.

Transfer the vegetables to large bowl. Stir in the walnuts, egg, curry powder, cumin, and a dash of sea salt. Mix the crabmeat into the mixture and stir well. Form into four patties and transfer to the baking sheet.

Stir together the ground flaxseed, onion powder, and garlic powder in a small bowl. Sprinkle the "breading" over the crab cakes. Bake the crab cakes until browned and heated through, about 25 minutes.

Serve on a bed of spinach or salad greens with a dollop of tartar sauce if desired.

GARLIC SHRIMP AND BROCCOLI WITH NOODLES

This is fresher, more flavorful, and way more delicious than any take-out. And you can make it in the time it takes to get carry-out. If you like, use broccolini or broccoli rabe instead of broccoli.

Makes 4 servings

3 tablespoons olive oil

3 to 4 large garlic cloves, thinly sliced

¼ to ½ teaspoon crushed red pepper flakes

1 pound medium peeled and deveined shrimp, tails left on

½ teaspoon salt

6 cups small broccoli florets

1 red bell pepper, cut into thin strips, strips cut in half

½ medium-size sweet white onion, sliced

1 package (8 ounces) tofu shirataki angel hair noodles, drained

½ cup slivered fresh basil

Bring a covered medium saucepan of water to a boil over high heat for the noodles.

Meanwhile, in a large nonstick skillet, combine 2 tablespoons of the oil, the garlic, and pepper flakes. Cook over medium-high heat, stirring for 2 to 4 minutes or until fragrant and lightly golden. Add the shrimp; sprinkle with ¼ teaspoon of the salt and cook, stirring often, for 4 minutes or until pink and just opaque in the thickest part. Transfer the shrimp to a bowl.

Add the remaining 1 tablespoon oil to the skillet. Add the broccoli, bell pepper, onion, and remaining ¼ teaspoon salt. Cook, stirring often, for 4 minutes, or until brightly colored. Add ¼ cup water and reduce the heat to medium. Cover and cook, stirring frequently, adding a tablespoon more water if the pan gets dry, for 5 to 6 minutes or until the vegetables are crisp-tender.

Meanwhile, stir the noodles into the saucepan of boiling water. Cook for 3 minutes; drain.

Add the shrimp and the noodles to the vegetables. Toss to heat through and distribute the noodles evenly. Sprinkle with the basil and serve.

HERB-ROASTED CHICKEN AND GRAVY

This gravy is thickened with arrowroot instead of flour or cornstarch and then whisked with a bit of butter. Use this technique for making gravy for any bird.

Makes 4 servings

1½ teaspoons dried sage

1 teaspoon kosher salt

½ teaspoon dried thyme

½ teaspoon pepper

One 4-pound chicken, giblets removed, rinsed and patted dry

1 large onion, halved and sliced

1 tablespoon olive oil

1¼ cups reduced-sodium, organic chicken broth

4 teaspoons arrowroot, dissolved in 2 tablespoons cold water

1 tablespoon unsalted butter, cut into pieces

Preheat the oven to 425°F. Set out a medium (about 13x9-inch) roasting pan.

In a cup, mix the sage, salt, thyme, and pepper, crumbling it with your fingers. Rub all over the chicken, inside and out. Tie the chicken legs together with kitchen string. Tuck the wing tips under the body. Strew the sliced onion in the roasting pan and place the chicken on top. Drizzle the chicken with the oil. Pour ½ cup of the broth into the pan.

Roast the chicken for 15 minutes. Reduce the oven temperature to 400°F. Continue roasting, basting the chicken a few times and adding 2 or 3 tablespoons water to pan if it gets dry, for about 1 hour and 15 minutes or until the chicken is browned, the juices run clear, and an instant-read thermometer inserted in the thickest part of the thigh (not touching bone) registers 170°F. Transfer the chicken to a warmed platter.

Tip the roasting pan and spoon off any fat. Place the roasting pan over medium heat and bring the juices to a boil, stirring to get up all the flavorful browned bits. Strain the mixture into a small saucepan, pressing down on the onions to get the juices. Stir in the remaining ¾ cup broth and the arrowroot mixture; bring to a boil over high heat, stirring constantly. Reduce the heat to low and simmer for 5 minutes, until slightly reduced.

Pour the chicken juices that have accumulated on the platter into the gravy. Whisk in the butter, a piece at a time, until it looks creamy.

Carve the chicken and serve with the gravy. Makes 4 generous servings, plus leftovers.

CHICKEN TETRAZZINI

Prepare this yummy casserole with leftover roast chicken or from a take-out rotisserie chicken. For ease, bake the squash a day ahead and shred the flesh and refrigerate. You'll need a 2-pound squash, or 3 cups cooked for this recipe. If your squash is larger, use the remainder in another dish or simply heat in the microwave and toss with a little olive oil and chopped fresh basil.

Makes 4 servings

1 spaghetti squash (about 2 pounds)

2 tablespoons olive oil

1 package (3½–4 ounces) baby shiitake mushrooms, sliced

1 red bell pepper, thinly sliced

1 can (13.5 oz) organic coconut milk

¼ cup chicken broth

1½ teaspoon dried thyme

½ teaspoon salt

¼ teaspoon pepper

2 cups shredded cooked chicken

1½ cups shredded Jarlsberg or Swiss cheese, divided

Preheat the oven to 400°F. Poke the squash several times with a fork and place in a pie plate or small baking dish. Bake for about 1 hour, or until a paring knife easily pierces the squash. Remove from the oven and let stand until cool enough to handle. Cut in half and scoop out and discard the seeds. With two forks, scrape out the pulp.

Reduce the oven to 375°F. Coat a 9-inch baking dish with cooking spray.

In a large skillet, heat the oil over medium-high heat. Cook the mushrooms and bell pepper for 7 minutes, stirring often, or until tender and lightly browned. Add the coconut milk, broth, thyme, and salt and pepper. Bring to a boil, stirring constantly. Remove from the heat. Stir in the chicken, squash, and 1 cup of the cheese, tossing gently until blended.

Place in the pan and sprinkle with the remaining ½ cup cheese. Bake for 35 to 40 minutes, or until hot and bubbly, and the top is lightly browned. Remove from the oven and let stand a few minutes before serving.

PECAN-ENCRUSTED CHICKEN WITH TAPENADE

This dish makes a great dinner entrée or a portable dish for lunch or another meal. And it can be whipped up in a hurry, especially if you have leftover chicken—just set aside a breast or two from last night's dinner. If you'd like, top the chicken with pesto (basil or sun-dried tomato) or eggplant caponata instead of the tapenade.

Makes 2 servings

2 four-ounce chicken breasts, boneless, skin removed

1 large egg

¼ cup coconut milk or dairy milk

½ cup ground pecans (can be purchased pre-ground)

3 tablespoons grated Parmesan cheese

2 teaspoons onion powder

1 teaspoon dried oregano

Fine sea salt and ground black pepper

4 tablespoons store-bought tapenade, caponata, or pesto

Preheat the oven to 350°F. Bake the chicken until cooked through, about 30 minutes.

Lightly beat the egg with a fork in a shallow bowl. Beat in the milk.

Stir together the ground pecans, Parmesan, onion powder, oregano, and salt and pepper to taste.

Roll the chicken in the egg, then in the pecan mixture. Place on a microwaveable plate and microwave on high power for 2 minutes.

Top with tapenade, caponata, or pesto and serve hot.

BEEF SLIDERS WITH THYME-SAUTÉED ONIONS

Either Bibb or Boston lettuce leaves take the place of buns for these yummy sliders. Continue the mini theme by serving them with baby cucumbers, mini peppers, and baby plum tomatoes.

Makes 4 servings

1   pound lean ground beef round

1   medium-size sweet white onion (12 ounces), halved and thinly sliced to make 2½ cups, then finely chop the other half to measure ¼ cup

¼   cup chopped fresh parsley

1   tablespoon grainy Dijon mustard

1   tablespoon horseradish

½   teaspoon salt

¼   teaspoon pepper

2   tablespoons olive oil

½   cup shredded carrot

½   teaspoon dried thyme

12   pieces Bibb or Boston lettuce, rinsed and spun dry

Preheat the broiler. Coat a broiler-pan rack with cooking oil spray.

In a medium bowl, combine the ground beef, chopped onion, parsley, mustard, horseradish, ¼ teaspoon of the salt, and the pepper. Mix lightly and shape into twelve 2-inch-round patties, using a scant 2 tablespoons for each. Place on the prepared broiler pan.

In large skillet, warm the oil over medium heat. Add the sliced onion, carrot, thyme, and the remaining ¼ teaspoon salt. Cook, stirring often, reducing heat if browning too fast, for 8 to 10 minutes or until tender and lightly golden. Remove from heat; cover to keep warm. Meanwhile, broil patties, turning once for 10 minutes or until browned and no longer pink in the center.

Place 3 lettuce leaves on each of 4 plates. Top each lettuce leaf with a patty on top and spoon some of the onions over.

PARMESAN-BREADED PORK CHOPS WITH BALSAMIC-ROASTED VEGETABLES

Ground nuts can be used as a stand-in for bread crumbs to make a tasty "breading" crust that can be easily herbed or spiced up any way you like.

Makes 4 servings

1   white onion, thinly sliced

1   small eggplant, unpeeled, cut into ½-inch cubes

1   green bell pepper, sliced

1   yellow or red bell pepper, sliced

2   garlic cloves, coarsely chopped

¼   cup extra-virgin olive oil or more as needed

¼   cup balsamic vinegar

Sea salt (fine or coarse) and ground black pepper

1   large egg

1   tablespoon coconut milk

½   cup ground almonds or pecans (can be purchased pre-ground)

¼   cup grated Parmesan cheese

1   teaspoon garlic powder

1   teaspoon onion powder

4   bone-in pork chops (about 6 ounces each)

1   lemon, thinly sliced

Preheat the oven to 350°F.

Combine the onion, eggplant, bell pepper, and garlic in a large baking pan. Drizzle with 2 tablespoons of the oil and the vinegar. Sprinkle with salt and black pepper to taste and toss to coat the vegetables. Cover the pan with foil and bake for 30 minutes.

Meanwhile, whisk together the egg and coconut milk in a shallow bowl. Combine the almond or pecan meal, Parmesan, garlic powder, and onion powder in another shallow bowl. Season with pepper and salt. Dip each pork chop into the egg, coating both sides. Then dredge both sides in the ground almond–Parmesan mix.

Heat 2 tablespoons of oil in a large skillet over medium-high heat. Add the pork chops and cook just until nicely browned, 2 to 3 minutes per side.

After the vegetables have been roasting for 30 minutes, remove the baking pan and place the pork chops on top. Top the pork chops with the lemon slices.

Return to the oven and baked, uncovered, until the pork chops are just cooked through (they should be very slightly pink at the center) and the vegetables are very soft, about 30 minutes.

PORK-FRIED WILD RICE

Pork tenderloins come two to package. Trim them both and wrap and freeze the other one for another meal. Crisp, fresh vegetables, ginger, and wild rice combine with tender pieces of pork to make a satisfying meal.

Makes 4 servings

1 pound trimmed pork tenderloin, cut crosswise into ¾-inch-thick slices, each slice cut in half

3 garlic cloves, minced

1 tablespoon grated peeled fresh ginger

¾ teaspoon salt

3 tablespoons olive oil

½ small red onion, thinly sliced

1 large carrot, cut into thin diagonal slices

6 tablespoons reduced-sodium organic chicken broth

1 medium zucchini, halved lengthwise and cut into thin diagonal slices

¼ pound snow peas, stringed

½ small Napa cabbage, thinly sliced (3½ cups)

2 cups cooked wild rice (can use quick cook)

Coat the pork with about 1 of the minced garlic cloves, about half the ginger, and ¼ teaspoon of the salt. In a large nonstick skillet, warm 2 tablespoons of the oil over medium-high heat until very hot but not smoking. Add half the pork; let it stand a minute, then cook for 2 to 3 minutes, turning once or twice, or until lightly browned and no longer pink in the center. With a slotted spoon, transfer to a clean bowl. Repeat with the remaining pork.

Add the remaining 1 tablespoon oil to the skillet. Add the red onion and the remaining garlic and ginger, and cook, stirring, for 1 minute or until the onion is lightly browned. Add the carrot and 2 tablespoons of the broth; stir-fry for 4 to 5 minutes, or until starting to get tender. Add the zucchini and another tablespoon broth; stir-fry for 2 minutes or until nearly tender. Add the Napa cabbage, snow peas, and remaining ½ teaspoon salt and stir-fry for 3 to 4 minutes, or until all vegetables are crisp-tender.

Return the pork and any juices to the pan. Add the rice and the remaining 3 tablespoons broth and cook, stirring often, for 1 to 2 minutes, or until heated through. Serve.

SPINACH AND MUSHROOM SALAD

This simple salad is easily prepared in larger quantities (using multiples of the specified quantities) or beforehand, to use in the near future (e.g., for tomorrow's breakfast). The dressing is best added just prior to serving. If you choose to use a store-bought salad dressing, read the label: They are often made with high-fructose corn syrup and/or sucrose. Low-fat or fat-free salad dressings, in particular, should be avoided like the plague. If a store-bought dressing is made with healthy oil and contains little or no sugar, use as much as you like: drizzle, pour, or drown your salad with dressing to your heart's content.

Makes 2 servings

8 cups baby spinach leaves

2 cups sliced mushrooms, your choice of variety

½ red or yellow bell pepper, chopped

½ cup chopped scallions or red onion

2 hard-boiled eggs, sliced

½ cup walnut halves

6 ounces cubed feta cheese

Homemade vinaigrette (extra-virgin olive oil plus your choice of vinegar) or store-bought dressing

Toss together the spinach, mushrooms, bell pepper, scallions, eggs, walnuts, and feta in a large bowl. Add the dressing and toss again, or divide the undressed salad between two airtight containers and refrigerate. Toss with dressing just before serving.

Variations: Play around with this salad formula by adding herbs, such as basil or cilantro; substituting goat cheese, creamy Gouda, or Swiss for the feta; adding whole pitted kalamata olives, or using a creamy dressing (with no added sugars or high-fructose corn syrup) such as the Worry-Free Ranch Dressing on page 301.

ASPARAGUS WITH ROASTED GARLIC
AND OLIVE OIL

Asparagus packs a lot of health benefits into a little package. The little bit of extra effort required to roast the garlic will be more than worth it to liven up a batch.

Makes 2 servings

1 head garlic

Extra-virgin olive oil

½ pound asparagus, trimmed and cut into 2-inch pieces

1 tablespoon ground pecans or almonds

½ teaspoon onion powder

Preheat the oven to 400°F.

Peel off the papery layers from the garlic head, then slice off the top ¼ inch to expose the garlic cloves. Place in the center of a square of foil and drizzle with olive oil. Seal the garlic in the foil and place in a shallow pan. Bake for 30 minutes. Remove from the foil and let cool.

Heat 1 tablespoon of oil in a large skillet over medium heat. Add the asparagus and cook, stirring, until bright green, 3 to 4 minutes. Sprinkle with the ground pecans or almonds and then the onion powder.

Squeeze the roasted garlic out of the skins into the pan. Continue to cook the asparagus, stirring, until the asparagus is crisp-tender, 1 to 2 minutes.

ORANGE-ROSEMARY SWEET POTATO FRIES

Rosemary and orange combine to make a most savory oven-baked "fry." They're perfect with plain grilled meats or fish or a broiled chicken breast. Leave the skins on for more nutrition, but if they're blemished, you can peel the potatoes. These sweet potato fries can be carbohydrate-rich, but they serve as a tasty side dish to liven up a meal; just go lightly with them.

Makes 4 servings

2 large sweet potatoes (about 12 ounces each), scrubbed and cut lengthwise into ½-inch-thick sticks

2 tablespoons olive oil

1 tablespoon chopped fresh rosemary

1 teaspoon grated orange zest

¼ teaspoon kosher salt

Pinch crushed red pepper flakes

Preheat the oven to 375°F. Coat a large rimmed baking sheet with cooking spray.

Put the sweet potatoes in a medium bowl. Add the oil, rosemary, orange zest, salt, and pepper flakes and toss to coat well. Arrange in a single layer on the prepared baking sheet. Bake, turning once, for 45 to 50 minutes, or until the potatoes are crisp at the edges and tender. Serve hot.

BAKED POTATO CRISPS
WITH CHIVE-SOUR CREAM DIP

These potatoes are sliced with a mandoline, a once professionals-only piece of kitchen equipment, now found at reasonable prices at houseware stores. It will easily slice these potatoes paper-thin. Lacking that, use the slicing blade of your food processor, the slicing blade of a four-sided box grater, or a sharp knife. Potatoes can trigger blood sugar spikes, so enjoy this as an occasional treat. But feel free to use the dip anytime—it's wonderful for veggies.

Makes 4 servings

2 large russet potatoes, scrubbed (about 8 ounces each)

2½ tablespoons olive oil

¼ teaspoon plus ⅛ teaspoon kosher salt

⅛ teaspoon pepper

½ cup sour cream

2 radishes, grated

2 tablespoons snipped fresh chives

1 teaspoon bottled white horseradish

½ teaspoon grated lemon zest

1 teaspoon lemon juice

Preheat the oven to 425°F. Coat two rimmed baking sheets with cooking spray.

Using a mandoline, food processor slicing blade, or a sharp knife, slice the potatoes into ⅛-inch-thick rounds. Place potatoes in a large bowl; add the oil, ¼ teaspoon of the salt, and the pepper and toss to coat well. Arrange the potato slices in single layers on the prepared baking sheets, crowding them a little if you have to.

Bake, turning once, and shifting pans around once while they bake, for 25 to 30 minutes, or until crisp and lightly browned. Blot lightly with paper towels and transfer to a serving plate.

Meanwhile, in a small bowl, stir together the sour cream, radishes, chives, horseradish, lemon zest and juice, and the remaining ⅛ teaspoon salt. Serve the crisps with the dipping sauce.

BAKED CHARD AND CARROT CHIPS

Whoever came up with the idea of transforming leafy greens into chips was one smart cookie. After baking, they become thin, brittle, and deliciously vegetal. The carrots add a sweet counterpoint, but they won't get as crisp. If the Swiss chard doesn't look good at the market, feel free to substitute leafy kale.

Makes 4 servings

4 large Swiss chard leaves

2 large carrots, thinly sliced on the diagonal (about 1¼ cups)

1 tablespoon olive oil

½ teaspoon ground cumin

¼ teaspoon kosher salt

Preheat the oven to 375°F. Coat two large rimmed baking sheets with olive oil cooking spray or healthy oil such as coconut oil, walnut oil, or olive oil.

Trim the stems and cut out the large center ribs from the chard. Tear the leaves into 3- to 4-inch pieces; you'll have about 6 cups, loosely packed.

In a bowl, toss the chard and carrots with the olive oil, cumin, and salt. Keeping the carrots together at one end of a baking sheet, spread the chard and carrots on the prepared baking sheets, trying to keep the chard in a single layer.

Bake, without turning, for 10 to 12 minutes, or until the chard is crisp and starting to brown at the edges. Transfer the chard to a serving plate. Spread the carrots out more on the baking sheet and return them to the oven. Bake for 8 to 10 minutes more, or until curled and lightly golden. Transfer to the plate with the chard and serve.

THREE-CHEESE EGGPLANT BAKE

If you love cheese, you'll love the combination of flavors in this three-cheese casserole. It is substantial enough to serve as an entrée, or in smaller portions as a side dish with a simple grilled steak or fish fillet. Leftovers are great for breakfast.

Makes 6 servings

1   eggplant, cut crosswise into ½-inch-thick slices

½   cup extra-virgin olive oil

1   yellow or Spanish onion, chopped

2   to 3 cloves garlic, minced

3   to 4 tablespoons sun-dried tomatoes

4   to 6 cups spinach leaves

2   tomatoes, cut into wedges

2   cups tomato sauce

1   cup ricotta cheese

1   cup shredded whole-milk mozzarella cheese (4 ounces)

½   cup grated Parmesan cheese (2 ounces)

4   to 5 fresh basil leaves, chopped

Preheat the oven to 325°F.

Place the eggplant slices in a baking pan. Brush both sides of the slices with most of the oil, reserving about 2 tablespoons. Bake for 20 minutes. Remove the eggplant but leave the oven on.

Heat the remaining 2 tablespoons oil in a large skillet over medium heat. Add the onion, garlic, sun-dried tomatoes, and spinach and cook until onion softens.

Scatter the tomato wedges over the eggplant. Spread the spinach mixture on top. Top the spinach with the tomato sauce.

Mix together the ricotta and mozzarella cheeses in a bowl. Spread the cheese mixture over the tomato sauce and sprinkle with the basil. Sprinkle the Parmesan cheese over the top.

Bake uncovered until bubbling and the cheese is melted, about 30 minutes.

SHIRATAKI FETTUCINE MARINARA WITH MEATBALLS

Shirataki noodles make a flavor-and vitamin-packed substitute for wheat-based noodles.

Makes 4 servings

4   packages shirataki fettucine, about 2 pounds

MEATBALLS AND SAUCE

2   tablespoons olive oil

1   large onion, finely chopped

3   garlic cloves, minced

1   teaspoon dried mixed Italian herbs

¼   teaspoon crushed red pepper flakes

¾   pound lean ground beef

8   tablespoons grated Parmesan cheese

½   teaspoon salt

¼   teaspoon black pepper

1   medium yellow or red bell pepper, coarsely chopped

2   cups crushed tomatoes in puree

In a large heavy saucepan, heat the oil over medium heat. Add the onion and garlic and cook, stirring often, for about 5 minutes or until tender. Stir in the herbs and crushed red pepper; remove from heat.

Coat a rimmed baking sheet with olive oil. Spoon ¼ cup of the sautéed onion mixture into a medium bowl. Add the ground beef, 4 tablespoons of the Parmesan, ¼ teaspoon of the salt, and ⅛ teaspoon of the black pepper. Mix well and form into 20 small meatballs, using 1 tablespoon of the mixture for each. Arrange on the prepared baking sheet.

Bake the meatballs in the oven, without turning, for 12 to 15 minutes. Remove from the oven and pour off any fat.

While the meatballs bake, put the saucepan with the remaining sautéed onion over medium heat. Add the bell pepper and cook, stirring often, for 5 minutes or until crisp-tender. Add the tomatoes, the remaining ¼ teaspoon salt and remaining ⅛ teaspoon black pepper. Bring to a boil; cover, reduce the heat to low and simmer for 10 minutes. Stir in the baked meatballs; cover and simmer for 10 minutes longer. Remove from the heat and cover to keep warm.

Cook shirataki fettucine according to package directions.

GREEK-STYLE QUINOA STUFFED PEPPERS

Make these with any color pepper you like, or mix them up! After the quinoa has cooked, fluff it with a fork to keep it from compacting. While quinoa is a carbohydrate-rich grain, the small amount contained split among four servings yields only a modest total carbohydrate exposure.

Makes 4 servings

- 2 tablespoons olive oil
- 4 large garlic cloves, minced
- 1 teaspoon dried oregano
- ¾ pound lean ground turkey
- 4 cups loosely packed baby spinach
- 1 can (14½ ounces) chopped tomatoes, drained, liquid reserved
- ½ teaspoon salt
- ¼ teaspoon black pepper
- ⅓ cup quinoa, cooked according to package directions (⅔ cup water, ⅛ teaspoon salt)
- 4 medium bell peppers cut in half through the stem end with stems, cores, ribs, and seeds removed
- ¾ cup crumbled feta cheese

Preheat the oven to 375°F. Set out a 13x9-inch glass baking dish.

In a large skillet, combine the oil, garlic, and oregano. Cook over medium-high heat, stirring for 2 to 3 minutes or until the garlic is fragrant but not browned. Add the ground turkey and cook, stirring often, for about 5 minutes, or until the meat loses its pink color. Add the spinach in 2 batches, and cook, stirring frequently, until wilted. Stir in the tomatoes, salt, and black pepper. Remove from heat. Stir in the quinoa. (Makes about 3 ¼ cups)

Arrange the bell peppers in the baking dish, cut sides up. Spoon a heaping ⅓ cup of the turkey mixture into each bell pepper and sprinkle 1½ tablespoons of the feta on top of each. Pour the tomato juice (about ½ cup) into the pan. Cover with foil and bake for 50 minutes, or the peppers are tender and the filling is heated. Serve hot with the pan juices.

APPLE WALNUT "BREAD"

Many people who embark on a wheat-free journey occasionally need to indulge a craving for bread, and this fragrant, high-protein loaf is just the ticket. Apple walnut bread is absolutely wonderful spread with cream cheese; peanut, sunflower seed, cashew, or almond butters; or regular, old-fashioned dairy butter (unsalted if you are salt sensitive). It will not, however, work well for a sandwich, due to its gluten-free tendency to crumble.

Despite the inclusion of carbohydrate sources like applesauce, the total carbohydrate gram count of a slice or two amounts to a modest exposure of around 5 grams per slice. Applesauce can be easily left out without sacrificing the quality of the bread.

Makes 10 to 12 servings

2 cups ground almonds (can be purchased pre-ground)

1 cup chopped walnuts

2 tablespoons ground flaxseeds (can be purchased pre-ground)

1 tablespoon ground cinnamon

2 teaspoons baking powder

½ teaspoon fine sea salt

2 large eggs

1 cup unsweetened applesauce

½ cup walnut oil, extra-light olive oil, melted coconut oil, or melted butter

¼ cup sour cream or coconut milk

Preheat the oven to 325°F. Coat a 9x5-inch loaf pan liberally with oil. (Coconut oil is ideal for this purpose.)

Combine the ground almonds, walnuts, ground flaxseeds, cinnamon, baking powder, and salt in a bowl and stir until thoroughly mixed.

Combine the eggs, applesauce, oil, and sour cream or coconut milk in a measuring cup. Pour the mixture into the dry ingredients and stir just until incorporated. If the mixture is very stiff, add 1 to 2 tablespoons of coconut milk. Press the "dough" into the pan and bake until a toothpick comes out dry, about 45 minutes. Allow to cool in the pan for 20 minutes, then turn out. Slice and serve.

Variations: Think of this recipe as a template for quick breads and loaves, such as banana bread, zucchini carrot bread, and so on. Replace applesauce, for instance, with 1½ cups canned pumpkin puree and add 1½ teaspoons nutmeg to make pumpkin bread, great for winter holidays.

BANANA-BLUEBERRY MUFFINS

Like most recipes made with healthy nonwheat ingredients, these muffins will be a bit coarser in texture than those made with wheat flour. Banana, a fruit known for its high carbohydrate content, gives the muffins some of its sweetness, but because it is distributed among 10 muffins, your carbohydrate exposure is kept to a minimum. Blueberries can be replaced by equivalent quantities of raspberries, cranberries, or other berries.

Makes 10 to 12 muffins

2 cups ground almonds (can be purchased pre-ground)

¼ cup ground flaxseeds (can be purchased pre-ground)

3 tablespoons xylitol

1 teaspoon baking powder

Dash of fine sea salt

1 ripe banana

2 large eggs, separated

½ cup sour cream or coconut milk

¼ cup walnut oil, coconut oil, or extra-light olive oil

1 cup blueberries, fresh or frozen

Preheat the oven to 325°F. Grease a 12-cup muffin tin with oil.

Combine the ground almonds, ground flaxseeds, xylitol, baking powder, and salt in a bowl and mix with a spoon.

In another bowl, mash the banana until smooth. Stir in the egg yolks, sour cream or coconut milk, and oil. Add the banana mixture to the almond meal mixture and mix thoroughly. Fold in the blueberries.

Beat egg whites to stiff peaks. Fold into batter.

Spoon the batter into the muffin cups, filling them halfway. Bake until a toothpick inserted in the center of a muffin comes out dry, about 35 minutes. Cool in the pans for 10 to 15 minutes, then turn out of the pan and transfer to a rack to cool completely.

PUMPKIN SPICE MUFFINS

I love having these muffins for breakfast in the fall and winter. Spread one with cream cheese and you will need little else to fill you up on a cold morning.

Makes 12 small muffins

2 cups ground almonds (can be purchased pre-ground)

1 cup chopped walnuts

¼ cup ground flaxseeds (can be purchased pre-ground)

½ cup Splenda

2 teaspoons ground cinnamon

1 teaspoon ground allspice

1 teaspoon grated nutmeg

1 teaspoon baking powder

Dash of fine sea salt

1 cup unsweetened pumpkin puree

½ cup sour cream or coconut milk

2 large eggs

¼ cup melted coconut oil, or extra-light olive oil

Preheat the oven to 325°F. Grease a 12-cup muffin tin with oil.

Stir together the almond meal, walnuts, ground flaxseeds, sweetener, cinnamon, allspice, nutmeg, baking powder, and salt in a large bowl. Stir together the pumpkin, sour cream or coconut milk, eggs, and oil in another large bowl.

Stir the pumpkin mixture into the almond meal mixture and mix thoroughly. Spoon the batter into the muffin cups, filling them about half full. Bake until a toothpick inserted in a muffin comes out dry, about 45 minutes.

Cool the muffins in the pans for 10 to 15 minutes, then turn out onto a rack to cool completely.

DARK CHOCOLATE TOFU MOUSSE

You will be hard-pressed to tell this dessert from a conventional mousse *and* it provides a generous quantity of the healthy flavonoids that cocoa products are coming to be recognized for. For anyone with a soy sensitivity, substitute 2 cups (16 ounces) plain Greek yogurt for both the tofu and soymilk.

Makes 4 servings

14 ounces silken tofu

⅓ cup unsweetened cocoa powder

¼ cup unsweetened almond milk, full-fat soymilk, or whole dairy milk

¼ cup Splenda

2 teaspoons pure vanilla extract

1 teaspoon pure almond extract

Whipped cream

3 to 4 strawberries, sliced, or 10 to 12 raspberries

Combine the tofu, cocoa, almond milk, sweetener, and vanilla and almond extracts in a blender and blend until smooth and creamy. Spoon the mixture into serving dishes.

Top with whipped cream and berries.

LEMON-RASPBERRY SOUFFLÉS

Think you can't have dessert on a wheat-free diet? Think again. Then make this light, lovely, and guilt-free dessert with the classic combination of lemon and raspberries. Straight-sided small 6- to 8-ounce soufflé dishes work best, but you can also bake these in glass custard cups of the same size.

Makes 4 servings

1 tablespoon unsalted butter, softened

3 large eggs, yolks and whites separated

3 tablespoons sour cream

1 tablespoon grated lemon zest

1 tablespoon fresh lemon juice

1½ teaspoons liquid stevia

⅛ teaspoon salt

¼ teaspoon cream of tartar

12 fresh or frozen raspberries

Preheat the oven to 400°F. Generously coat four 6- to 8-ounce soufflé dishes or ovenproof custard cups with the butter and place on a rimmed baking sheet.

In a large bowl, put the egg yolks. Whisk in the sour cream, lemon zest and juice, stevia, and salt until well blended. In a medium bowl, with an electric mixer at medium speed, beat the egg whites and cream of tartar until frothy. Increase the mixer speed to high and beat just until stiff but not dry peaks form when the beaters are lifted. Gently stir ¼ of the beaten whites into the yolk mixture. With a spatula, fold in the remainder until just blended. Evenly spoon the mixture into the prepared dishes (they will be very full). Press 4 raspberries into each. Run your finger through the batter in a circular manner to even it.

Bake for 12 to 14 minutes, or until well risen, golden brown, and just firm to the touch. With a metal spatula, transfer each to a small plate and serve at once.

GINGER SPICE COOKIES

These wheat-free cookies will satisfy your occasional craving. Replacing wheat flour with coconut flour yields a somewhat heavier, less cohesive cookie. But once your friends and family get familiar with the somewhat unusual texture, they will ask for more. Like several of the other recipes here, this is a basic cookie recipe that can be modified in any number of delicious ways. Chocolate lovers, for instance, can add semisweet chocolate chips and leave out the allspice, nutmeg, and ginger to make a healthy wheat-free equivalent to chocolate chip cookies.

Makes about 30 (2½-inch) cookies

2 cups coconut flour

1 cup finely chopped walnuts

3 tablespoons desiccated coconut

¼ cup xylitol

2 teaspoons ground cinnamon

1 teaspoon ground allspice

1 teaspoon ground ginger

1 teaspoon grated nutmeg

1 teaspoon baking soda

1 cup sour cream or coconut milk

1 cup extra-light olive oil, melted coconut oil, or melted butter

½ cup sugar-free vanilla syrup (DaVinci and Torani make good ones)

3 large eggs, lightly beaten

1 tablespoon grated lemon zest

1 teaspoon pure almond extract

Milk, unsweetened almond milk, or soymilk (optional)

Preheat the oven to 325°F. Grease a baking sheet or line sheet with parchment paper.

Stir together the coconut flour, walnuts, shredded coconut, xylitol, cinnamon, allspice, ginger, nutmeg, and baking soda in a large bowl.

Whisk together the sour cream or coconut milk, oil or butter, vanilla syrup, eggs, lemon zest, and almond extract in a 4-cup measuring cup. Add the egg mixture to the coconut flour mixture and stir just until incorporated. (If the mixture is too thick to stir easily, add the milk, unsweetened almond milk, or soymilk 1 tablespoon at a time until the consistency of cake batter.)

Drop 1-inch mounds onto the baking sheet and flatten. Bake for 20 minutes, or until a toothpick comes out clean. Cool on racks.

CARROT CAKE

Of all the recipes here, this one comes closest in taste to the wheat-containing original to satisfy even the most demanding wheat-lover's craving.

Makes 8 to 10 servings

CAKE

1 cup coconut flour
½ cup Splenda
2 tablespoons grated orange zest
1 tablespoon ground flaxseeds
2 teaspoons ground cinnamon
1 teaspoon ground allspice
1 teaspoon grated nutmeg
1 teaspoon baking powder
   Dash of fine sea salt
4 large eggs
½ cup coconut oil, melted
1 cup sour cream
½ cup coconut milk
2 teaspoons pure vanilla extract
1 (3.5 oz) jar baby carrots
1 cup finely grated carrots
1 cup chopped pecans
1 cup golden raisins

ICING

8 ounces ⅓-less-fat cream cheese (Neufchâtel), at room temperature
1 teaspoon fresh lemon juice
1 tablespoon Splenda

Preheat the oven to 325°F. Grease a 9x9-inch or 10x10-inch baking pan.

To make the cake: Combine the coconut flour, sweetener, orange zest, ground flaxseed, cinnamon, allspice, nutmeg, baking powder, and salt in a large bowl and mix by hand.

Beat together the eggs, melted butter or coconut oil, sour cream, coconut milk, baby food, and vanilla in a medium bowl. Pour the egg mixture into the coconut flour mixture. Using an electric mixer, beat until thoroughly mixed. Stir in the carrots, pecans, and raisins by hand. Pour the mixture into the baking pan.

Bake for 1 hour, or until toothpick comes out clean. Let cool.

To make the icing, combine the cream cheese, lemon juice, and xylitol in a bowl and blend thoroughly.

Spread the icing over the cooled cake.

FLOURLESS ORANGE-ALMOND CAKE

The orange segments on top of this cake add a fresh element. You could also add a bit of finely chopped mint if you have any growing in your garden. Serve this the day it is made.

Makes 6 servings

2 large oranges

4 large eggs, yolks and whites separated

1⅓ cups almond meal

2 teaspoons liquid stevia

¼ teaspoon almond extract

⅛ teaspoon salt

¼ teaspoon cream of tartar

¼ cup slivered almonds

Preheat the oven to 350°F. Coat an 8-inch glass baking dish with olive oil cooking spray or coconut, walnut, or olive oil.

From the oranges, grate 1 tablespoon zest. With a serrated knife, remove the peel and white pith from the oranges. Working over a medium bowl, cut out the orange segments from in between the membranes, letting them drop into the bowl. Squeeze the membranes. Cover and refrigerate for serving.

In a large bowl, stir together the egg yolks, almond meal, stevia, almond extract, salt, and orange zest. This will be thick. Stir in 4 to 5 table-spoons water to loosen it.

In a medium bowl, with an electric mixer at medium speed, beat the egg whites and cream of tartar until frothy. Increase the mixer speed to high and beat just until stiff but not dry peaks form when the beaters are lifted. Gently stir ¼ of the beaten whites into the yolk mixture. With a spatula, fold in the remainder until just blended. Scrape into the prepared pan. Sprinkle with the slivered almonds.

Bake for 20 to 25 minutes, or until the cake is browned, puffed, and a toothpick inserted in the center comes out clean. Cool in the pan on a wire rack. Arrange orange seg-ments over slices of cake.

CLASSIC CHEESECAKE WITH WHEATLESS CRUST

This is a cause for celebration: cheesecake without undesirable health or weight consequences! Ground pecans serve as the wheatless base for this decadent cheesecake, though you could use ground walnuts or almonds instead.

Makes 6 to 8 servings

CRUST

- 1½ cups ground pecans
- Sweetener such as Truvia, stevia extract, or Splenda equivalent to ½ cup sucrose
- 1½ teaspoons ground cinnamon
- 6 tablespoons unsalted butter, melted and cooled

FILLING

- 16 ounces ⅓-less-fat cream cheese, at room temperature
- ¾ cup sour cream
- 3 tablespoons xylitol
- Dash of fine sea salt
- 3 large eggs
- Juice of 1 small lemon and 1 tablespoon grated lemon zest
- 2 teaspoons pure vanilla extract

Preheat the oven to 325°F.

To make the crust: Combine the ground pecans and cinnamon in a large bowl. Stir in the melted butter and mix thoroughly.

Press the crumb mixture into the bottom and 1½ to 2 inches up the sides of a 10-inch or 9-inch deep dish pie pan.

To make the filling: Combine the cream cheese, sour cream, xylitol, and salt in a bowl. Using an electric mixer, beat at low speed to blend. Beat in the eggs, lemon juice, lemon zest, and vanilla. Beat at medium speed for 1 minute.

Pour the filling into the crust. Bake until nearly firm in the center, about 50 minutes. Cool the cheesecake on a rack. Refrigerate to chill before serving.

Variations: The filling can be modified in dozens of ways. Try adding ½ cup cocoa powder and topping with shaved dark chocolate; or substitute lime juice and zest for the lemon; or top with berries, mint leaves, and whipped cream.

CHOCOLATE PEANUT BUTTER FUDGE

There is probably no such thing as truly healthy fudge, but this is about as close as it gets. Keep a supply of this decadent dessert handy to satisfy those occasional cravings for chocolate or sweets.

Makes 12 servings

FUDGE

2 teaspoons coconut oil, melted

8 ounces unsweetened chocolate

1 cup natural peanut butter, at room temperature

4 ounces ⅓-less-fat cream cheese, at room temperature

Sweetener such as Truvia, stevia extract, or Splenda equivalent to 1 cup sucrose

1 teaspoon pure vanilla extract

Pinch of salt

½ cup chopped unsalted dry-roasted peanuts or walnuts

TOPPING (OPTIONAL)

½ cup natural peanut butter, at room temperature

½ cup chopped unsalted dry-roasted peanuts

Coat 8x8-inch pan with the melted coconut oil.

To make the fudge: Place the chocolate in a microwaveable bowl and microwave 1½ to 2 minutes in 30-second intervals until just melted. (Stir after 1 minute to check since the chocolate will hold its shape even when melted.)

In a separate microwaveable bowl, combine the peanut butter, cream cheese, sweetener, vanilla, and salt. Microwave about 1 minute to soften, then stir to thoroughly blend. Stir the peanut butter mixture into the melted chocolate and stir well. (If the mix becomes too stiff, microwave another 30 to 40 seconds.)

Spread the fudge into the prepared pan and set aside to cool. If desired, spread the fudge with a layer of peanut butter and sprinkle with the chopped peanuts.

CHOCOLATE FLOURLESS TORTE

A favorite among chocoholics, it's naturally wheat free since it's made without flour (hence, the title). But this version also keeps blood sugar in check by using xylitol instead of the usual cups of sugar.

Makes 16 servings

1 tablespoon cocoa powder

¾ cup ground almonds

⅓ cup xylitol

6 eggs, yolks and whites separated

½ teaspoon cream of tartar

½ cup reduced fat sour cream

6 ounces bittersweet chocolate, melted

1 teaspoon cinnamon

Preheat the oven to 350°F. Coat a 9-inch springform pan with cooking spray and dust with 1 tablespoon cocoa powder.

Combine the almonds and 2 tablespoons xylitol in a blender or food processor until ground finely. Set aside.

Beat the egg whites and cream of tartar in a large bowl with an electric mixer on high until foamy. Gradually add the remaining xylitol, beating until stiff peaks form.

With the same beaters, beat the egg yolks in another bowl until thick. Add the sour cream, chocolate, cinnamon and beat to blend well. Fold in the almonds. Stir ¼ of the egg whites into the chocolate mixture. Fold the remaining whites in 2 batches.

Pour into the pan and bake for about 45 to 50 minutes or until a knife inserted comes out clean. Cool the cake completely.

WASABI SAUCE

If you haven't yet tried wasabi, be warned: It can be awfully pungent, but in a unique, indescribable way. The "heat" of the sauce can be tempered by decreasing the amount of wasabi powder used. (Err on the side of caution and use 1 teaspoon at first until you have a chance to gauge the hotness of your wasabi, as well as your tolerance.) Wasabi sauce makes a great accompaniment to fish and chicken. It can also be used as a sauce in wheat-free wraps (page 263). For a more Asian variation, substitute 2 tablespoons sesame oil and 1 tablespoon (wheat-free) soy sauce for the mayonnaise.

Makes 2 servings

3 tablespoons mayonnaise

1 to 2 teaspoons wasabi powder

1 teaspoon finely minced fresh or dried ginger

1 teaspoon rice vinegar or water

Mix all the ingredients in a small bowl. Store tightly covered in the refrigerator for up to 5 days.

VINAIGRETTE DRESSING

This recipe for a basic vinaigrette is extremely versatile and can be modified in dozens of ways by adding such ingredients as Dijon mustard, chopped herbs (basil, oregano, parsley), or finely chopped sun-dried tomatoes. If you choose balsamic vinegar for this dressing, read the label carefully, as many have added sugar. Distilled white, rice, white wine, red wine, and apple cider vinegars are other good choices.

Makes 1 cup

¾ cup extra-virgin olive oil

¼ cup vinegar, your choice

1 garlic clove, finely minced

1 teaspoon onion powder

½ teaspoon freshly ground white or black pepper

Pinch of sea salt

Combine the ingredients in a 12-ounce jar with a lid. Cover the jar tightly and shake to combine. Store in the refrigerator for up to 1 week; shake well before using.

WORRY-FREE RANCH DRESSING

When you make your own salad dressing, even using some prepared ingredients like mayonnaise, you have more control over what goes into it. Here's a quick ranch dressing that contains no unhealthy ingredients, provided you choose a mayonnaise that includes no wheat, cornstarch, high-fructose corn syrup, sucrose, or hydrogenated oils. (Most do not.)

Makes about 2 cups

1 cup sour cream

½ cup mayonnaise

1 tablespoon distilled white vinegar

½ cup grated Parmesan cheese (2 ounces)

1 teaspoon garlic powder or finely minced garlic

1½ teaspoons onion powder

Pinch of sea salt

Mix the sour cream, mayonnaise, vinegar, and 1 tablespoon water in bowl. Stir in the Parmesan, garlic powder, onion powder, and salt. Add up to another tablespoon of water if you want a thinner dressing. Store in the refrigerator.

CHAPTER 16

THE WHEAT-FREE EATING-OUT GUIDE

EATING OUTSIDE THE home does not have to be an exercise in hassling the waitstaff at a restaurant or a tortured experience in deprivation. Eating wheat-free can be every bit as interesting and delicious as eating a diet that includes wheat. In fact, it can be *more* interesting, since people who are wheat-free enjoy their food more, tend to develop a heightened sense of taste, do not suffer through the sleepiness and lethargy that follow a wheat-containing meal, and don't have to suffer through days of remorse afterwards flogging themselves for overconsumption. Remember: Being wheat-free sets you free.

The struggle, of course, is to follow this healthy lifestyle in a world hell-bent on feeding you wheat and plenty of it. So here are some practical tips on how to enjoy a dinner at a restaurant and minimize the likelihood of an inadvertent wheat exposure.

Be wary of gluten-free menus. Though the trend is still in its infancy, gluten-free restaurants and restaurants with a gluten-free menu are cropping up in more and more cities. The worst that might happen in a restaurant with a gluten-free menu is cross-contamination if wheat-gluten dishes are also served, an issue only for the most gluten-sensitive. Recall that many gluten-free dishes are prepared using starchy carbohydrate substitutes, such as cornstarch, potato flour, tapioca starch, or rice starch, ingredients that still trigger excessive blood sugar rises and weight gain—no different from substituting jelly beans for your wheat pasta or bread. An occasional treat—e.g., a gluten-free tiramisu—might be fine. But habitual consumption of gluten-free foods made with these substitutes will result in having to buy new dresses a few sizes larger.

More often than not, you will be disappointed by the lack of knowledge about wheat and gluten in restaurant personnel, head chef on down. They are in the business of providing tasty, visually appealing dishes; they are not necessarily in the business of providing healthy dishes or those suited to those of us with "special" needs. (There's the horror story of a New York chef who, believing that all gluten intolerance was a fairy tale, served gluten-containing noodles, breads, and other dishes to his gluten-avoiding clientele, proclaiming them gluten-free and then boasting about his defiant experiment on Facebook.)

Watch for the key words. For anyone who is *not* exceptionally wheat sensitive, avoiding wheat land mines is relatively straightforward. There's the easy stuff—pass on the bread basket, don't order anything on a bun or roll, skip the pasta dishes. But you also have to remember that chef's use wheat in many dishes beyond bread. So avoid breaded items such as veal or chicken Parmesan; skip fried foods (which you should do anyway) such as chicken fingers or onion rings, since they are nearly always breaded; pass over meatloaf, meatballs, and other foods made with bread crumbs; order your salad without the croutons.

Gravies and sauces are another potential problem area, since flour is often used for thickening. White sauces, Béchamel, and Mornay sauces are nearly always made with wheat flour and should be avoided, while Alfredo, Béarnaise, Florentine, hollandaise, Normandy, peanut, and tartar sauces are usually safe. Ironically, though, the most common toppings for wheat-based pasta, tomato or marinara sauces, are usually gluten-free. If you can't figure out what's in the sauce, make sure to ask the chef. You may need to request your meat, poultry, or fish *without* sauce.

Figure out fast food. Almost all fast food contains wheat. Cooking surfaces and oils in fast food restaurants are nearly always shared with wheat-containing or flour-coated foods. In general, it is best to avoid fast food restaurants (for plenty of other reasons beyond wheat exposure). In a pinch, fast food salads (without croutons) are usually safe, though examine the dressing closely for hidden gluten sources. Wendy's is an exception, with a fairly broad selection of gluten-free items listed on their website and updated periodically. Burger King maintains a smaller list. Subway, Arbys, Wendy's, and Chipotle claim that many of their products are confidently gluten-free and/or offer a gluten-free menu.

McDonald's, partly due to the media scrutiny it has endured, works hard to disclose the ingredients in various menu items, but it means examining each one by one. You'll be left mostly with soft drinks and condiments, however. While McDonald's French fries were originally declared gluten-free by the company in 2006, they were taken off the list because the beef flavor used in the frying oil contains hydrolyzed wheat protein. It's also unrealistic to expect the high school kid behind the counter to have any understanding of your gluten-free needs.

At many fast food restaurants, the oil used to fry French fries may be the same oil used to fry bread-crumb-coated chicken patties. Likewise, cooking surfaces may be shared. It is therefore difficult to obtain wheat- and gluten-free foods at fast food restaurants. (You probably shouldn't be eating there anyway!) But all of these items have wheat or gluten in them.

- Breakfast steak
- Burritos
- Chicken McNuggets
- French fries and other fried foods (contain wheat and/or fried in oil shared with gluten-containing products; beer-battered)
- Fried chicken, fish
- Fruit and yogurt parfait
- Hash browns
- KFC fried chicken, Colonel's sauce, hot wings
- Mozzarella sticks
- Onion rings
- Sausage
- Scrambled eggs (made with pancake batter)
- Taco Bell taco meat
- Tortillas

Dig into dessert carefully. Desserts that are assuredly wheat free sadly form a short list. Pies, cakes, and cheesecake are out, of course (unless, of course, the chef got the recipe from *Lose the Wheat, Lose the Weight!* recipe choices!). Some familiar desserts are nearly always wheat and gluten-free, including fresh berries, crème brûlée, flourless chocolate cake, fudge, ice creams (except those with wheat- or gluten-containing ingredients added, such as Oreo cookies, cake batter, or cookie dough), and rice pudding.

Watch your drink order too. For alcoholic beverages, absolute no-nos include ales, most beers, malt liquors, and lagers; bloody Mary mixes; vodkas distilled from wheat including Absolut, Grey Goose, Ketel One, and Stolichnaya (an issue only for the most gluten-sensitive, since the distillation process removes nearly all wheat proteins); wine coolers (containing barley malt); and whiskey distilled from wheat or barley. Wines are nearly always safe, regardless of varietal or vintage. A growing list of gluten-free beers, usually brewed from sorghum, millet, and buckwheat, are also appearing on the menu. Be aware that some fermented ciders brewed from apple and other fruits are sometimes labeled "gluten-free beer," but truly taste more like ciders.

Learn the wheat hiding places. Like we said, many items are made with wheat or gluten that you'd never even consider to have it. Keep these in mind when ordering out:

- Avoid salad dressings unless they are also gluten-free. If simple oil and vinegar are available (they nearly always are), they are the safest option.
- If gluten-free pasta or noodles are available, ask whether they have been cooked in water using utensils not shared with wheat noodles.
- Soy sauce in Asian dishes is nearly always wheat-containing and should therefore be avoided.
- Be suspicious of exotic-sounding ingredients, particularly in sauces. Farro, panko, roux, and durum all contain wheat or are entirely wheat, added for the sound of an unusual ingredient. Beware if the dish contains anything obscure or unrecognizable: It may be nothing more than an exotic name for wheat.
- Ask, but be skeptical. The twenty-one-year old college student serving as your waiter tries to preserve face by answering your pointed questions, whether or not he knows the answer. All you can do is say something like "I get *really* sick if I eat anything containing wheat. I just need to know for certain."
- Keep the *Lose the Wheat, Lose the Weight!* Shopping List (on page 243) in your purse or wallet. This exhaustive list may also help you steer clear of foods containing wheat.

ETHNIC FOODS FOR
THE WHEAT BELLY BELIEVER

If you are like me, you like to venture out into some unique ethnic cuisine and sample some of the wonderfully creative ways other cultures treat their food. Here are some issues to consider:

Italian. Italian restaurants can be among the most difficult, since wheat flour serves as the main course, side dish, or breading in so many recipes—pasta, bread, and bread crumbs dominate or adorn so many Italian dishes. Some dishes, such as veal Parmesan, can be made gluten-free simply by asking for the veal without breading. (You may have to ask about the potential for cross-contamination, however.) You can opt for salads (ask to omit the croutons), soups (without noodles), risotto (rice), polenta (cornmeal), and meat dishes that you may have to request without bread crumbs or flour. All sauces are potential wheat and gluten sources, so ask first. Beware of meatballs, which are nearly always made with bread crumbs.

French. French, like Italian foods, are built around wheat products and can be tough places to safely enjoy a meal, especially for the most sensitive. French sauces, in particular, such as béchamel, mornay, and roux, are a land mine of gluten ingredients. Though you will undoubtedly raise eyebrows when you place your order, you will nearly always have to ask for your meat or other dish without sauce. Butter and cheese sauces are generally safe, however.

Mediterranean and Middle Eastern. Mediterranean and Middle Eastern restaurants are among the easiest to navigate gluten-free. However, there are several important wheat hazards. Pita bread is out, of course, as are moussaka, tabbouleh, couscous, and baklava. Olives, olive oil, hummus, tahini, and dawali, as well as the variety of salads and vegetables that Mediterranean restaurants prepare so well, are nearly always safe.

Chinese. Chinese restaurants are, in my experience, among the most difficult to navigate for the gluten-free. If there is a language barrier (how's your Mandarin?), then you may be out of luck entirely. Soy sauce is the most common problem in Chinese food, since it is usually made with wheat flour. In my experience, rarely will gluten-free soy sauce be available unless you bring it yourself (available in bottles and single-serve packets). Avoid the egg rolls, pot stickers, chicken and other meats breaded before frying, fried foods (fried in oils shared with wheat-containing foods), wontons, noodles, and fortune cookies. This leaves very few foods on the menu in most Chinese restaurants beyond white rice that are confidently wheat- and gluten-free. Some tofu dishes, rice noodles, egg drop soup, and vegetable dishes are safe. Cross-contamination is the rule and is essentially unavoidable.

Japanese. Japanese restaurants are among the more safe, though, as always, some caution needs to be exercised. The soy sauce issue applies equally well to Japanese fare and usually necessitates supplying your own gluten-free soy sauce. Soy sauce maker Kikkoman makes a Japanese variety gluten-free version. The many varieties of sushi are gluten-free, provided no tempura is included. (Tempura is flour-coated and fried. The tempura provides a potential cross-contamination risk, however.) Most of the condiments and non-fish ingredients used—for example, pickled radish, seaweed, tsukemono (pickled vegetables), and tofu—are safe. The various seaweeds, including kombu, wakame, and nori, are also safe, as is the edamame. Be careful with wasabi, imitation crab, and some of the sauces, all of which may contain wheat or gluten. Steer clear of anything with "fu," which is pure gluten.

Thai. Thai cuisine can fit very nicely into a wheat- and gluten-free lifestyle. Potential problem areas are, as in other restaurants, noodles and sauces. Fish, curry, and peanut sauces are usually safe, but it needs to be verified by the server, since flour is occasionally added. Soy sauce containing gluten is another problem area. Many Thai noodle dishes use rice noodles that are safe from a wheat standpoint. The most sensitive may encounter cross-contamination, a hurdle that can be impossible if a language barrier stands in the way.

Mexican. While some Mexican restaurants will use pure cornmeal in their tortillas and burritos (recall that cornmeal is not necessarily healthy, either, as it is a readily digested carbohydrate, but it does not contain gluten proteins), many use wheat flour and should therefore be avoided unless you are confident that they are pure corn. Salsas, nachos, beans, cheeses, and meats are generally safe.

CHAPTER 17

LOSE THE WHEAT, LOSE THE WEIGHT! JOURNAL

IT'S TIME TO put the *Lose the Wheat, Lose the Weight!* plan in motion! I encourage you to use the following journal pages to record your daily meals, markers and feelings. Documenting these things is a great way to track your progress, keep you motivated, and create a reference for the future. How you use the log is up to you, but below are some general tips on what to look for and record in each category.

Weight: Record your weight as often as you'd like—daily, weekly, whatever! Keep in mind, however, that tracking your weight daily can be an amazing motivator as you watch the number fall. If stepping on the scale every day feels too neurotic for you, do it every other day, once a week, or however often works for you.

Blood pressure/blood sugar: Tests for measuring these markers are widely available and will certainly show major progress as you embark on the plan. These measurements are totally optional, but very helpful—especially if you're using my plan to reverse or prevent diabetes or high LDL levels.

Meals: No need to record how many calories you consume at each meal—remember, my plan has no restrictions in this regard.

Use the specific meal categories, however, to record what you ate at meal and snack times (even if it wasn't program-compliant!) and if you enjoyed the recipe.

Other markers: The other markers in the log pages—temptations, mood, sleep quality—are additional ways to measure progress. You're the only person who knows your body completely, so use whatever guidelines you'd like to measure your mood, how well you slept and how strong your wheat temptations were. You'll be pleasantly surprised at how quickly these markers will improve!

Additional comments: How you use this space is, again, totally up to you. Was there a specific pain or problem—joint pain, a cloudy mind, acne, etc.—that motivated you to try this program? How is that problem improving? Maybe you're finding that the plan has had some unexpected benefits that you hadn't originally thought of, or you'd like to record a specific aspect of your health that you'd like to discuss with your doctor. I've included these lines so that you can tailor your journal to aid you in the best possible way.

Date: _____   **Weight:** _____

Blood Pressure: _____   **Blood Sugar:** _____

Rate quality of sleep: (1 being poorest and 5 being best)

1   2   3   4   5

Breakfast (time) _____

_____

_____

Mid-Morning Snack (time) _____

_____

Lunch (time) _____

_____

_____

Mid-Afternoon Snack (time) _____

_____

Dinner (time) _____

_____

_____

Nighttime Snack (time) _____

_____

Rate today's wheat temptation: (5 being very strong cravings and 1 being no cravings at all)

1   2   3   4   5

Rate overall mood: (1 being poorest and 5 being best)

1   2   3   4   5

Additional comments/progress:

_____

_____

_____

Date: _____   **Weight:** _____
Blood Pressure: _____   **Blood Sugar:** _____

Rate quality of sleep: (1 being poorest and 5 being best)
1   2   3   4   5

Breakfast (time)_____

_____

_____

Mid-Morning Snack (time)_____

_____

Lunch (time)_____

_____

_____

Mid-Afternoon Snack (time)_____

_____

Dinner (time)_____

_____

_____

Nighttime Snack (time)_____

_____

Rate today's wheat temptation: (5 being very strong cravings and 1 being no cravings at all)
1   2   3   4   5

Rate overall mood: (1 being poorest and 5 being best)
1   2   3   4   5

Additional comments/progress:

_____

_____

_____

Date: _____   **Weight:** _____

Blood Pressure: _____   **Blood Sugar:** _____

Rate quality of sleep: (1 being poorest and 5 being best)

1   2   3   4   5

Breakfast (time)_____

_____

_____

Mid-Morning Snack (time)_____

_____

Lunch (time)_____

_____

_____

Mid-Afternoon Snack (time)_____

_____

Dinner (time)_____

_____

_____

Nighttime Snack (time)_____

_____

Rate today's wheat temptation: (5 being very strong cravings and 1 being no cravings at all)

1   2   3   4   5

Rate overall mood: (1 being poorest and 5 being best)

1   2   3   4   5

Additional comments/progress:

_____

_____

_____

Date: _____   **Weight:** _____

Blood Pressure: _____   **Blood Sugar:** _____

Rate quality of sleep: (1 being poorest and 5 being best)

1   2   3   4   5

Breakfast (time) _____

_____

_____

Mid-Morning Snack (time) _____

_____

Lunch (time) _____

_____

_____

Mid-Afternoon Snack (time) _____

_____

Dinner (time) _____

_____

_____

Nighttime Snack (time) _____

_____

Rate today's wheat temptation: (5 being very strong cravings and 1 being no cravings at all)

1   2   3   4   5

Rate overall mood: (1 being poorest and 5 being best)

1   2   3   4   5

Additional comments/progress:

_____

_____

_____

Date: _____   **Weight:** _____

Blood Pressure: _____   **Blood Sugar:** _____

Rate quality of sleep: (1 being poorest and 5 being best)

1   2   3   4   5

Breakfast (time)_____

_____

_____

Mid-Morning Snack (time)_____

_____

Lunch (time)_____

_____

_____

Mid-Afternoon Snack (time)_____

_____

Dinner (time)_____

_____

_____

Nighttime Snack (time)_____

_____

Rate today's wheat temptation: (5 being very strong cravings and 1 being no cravings at all)

1   2   3   4   5

Rate overall mood: (1 being poorest and 5 being best)

1   2   3   4   5

Additional comments/progress:

_____

_____

_____

Date: _____   **Weight:** _____

Blood Pressure: _____   **Blood Sugar:** _____

Rate quality of sleep: (1 being poorest and 5 being best)

1   2   3   4   5

Breakfast (time)_____

_____

_____

Mid-Morning Snack (time)_____

_____

Lunch (time)_____

_____

_____

Mid-Afternoon Snack (time)_____

_____

Dinner (time)_____

_____

_____

Nighttime Snack (time)_____

_____

Rate today's wheat temptation: (5 being very strong cravings and 1 being no cravings at all)

1   2   3   4   5

Rate overall mood: (1 being poorest and 5 being best)

1   2   3   4   5

Additional comments/progress:

_____

_____

_____

Date: _____   **Weight:** _____

Blood Pressure: _____   **Blood Sugar:** _____

Rate quality of sleep: (1 being poorest and 5 being best)

1   2   3   4   5

Breakfast (time)_____

_____

_____

Mid-Morning Snack (time)_____

_____

Lunch (time)_____

_____

_____

Mid-Afternoon Snack (time)_____

_____

Dinner (time)_____

_____

_____

Nighttime Snack (time)_____

_____

Rate today's wheat temptation: (5 being very strong cravings and 1 being no cravings at all)

1   2   3   4   5

Rate overall mood: (1 being poorest and 5 being best)

1   2   3   4   5

Additional comments/progress:

_____

_____

_____

Date: _____ **Weight:** _____

Blood Pressure: _____ **Blood Sugar:** _____

Rate quality of sleep: (1 being poorest and 5 being best)

1   2   3   4   5

Breakfast (time)_____

_____

_____

Mid-Morning Snack (time)_____

_____

Lunch (time)_____

_____

_____

Mid-Afternoon Snack (time)_____

_____

Dinner (time)_____

_____

_____

Nighttime Snack (time)_____

_____

Rate today's wheat temptation: (5 being very strong cravings and 1 being no cravings at all)

1   2   3   4   5

Rate overall mood: (1 being poorest and 5 being best)

1   2   3   4   5

Additional comments/progress:

_____

_____

_____

Date: _____   **Weight:** _____

Blood Pressure: _____   **Blood Sugar:** _____

Rate quality of sleep: (1 being poorest and 5 being best)

1   2   3   4   5

Breakfast (time)_____

_____

_____

Mid-Morning Snack (time)_____

_____

Lunch (time)_____

_____

_____

Mid-Afternoon Snack (time)_____

_____

Dinner (time)_____

_____

_____

Nighttime Snack (time)_____

_____

Rate today's wheat temptation: (5 being very strong cravings and 1 being no cravings at all)

1   2   3   4   5

Rate overall mood: (1 being poorest and 5 being best)

1   2   3   4   5

Additional comments/progress:

_____

_____

_____

Date: _____   Weight: _____

Blood Pressure: _____   Blood Sugar: _____

Rate quality of sleep: (1 being poorest and 5 being best)

1   2   3   4   5

Breakfast (time)_____

_____

_____

Mid-Morning Snack (time)_____

_____

Lunch (time)_____

_____

_____

Mid-Afternoon Snack (time)_____

_____

Dinner (time)_____

_____

_____

Nighttime Snack (time)_____

_____

Rate today's wheat temptation: (5 being very strong cravings and 1 being no cravings at all)

1   2   3   4   5

Rate overall mood: (1 being poorest and 5 being best)

1   2   3   4   5

Additional comments/progress:

_____

_____

_____

Date: _____   **Weight:** _____

Blood Pressure: _____   **Blood Sugar:** _____

Rate quality of sleep: (1 being poorest and 5 being best)

1   2   3   4   5

Breakfast (time)_____

_____

_____

Mid-Morning Snack (time)_____

_____

Lunch (time)_____

_____

_____

Mid-Afternoon Snack (time)_____

_____

Dinner (time)_____

_____

_____

Nighttime Snack (time)_____

_____

Rate today's wheat temptation: (5 being very strong cravings and 1 being no cravings at all)

1   2   3   4   5

Rate overall mood: (1 being poorest and 5 being best)

1   2   3   4   5

Additional comments/progress:

_____

_____

_____

Date: _____   **Weight:** _____

Blood Pressure: _____   **Blood Sugar:** _____

Rate quality of sleep: (1 being poorest and 5 being best)

1   2   3   4   5

Breakfast (time)_____

_____

_____

Mid-Morning Snack (time)_____

_____

Lunch (time)_____

_____

_____

Mid-Afternoon Snack (time)_____

_____

Dinner (time)_____

_____

_____

Nighttime Snack (time)_____

_____

Rate today's wheat temptation: (5 being very strong cravings and 1 being no cravings at all)

1   2   3   4   5

Rate overall mood: (1 being poorest and 5 being best)

1   2   3   4   5

Additional comments/progress:

_____

_____

_____

Date: _____   **Weight:** _____

Blood Pressure: _____   **Blood Sugar:** _____

Rate quality of sleep: (1 being poorest and 5 being best)

1   2   3   4   5

Breakfast (time)_____

_____

_____

Mid-Morning Snack (time)_____

_____

Lunch (time)_____

_____

_____

Mid-Afternoon Snack (time)_____

_____

Dinner (time)_____

_____

_____

Nighttime Snack (time)_____

_____

Rate today's wheat temptation: (5 being very strong cravings and 1 being no cravings at all)

1   2   3   4   5

Rate overall mood: (1 being poorest and 5 being best)

1   2   3   4   5

Additional comments/progress:

_____

_____

_____

Date: _____   **Weight:** _____

Blood Pressure: _____   **Blood Sugar:** _____

Rate quality of sleep: (1 being poorest and 5 being best)

1   2   3   4   5

Breakfast (time)_____

_____

_____

Mid-Morning Snack (time)_____

_____

Lunch (time)_____

_____

_____

Mid-Afternoon Snack (time)_____

_____

Dinner (time)_____

_____

_____

Nighttime Snack (time)_____

_____

Rate today's wheat temptation: (5 being very strong cravings and 1 being no cravings at all)

1   2   3   4   5

Rate overall mood: (1 being poorest and 5 being best)

1   2   3   4   5

Additional comments/progress:

_____

_____

EPILOGUE

THERE IS NO QUESTION that the cultivation of wheat in the Fertile Crescent 10,000 years ago marked a turning point in the course of civilization, planting the seeds for the Agricultural Revolution. Cultivation of wheat was the pivotal step that converted nomadic hunter-gatherers to fixed, nonmigratory societies that grew into villages and cities, yielded food surplus, and allowed occupational specialization. Without wheat, life today would surely be quite different.

So, in many ways, we owe wheat a debt of gratitude for having propelled human civilization on a course that has led us to our modern technological age. Or do we?

Jared Diamond, professor of geography and physiology at UCLA and author of the Pulitzer Prize–winning book, *Guns, Germs, and Steel*, believes that "the adoption of agriculture, supposedly our most decisive step toward a better life, was in many ways a catastrophe from which we have never recovered."[1] Dr. Diamond points out that, based on lessons learned through modern paleopathology, the conversion from hunter-gatherer to agricultural society was accompanied by reduced stature, a rapid spread of infectious diseases such as tuberculosis and bubonic plague, and a class structure from peasantry to royalty, and it also set the stage for sexual inequality.

In his books *Paleopathology at the Origins of Agriculture* and *Health and the Rise of Civilization*, anthropologist Mark Cohen of the State University of New York argues that, while agriculture yielded surplus and allowed division of labor, it also entailed working harder and longer hours. It meant narrowing the wide variety of gathered plants down to the few crops that could be cultivated. It also introduced an entirely new collection of diseases that had previously been uncommon. "I don't think most hunter-gatherers farmed until they had to, and when they switched to farming they traded quality for quantity," he writes.

The standard modern notion of preagricultural hunter-gatherer life as short, brutish, desperate, and a nutritional dead end may be incorrect. The adoption of agriculture in this revisionist line of thinking can be viewed as a compromise in which convenience, societal evolution, and food abundance were traded for health.

We have taken this paradigm to the extreme, narrowing our dietary variety down to popular catchphrases such as "Eat more healthy whole grains." Convenience, abundance, and inexpensive accessibility have all been achieved to a degree inconceivable even a century ago. Fourteen-chromosome wild grass has been transformed into the forty-two-chromosome, nitrate-fertilized, top-heavy, ultra-high-yield variety that now enables us to buy bagels by the dozen, pancakes by the stack, and pretzels by the "family size" bag.

Such extremes of accessibility are therefore accompanied by extremes of health sacrifice—obesity, arthritis, neurological incapacity, even death from increasingly common diseases such as celiac. We have unwittingly struck a Faustian bargain with nature, trading abundance for health.

This idea that wheat is not only making people ill, but killing some of us—some quickly, others more slowly—raises unsettling questions: What do we say to the millions of people in Third World countries who, if deprived of high-yield wheat, might have less chronic illness but greater likelihood of near-term starvation? Should we just accept that our far-from-perfect means justifies the net reduced mortality end?

Can the shaky United States economy endure the huge shake-down that would be required if wheat were to experience a down-turn in demand to make way for other crops and food sources? Is it even possible to maintain access to cheap, high-volume food for the tens of millions of people who presently rely on high-yield wheat for $5.00 pizza and $1.29 loaves of bread?

Should einkorn or emmer, primordial wheat that predates the thousands of hybridizations leading to modern wheat, replace our modern version but at the price of reduced yield and increased cost?

I won't pretend to have the answers. In fact, it may be decades before all these questions can be adequately answered. I believe that resurrecting ancient grains (as Eli Rogosa is doing in western Massachusetts) may provide a small part of the solution, one that will grow in importance over many years in the same way that cage-free eggs have gained some economic traction. For many people, I suspect that ancestral wheat represents a reasonable solu-tion, not necessarily entirely free of human health implications, but at least far safer. And, in an economy in which demand ulti-mately drives supply, reduced consumer interest in modern genet-ically altered wheat products will cause agricultural production to gradually shift to accommodate changing tastes.

What to do with the thorny issue of helping to feed the Third World? I can only hope that improved conditions in the coming years will also introduce wider choice in food that will allow peo-ple to move away from the "It's better than nothing" mentality that presently dominates.

In the meantime, you have the freedom to exert your procla-mation of wheat belly emancipation with the power of your con-sumer dollars.

The message to "eat more healthy whole grains" should accom-pany other mistakes, such as substituting hydrogenated and poly-unsaturated fats for saturated fats, substituting margarine for butter, and substituting high-fructose corn syrup for sucrose, in the graveyard of misguided nutritional advice that has confused, misled, and fattened the American public.

Wheat is *not* just another carbohydrate, no more than nuclear fission is just another chemical reaction.

It is the ultimate hubris of modern humans that we can change and manipulate the genetic code of another species to suit our needs. Perhaps that will be possible in a hundred years, when the genetic code may be as readily manipulated as your checking account. But today, genetic modification and hybridization of the plants we call food crops remain crude science, still fraught with unintended effects on both the plant itself and the animals consuming them.

Earth's plants and animals exist in their current form because of the end result of millions of years of evolutionary coddling. We step in and, in the absurdly brief period of the past half century, alter the course of evolution of a plant that thrived alongside humans for millennia, only now to suffer the consequences of our shortsighted manipulations.

In the 10,000-year journey from innocent, low-yield, not-so-baking-friendly einkorn grass to high-yield, created-in-a-laboratory, unable-to-survive-in-the-wild, suited-to-modern-tastes dwarf wheat, we've witnessed a human engineered transformation that is no different than pumping livestock full of antibiotics and hormones while confining them in a factory warehouse. Perhaps we *can* recover from this catastrophe called agriculture, but a big first step is to recognize what we've done to this thing called "wheat."

See you in the produce aisle.

ACKNOWLEDGMENTS

THE PATH I TOOK to wheat-free enlightenment was anything but a straight line. It was, in truth, a zigzagging, up-and-down struggle to come to terms with what has got to be one of the biggest nutritional blunders conducted on an international scale. A number of people were instrumental in helping me understand these issues and deliver this crucial message to a larger audience.

I owe my agent and friend, Rick Broadhead, a debt of gratitude for hearing me out on what, I knew from the start, sounded like a kooky idea. Within the first few moments, Rick was behind this project 100 percent. He catapulted my proposal from speculation to full-fledged, full-steam-ahead plan. Rick was more than a dedicated agent; he also offered advice on how to craft the message and how to most effectively deliver it, not to mention unwavering moral support.

Pam Krauss, my editor at Rodale, kept me on my toes, transforming my rambling prose into its current form. I'm sure Pam spent many long nights poring over my musings, pulling out her hair, brewing up yet another pot of late-night coffee while wielding her green-inked pen on my rough draft. I owe you a year's worth of evening toasts, Pam!

There is a list of people who deserve thanks for providing unique insights. Elisheva Rogosa of the Heritage Wheat Foundation (www.growseed.org) not only helped me understand the role of ancient wheat in this 10,000-year-long trek, but also provided the actual einkorn grain that allowed me to experience firsthand what it meant to consume the direct ancestor of grain consumed by Natufian hunter-gatherers. Dr. Allan Fritz, professor of wheat breeding at Kansas State University, and USDA agricultural statistician and lead wheat analyst, Gary Vocke, PhD, both assisted in providing data on their perspectives on the modern wheat phenomenon.

Dr. Peter Green, director of the Celiac Disease Center of Columbia University in New York City, through both his groundbreaking clinical studies as well as his personal communications, provided the groundwork that helped me understand how celiac disease fits into the larger issue of wheat intolerance. The Mayo Clinic's Dr. Joseph Murray not only provided enormously clever clinical studies that have helped make a damning case against the modern version of agribusiness-generated wheat, but offered a helping hand to assist in my understanding of issues that, I believe, will prove the ultimate undoing of this Frankengrain that has infiltrated every aspect of American culture.

Two groups of people, too many to name but nonetheless near and dear to my heart, are my patients and the followers of my online heart disease prevention program, Track Your Plaque (www.trackyourplaque.com). These are the real-life people who have taught me many lessons along the way that helped mold and refine these ideas. These are the people who demonstrated to me, over and over again, what wonderful health effects develop on removal of wheat.

My friend and chief IT guru, Chris Kliesmet, saw me through this effort, allowing me to bounce ideas off him for his nobody-else-thinks-like-this brand of thinking.

Of course, I owe an infinite number of reminders to my wonderful wife, Dawn, that I will indeed take her on many well-deserved getaways after I sacrificed many family outings and evenings together during my preoccupation with this effort.

Sweetie, I love you and I am grateful that you allowed me to undertake this very, very important project.

Thanks to my son, Bill, just starting his first year of college, who patiently listened to my chattering on about this issue. I am impressed with your courage to argue these ideas with your professors! To my daughter, Lauren, who declared her professional tennis status while I was laboring away at this book, I will be sure to now be courtside at more of your matches. Forty-love! Finally, I offer a piece of gentle advice to Jacob, my stepson, who endured my endless admonitions to "Put down that bread stick!": It is my desire to see you succeed, prosper, while enjoying the moment and not suffer through decades of stupor, sleepiness, and emotional turmoil due to nothing more than the ham sandwich you just ate. Swallow hard and move on.

REFERENCES

CHAPTER 2

1. Rollo F, Ubaldi M, Ermini L, Marota I. Ötzi's last meals: DNA analysis of the intestinal content of the Neolithic glacier mummy from the Alps. *Proc Nat Acad Sci* 2002 Oct 1;99(20):12594–9.
2. Shewry PR. Wheat. *J Exp Botany* 2009;60(6):1537–53.
3. Ibid.
4. Ibid.
5. Song X, Ni Z. Yao Y et al. Identification of differentially expressed proteins between hybrid and parents in wheat (*Triticum aestivum L.*) seedling leaves. *Theor Appl Genet* 2009 Jan;118(2):213–25.
6. Gao X, Liu SW, Sun Q, Xia GM. High frequency of HMW-GS sequence variation through somatic hybridization between *Agropyron elongatum* and common wheat. *Planta* 2010 Jan;23(2):245–50.
7. Van den Broeck HC, de Jong HC, Salentijn EM et al. Presence of celiac disease epitopes in modern and old hexaploid wheat varieties: wheat breeding may have contributed to increased prevalence of celiac disease. *Theor Appl Genet* 2010 Jul 28.
8. Shewry. *J Exp Botany* 2009;60(6):1537–53.
9. Magaña-Gómez JA, Calderón de la Barca AM. Risk assessment of genetically modified crops for nutrition and health. *Nutr Rev* 2009;67(1):1–16.
10. Dubcovsky J, Dvorak J. Genome plasticity a key factor in the success of polyploidy wheat under domestication. *Science* 2007 June 29;316:1862–6.

CHAPTER 3

1. Raeker RÖ, Gaines CS, Finney PL, Donelson T. Granule size distribution and chemical composition of starches from 12 soft wheat cultivars. *Cereal Chem* 1998 75(5):721–8.
2. Avivi L. High grain protein content in wild tetraploid wheat, *Triticum dicoccoides*. In Fifth International Wheat Genetics Symposium, New Delhi, India 1978, Feb 23–28;372–80.
3. Cummings JH, Englyst HN. Gastrointestinal effects of food carbohydrate. *Am J Clin Nutr* 1995; 61:938S–45S.

4. Foster-Powell, Holt SHA, Brand-Miller JC. International table of glycemic index and glycemic load values: 2002. *Am J Clin Nutr* 2002;76(1):5–56.

5. Jenkins DJH, Wolever TM, Taylor RH et al. Glycemic index of foods: a physiological basis for carbohydrate exchange. *Am J Clin Nutr* 1981 Mar;34(3):362–6.

6. Juntunen KS, Niskanen LK, Liukkonen KH et al. Postprandial glucose, insulin, and incretin responses to grain products in healthy subjects. *Am J Clin Nutr* 2002 Feb;75(2):254–62.

7. Järvi AE, Karlström BE, Granfeldt YE et al. The influence of food structure on postprandial metabolism in patients with non-insulin-dependent diabetes mellitus. *Am J Clin Nutr* 1995 Apr;61(4):837–42.

8. Juntunen et al. *Am J Clin Nutr* 2002 Feb;75(2):254–62.

9. Järvi et al. *Am J Clin Nutr* 1995 Apr;61(4):837–42.

10. Yoshimoto Y, Tashiro J, Takenouchi T, Takeda Y. Molecular structure and some physiochemical properties of high-amylose barley starches. *Cereal Chemistry* 2000;77:279–85.

11. Murray JA, Watson T, Clearman B, Mitros F. Effect of a gluten-free diet on gastrointestinal symptoms in celiac disease. *Am J Clin Nutr* 2004 Apr;79(4):669–73.

12. Cheng J, Brar PS, Lee AR, Green PH. Body mass index in celiac disease: beneficial effect of a gluten-free diet. *J Clin Gastroenterol* 2010 Apr;44(4):267–71.

13. Shewry PR, Jones HD. Transgenic wheat: Where do we stand after the first 12 years? *Ann App Biol* 2005;147:1–14.

14. Van Herpen T, Goryunova SV, van der Schoot J et al. Alpha-gliadin genes from the A, B, and D genomes of wheat contain different sets of celiac disease epitopes. *BMC Genomics* 2006 Jan 10;7:1.

15. Molberg Ø, Uhlen AK, Jensen T et al. Mapping of gluten T-cell epitopes in the bread wheat ancestors: implications for celiac disease. *Gastroenterol* 2005;128:393–401.

16. Shewry PR, Halford NG, Belton PS, Tatham AS. The structure and properties of gluten: an elastic protein from wheat grain. *Phil Trans Roy Soc London* 2002;357:133–42.

17. Molberg et al. *Gastroenterol* 2005;128:393–401.

18. Tatham AS, Shewry PR. Allergens in wheat and related cereals. *Clin Exp Allergy* 2008;38:1712–26.

CHAPTER 4

1. Dohan FC. Wheat "consumption" and hospital admissions for schizophrenia during World War II. A preliminary report. 1966 Jan;18(1):7–10.

2. Dohan FC. Coeliac disease and schizophrenia. *Brit Med J* 1973 July 7; 51–52.

3. Dohan, F.C. Hypothesis: Genes and neuroactive peptides from food as cause of schizophrenia. In: Costa E and Trabucchi M, eds. *Advances in Biochemical Psychopharmacology*, New York: Raven Press 1980;22:535–48.

4. Vlissides DN, Venulet A, Jenner FA. A double-blind gluten-free/gluten-load controlled trial in a secure ward population. *Br J Psych* 1986;148:447–52.

5. Kraft BD, West EC. Schizophrenia, gluten, and low-carbohydrate, ketogenic diets: a case report and review of the literature. *Nutr Metab* 2009;6:10.
6. Cermak SA, Curtin C, Bandini LG. Food selectivity and sensory sensitivity in children with autism spectrum disorders. *J Am Diet Assoc* 2010 Feb;110(2):238–46.
7. Knivsberg AM, Reichelt KL, Hoien T, Nodland M. A randomized, controlled study of dietary intervention in autistic syndromes. *Nutr Neurosci* 2002;5:251–61.
8. Millward C, Ferriter M, Calver S et al. Gluten- and casein-free diets for autistic spectrum disorder. *Cochrane Database Syst Rev* 2008 Apr 16;(2):CD003498.
9. Whiteley P, Haracopos D, Knivsberg AM et al. The ScanBrit randomised, controlled, single-blind study of a gluten- and casein-free dietary intervention for children with autism spectrum disorders. *Nutr Neurosci* 2010 Apr;13(2):87–100.
10. Niederhofer H, Pittschieler K. A preliminary investigation of ADHD symptoms in persons with celiac disease. *J Atten Disord* 2006 Nov;10(2):200–4.
11. Zioudrou C, Streaty RA, Klee WA. Opioid peptides derived from food proteins. The exorphins. *J Biol Chem* 1979 Apr 10;254(7):2446–9.
12. Pickar D, Vartanian F, Bunney WE Jr et al. Short-term naloxone administration in schizophrenic and manic patients. A World Health Organization Collaborative Study. *Arch Gen Psychiatry* 1982 Mar;39(3):313–9.
13. Cohen MR, Cohen RM, Pickar D, Murphy DL. Naloxone reduces food intake in humans. *Psychosomatic Med* 1985 March/April;47(2):132–8.
14. Drewnowski A, Krahn DD, Demitrack MA et al. Naloxone, an opiate blocker, reduces the consumption of sweet high-fat foods in obese and lean female binge eaters. *Am J Clin Nutr* 1995;61:1206–12.

CHAPTER 5

1. Flegal KM, Carroll MD, Ogden CL, Curtin LR. Prevalence and trends in obesity among US adults, 1999–2008. *JAMA* 2010;303(3):235–41.
2. Flegal KM, Carroll MD, Kuczmarski RJ, Johnson CL. Overweight and obesity in the United States: prevalence and trends, 1960–1994. *Int J Obes Relat Metab Disord* 1998;22(1):39–47.
3. Costa D, Steckel RH. Long-term trends in health, welfare, and economic growth in the United States, in Steckel RH, Floud R (eds): *Health and Welfare during Industrialization*. Univ Chicago Press 1997: 47–90.
4. Klöting N, Fasshauer M, Dietrich A et al. Insulin sensitive obesity. *Am J Physiol Endocrinol Metab* 2010 Jun 22. [Epub ahead of print]
5. DeMarco VG, Johnson MS, Whaley-Connell AT, Sowers JR. Cytokine abnormalities in the etiology of the cardiometabolic syndrome. *Curr Hypertens Rep* 2010 Apr;12(2):93–8.
6. Matsuzawa Y. Establishment of a concept of visceral fat syndrome and discovery of adiponectin. *Proc Jpn Acad Ser B Phys Biol Sci* 2010;86(2):131–41.
7. Ibid.
8. Funahashi T, Matsuzawa Y. Hypoadiponectinemia: a common basis for diseases associated with overnutrition. *Curr Atheroscler Rep* 2006 Sep;8(5):433–8.

9. Deprés J, Lemieux I, Bergeron J et al. Abdominal obesity and the metabolic syndrome: contributions to global cardiometabolic risk. *Arterioscl Thromb Vasc Biol* 2008;28:1039–49.
10. Lee Y, Pratley RE. Abdominal obesity and cardiovascular disease risk: the emerging role of the adipocyte. *J Cardiopulm Rehab Prev* 2007;27:2–10.
11. Lautenbach A, Budde A, Wrann CD. Obesity and the associated mediators leptin, estrogen and IGF-I enhance the cell proliferation and early tumorigenesis of breast cancer cells. *Nutr Cancer* 2009;61(4):484–91.
12. Endogenous Hormones and Breast Cancer Collaborative Group. Endogenous sex hormones and breast cancer in postmenopausal women: reanalysis of nine prospective studies. *J Natl Cancer Inst* 2002;94:606–16.
13. Johnson RE, Murah MH. Gynecomastia: pathophysiology, evaluation, and management. *Mayo Clin Proc* 2009 Nov;84(11):1010–5.
14. Pynnönen PA, Isometsä ET, Verkasalo MA et al. Gluten-free diet may alleviate depressive and behavioural symptoms in adolescents with celiac disease: a prospective follow-up case-series study. *BMC Psychiatry* 2005;5:14.
15. Green P, Stavropoulos S, Panagi S et al. Characteristics of adult celiac disease in the USA: results of a national survey. *Am J Gastroenterol* 2001;96:126–31.
16. Cranney A, Zarkadas M, Graham ID et al. The Canadian Celiac Health Survey. *Dig Dis Sci* 2007 Apr; (5294):1087–95.
17. Barera G, Mora S, Brambill a P et al. Body composition in children with celiac disease and the effects of a gluten-free diet: a prospective case-control study. *Am J Clin Nutr* 2000 Jul;72(1):71–5.
18. Cheng J, Brar PS, Lee AR, Green PH. Body mass index in celiac disease: beneficial effect of a gluten-free diet. *J Clin Gastroenterol* 2010 Apr;44(4):267–71.
19. Dickey W, Kearney N. Overweight in celiac disease: prevalence, clinical characteristics, and effect of a gluten-free diet. *Am J Gastroenterol* 2006 Oct;101(10):2356–9.
20. Murray JA, Watson T, Clearman B, Mitros F. Effect of a gluten-free diet on gastrointestinal symptoms in celiac disease. *Am J Clin Nutr* 2004 Apr;79(4):669–73.
21. Cheng et al. *J Clin Gastroenterol* 2010 Apr;44(4):267–71.
22. Barera G et al. *Am J Clin Nutr* 2000 Jul;72(1):71–5.
23. Venkatasubramani N, Telega G, Werlin SL. Obesity in pediatric celiac disease. *J Pediat Gastrolenterol Nutr* 2010 May 12 [Epub ahead of print].
24. Bardella MT, Fredella C, Prampolini L et al. Body composition and dietary intakes in adult celiac disease patients consuming a strict gluten-free diet. *Am J Clin Nutr* 2000 Oct;72(4):937–9.
25. Smecuol E, Gonzalez D, Mautalen C et al. Longitudinal study on the effect of treatment on body composition and anthropometry of celiac disease patients. *Am J Gastroenterol* 1997 April;92(4):639–43.
26. Green P, Cellier C. Celiac disease. *New Engl J Med* 2007 October 25;357:1731–43.
27. Foster GD, Wyatt HR, Hill JO et al. A randomized trial of a low–carbohydrate diet for obesity. *N Engl J Med* 2003;348:2082–90.
28. Samaha FF, Iqbal N, Seshadri P et al. A low-carbohydrate as compared with a low-fat diet in severe obesity. *N Engl J Med* 2003;348:2074–81.

CHAPTER 6

1. Paveley WF. From Aretaeus to Crosby: a history of coeliac disease. *Brit Med J* 1988 Dec 24–31;297:1646–9.
2. Van Berge-Henegouwen, Mulder C. Pioneer in the gluten free diet: Willem-Karel Dicke 1905-1962, over 50 years of gluten free diet. *Gut* 1993;34:1473–5.
3. Barton SH, Kelly DG, Murray JA. Nutritional deficiencies in celiac disease. *Gastroenterol Clin N Am* 2007;36:93–108.
4. Fasano A. Systemic autoimmune disorders in celiac disease. *Curr Opin Gastroenterol* 2006;22(6):674–9.
5. Fasano A, Berti I, Gerarduzzi T et al. Prevalence of celiac disease in at-risk and not-at-risk groups in the United States: a large multicenter study. *Arch Intern Med* 2003 Feb 10;163(3):286–92.
6. Farrell RJ, Kelly CP. Celiac sprue. *N Engl J Med* 2002;346(3):180–8.
7. Garampazzi A, Rapa A, Mura S et al. Clinical pattern of celiac disease is still changing. *J Ped Gastroenterol Nutr* 2007;45:611–4.
8. Steens R, Csizmadia C, George E et al. A national prospective study on childhood celiac disease in the Netherlands 1993–2000: An increasing recognition and a changing clinical picture. *J Pediatr* 2005;147–239–43.
9. McGowan KE, Castiglione DA, Butzner JD. The changing face of childhood celiac disease in North America: impact of serological testing. *Pediatrics* 2009 Dec;124(6):1572–8.
10. Rajani S, Huynh HQ, Turner J. The changing frequency of celiac disease diagnosed at the Stollery Children's Hospital. *Can J Gastrolenterol* 2010 Feb;24(2):109–12.
11. Bottaro G, Cataldo F, Rotolo N et al. The clinical pattern of subclinical/silent celiac disease: an analysis on 1026 consecutive cases. *Am J Gastrolenterol* 1999 Mar;94(3):691–6.
12. Van der Windt D, Jellema P, Mulder CJ et al. Diagnostic testing for celiac disease among patients with abdominal symptoms: a systematic review. *J Am Med Assoc* 2010;303(17):1738–46.
13. Johnston SD, McMillan SA, Collins JS et al. A comparison of antibodies to tissue transglutaminase with conventional serological tests in the diagnosis of coeliac disease. *Eur J Gastroenterol Hepatol* 2003 Sep;15(9):1001–4.
14. Van der Windt et al. *J Am Med Assoc* 2010;303(17):1738–46.
15. Johnston SD et al. *Eur J Gastroenterol Hepatol* 2003 Sep;15(9):1001–4.
16. Van der Windt et al. *J Am Med Assoc* 2010;303(17):1738–46.
17. NIH Consensus Development Conference on Celiac Disease. *NIH Consens State Sci Statements* 2004 Jun 28–30;21(1):1–23.
18. Mustalahti K, Lohiniemi S, Collin P et al. Gluten-free diet and quality of life in patients with screen-detected celiac disease. *Eff Clin Pract* 202 May–Jun;5(3):105–13.
19. Ensari A, Marsh MN, Morgan S et al. Diagnosing coeliac disease by rectal gluten challenge: a prospective study based on immunopathology, computer-ized image analysis and logistic regression analysis. *Clin Sci* (Lond) 2001 Aug; 101(2):199–207.

20. Rubio-Tapia A, Kyle RA, Kaplan E et al. Increased prevalence and mortality in undiagnosed celiac disease. *Gastroenterol* 2009 July;137(1):88–93.

21. Lohi S, Mustalahti K, Kaukinen K et al. Increasing prevalence of celiac disease over time. *Aliment Pharmacol Ther* 2007;26:1217–25.

22. Bach JF. The effect of infections on susceptibility to autoimmune and allergic disease. *N Engl J Med* 2002;347:911–20.

23. Van den Broeck HC, de Jong HC, Salentijn EM et al. Presence of celiac disease epitopes in modern and old hexaploid wheat varieties: Wheat breeding may have contributed to increased prevalence of celiac disease. *Theor Appl Genet* 2010 July 28 [Epub ahead of print].

24. Drago S, El Asmar R, Di Pierro M et al. Gliadin, zonulin and gut permeability: effects on celiac and nonceliac intestinal mucosa and intestinal cell lines. *Scand J Gastroenterol* 2006;41:408–19.

25. Guttman JA, Finlay BB. Tight junctions as targets of infectious agents. *Biochim Biophys Acta* 2009 Apr;1788(4):832–41.

26. Parnell N, Ciclitira PJ. Celiac disease. *Curr Opin Gastroenterol* 1999 Mar;15(2):120–4.

27. Peters U, Askling J, Gridley G et al. Causes of death in patients with celiac disease in a population-based Swedish cohort. *Arch Intern Med* 2003;163:1566–72.

28. Hafström I, Ringertz B, Spängberg A et al. A vegan diet free of gluten improves the signs and symptoms of rheumatoid arthritis: the effects on arthritis correlate with a reduction in antibodies to food antigens. *Rheumatology* (Oxford) 2001 Oct;40(10):1175–9.

29. Peters et al. *Arch Intern Med* 2003;163:1566–72.

30. Barera G, Bonfanti R, Viscardi M et al. Occurrence of celiac disease after onset of type 1 diabetes: a 6-year prospective longitudinal study. *Pediatrics* 2002;109:833–8.

31. Ascher H. Coeliac disease and type 1 diabetes: an affair still with much hidden behind the veil. *Acta Paediatr* 2001;90;1217–25.

32. Hadjivassiliou M, Sanders DS, Grünewald RA et al. Gluten sensitivity: from gut to brain. *Lancet* 2010 March;9:318–30.

33. Hadjivassiliou M, Grünewald RA, Lawden M et al. Headache and CNS white matter abnormalities associated with gluten sensitivity. *Neurology* 2001 Feb 13;56(3):385–8.

34. Barton SH, Kelly DG, Murray JA. *Gastroenterol* Clin N Am 2007;36:93–108.

35. Ludvigsson JF, Montgomery SM, Ekbom A et al. Small-intestinal histopathology and mortality risk in celiac disease. *J Am Med Assoc* 2009;302(11):1171–8.

36. West J, Logan R, Smith C et al. Malignancy and mortality in people with celiac disease: population based cohort study. *Brit Med J* 2004 July 21;doi:10.1136/bmj.38169.486701.7C.

37. Askling J, Linet M, Gridley G et al. Cancer incidence in a population-based cohort of individuals hospitalized with celiac disease or dermatitis herpetiformis. *Gastroenterol* 2002 Nov;123(5):1428–35.

38. Peters et al. *Arch Intern Med* 2003;163:1566–72.

39. Ludvigsson et al. *J Am Med Assoc* 2009;302(11):1171–8.

40. Holmes GKT, Prior P, Lane MR et al. Malignancy in celiac disease—effect of a gluten free diet. *Gut* 1989;30:333–8.
41. Ford AC, Chey WD, Talley NJ et al. Yield of diagnostic tests for celiac disease in individuals with symptoms suggestive of irritable bowel syndrome: systematic review and meta-analysis. *Arch Intern Med* 2009 April 13;169(7):651–8.
42. Ibid.
43. Bagci S, Ercin CN, Yesilova Z et al. Levels of serologic markers of celiac disease in patients with reflux esophagitis. *World J Gastrolenterol* 2006 Nov 7;12(41):6707–10.
44. Usai P, Manca R, Cuomo R et al. Effect of gluten-free diet and co-morbidity of irritable bowel syndrome-type symptoms on health-related quality of life in adult coeliac patients. *Dig Liver Dis* 2007 Sep;39(9):824–8.
45. Collin P, Mustalahti K, Kyrönpalo S et al. Should we screen reflux oesophagitis patients for coeliac disease? *Eur J Gastroenterol Hepatol* 2004 Sep;16(9):917–20.
46. Cuomo A, Romano M, Rocco A et al. Reflux oesophagitis in adult coeliac disease: beneficial effect of a gluten free diet. *Gut* 2003 Apr;52(4):514–7.
47. Ibid.
48. Verdu EF, Armstrong D, Murray JA. Between celiac disease and irritable bowel syndrome: the "no man's land" of gluten sensitivity. *Am J Gastroenterol* 2009 Jun;104(6):1587–94.

CHAPTER 7

1. Zhao X. 434-PP. Presented at the American Diabetes Association 70th Scientific Sessions; June 25, 2010.
2. Franco OH, Steyerberg EW, Hu FB et al. Associations of diabetes mellitus with total life expectancy and life expectancy with and without cardiovascular disease. *Arch Intern Med* 2007 Jun 11;167(11):1145–51.
3. Daniel M, Rowley KG, McDermott R et al. Diabetes incidence in an Australian aboriginal population: an 8-year follow-up study. *Diabetes Care* 1999;22:1993–8.
4. Ebbesson SO, Schraer CD, Risica PM et al. Diabetes and impaired glucose tolerance in three Alaskan Eskimo populations: the Alaska-Siberia Project. *Diabetes Care* 1998;21:563–9.
5. Cordain L. Cereal grains: Humanity's double-edged sword. In Simopoulous AP (ed), Evolutionary aspects of nutrition and health. *World Rev Nutr Diet* 1999;84:19–73.
6. Reaven GM. Banting Lecture 1988: Role of insulin resistance in human disease. *Diabetes* 1988;37:1595–607.
7. Crawford EM. Death rates from diabetes mellitus in Ireland 1833–1983: a historical commentary. *Ulster Med J* 1987 Oct;56(2):109–15.
8. Ginsberg HN, MacCallum PR. The obesity, metabolic syndrome, and type 2 diabetes mellitus pandemic: Part I. Increased cardiovascular disease risk and the importance of atherogenic dyslipidemia in persons with the metabolic syndrome and type 2 diabetes mellitus. *J Cardiometab Syndr* 2009;4(2):113–9.

9. Centers fpr Disease Control. National diabetes fact sheet 2011, at http://apps. nccd.cdc.gov/DDTSTRS/FactSheet.aspx.

10. Ginsberg et al. *J Cardiometab Syndr* 2009;4(2):113–9.

11. Centers for Disease Control. Overweight and obesity trends among adults 2011, at http://www.cdc.gov/obesity/data/index.html.

12. Wang Y, Beydoun MA, Liang L et al. Will all Americans become overweight or obese? Estimating the progression and cost of the US obesity epidemic. *Obesity* (Silver Spring) 2008 Oct;16(10):2323–30.

13. USDA. U.S. Per capita wheat use, at http://www.ers.usda.gov/amberwaves/september08/findings/wheatflour.htm.

14. Macor C, Ruggeri A, Mazzonetto P et al. Visceral adipose tissue impairs insulin secretion and insulin sensitivity but not energy expenditure in obesity. *Metabolism* 1997 Feb;46(2):123–9.

15. Marchetti P, Lupi R, Del Guerra S et al. The beta-cell in human type 2 diabetes. *Adv Exp Med Biol* 2010;654:501–14.

16. Ibid.

17. Wajchenberg BL. Beta-cell failure in diabetes and preservation by clinical treatment. *Endocr Rev* 2007 Apr;28(2):187–218.

18. Banting FG, Best CH, Collip JB et al. Pancreatic extracts in the treatment of diabetes mellitus: preliminary report. *Can Med Assoc J* 1922 March;12(3): 141–6.

19. Westman EC, Vernon MC. Has carbohydrate-restriction been forgotten as a treatment for diabetes mellitus? A perspective on the ACCORD study design. *Nutr Metab* 2008;5:10.

20. Volek JS, Sharman M, Gómez A et al. Comparison of energy-restricted very low-carbohydrate and low-fat diets on weight loss and body composition in overweight men and women. *Nutr Metab* (Lond); 2004 Nov 8;1(1):13.

21. Volek JS, Phinney SD, Forsythe CE et al. Carbohydrate restriction has a more favorable impact on the metabolic syndrome than a low fat diet. *Lipids* 2009 Apr;44(4):297–309.

22. Stern L, Iqbal N, Seshadri P et al. The effects of a low-carbohydrate versus conventional weight loss diets in severely obese adults: one-year follow-up of a randomized trial. *Ann Intern Med* 2004;140:778–85.

23. Samaha FF, Iqbal N, Seshadri P et al. A low-carbohydrate as compared with a low-fat diet in severe obesity. *N Engl J Med* 2003;348:2074–81.

24. Gannon MC, Nuttall FQ. Effect of a high-protein, low-carbohydrate diet on blood glucose control in people with type 2 diabetes. *Diabetes* 2004;53:2375–82.

25. Stern et al. *Ann Intern Med* 2004;140:778–85.

26. Boden G, Sargrad K, Homko C et al. Effect of a low-carbohydrate diet on appetite, blood glucose levels and insulin resistance in obese patients with type 2 diabetes. *Ann Intern Med* 2005;142:403–11.

27. Ventura A, Neri E, Ughi C et al. Gluten-dependent diabetes-related and thyroid related autoantibodies in patients with celiac disease. *J Pediatr* 2000;137:263–5.

28. Vehik K, Hamman RF, Lezotte D et al. Increasing incidence of type 1 diabetes in 0- to 17-year-old Colorado youth. *Diabetes Care* 2007 Mar;30(3):503–9.

29. DIAMOND Project Group. Incidence and trends of childhood type 1 diabetes worldwide 1990-1999. *Diabet Med* 2006 Aug;23(8):857–66.
30. Hansen D, Bennedbaek FN, Hansen LK et al. High prevalence of coeliac disease in Danish children with type 1 diabetes mellitus. *Acta Paediatr* 2001 Nov;90(11):1238–43.
31. Barera G, Bonfanti R, Viscsrdi M et al. Occurrence of celiac disease after onset of type 1 diabetes: A 6-year prospective longitudinal study. *Pediatrics* 2002;109:833–8.
32. Ibid.
33. Funda DP, Kaas A, Bock T et al. Gluten-free diet prevents diabetes in NOD mice. *Diabetes Metab Res Rev* 1999;15:323–7.
34. Maurano F, Mazzarella G, Luongo D et al. Small intestinal enteropathy in non-obese diabetic mice fed a diet containing wheat. *Diabetologia* 2005 May;48(5):931–7.
35. Westman EC, Yancy WS, Mavropoulos JC et al. The effect of a low-carbohydrate, ketogenic diet versus a low-glycemic index diet on glycemic control in type 2 diabetes mellitus. *Nutr Metab* 2008 Dec 9;5:36.

CHAPTER 8

1. Wyshak G. Teenaged girls, carbonated beverage consumption, and bone fractures. *Arch Pediatr Adolesc Med* 2000 Jun;154(6):610–3.
2. Remer T, Manz F. Potential renal acid load of foods and its influence on urine pH. *J Am Diet Assoc* 1995;95:791–7.
3. Alexy U, Remer T, Manz F et al. Long-term protein intake and dietary potential renal acid load are associated with bone modeling and remodeling at the proximal radius in healthy children. *Am J Clin Nutr* 2005 Nov;82(5):1107–14.
4. Sebastian A, Frassetto LA, Sellmeyer DE et al. Estimation of the net acid load of the diet of ancestral preagricultural *Homo sapiens* and their hominid ancestors. *Am J Clin Nutr* 2002;76:1308–16.
5. Kurtz I, Maher T, Hulter HN et al. Effect of diet on plasma acid-base composition in normal humans. *Kidney Int* 1983;24:670–80.
6. Frassetto L, Morris RC, Sellmeyer DE et al. Diet, evolution and aging. *Eur J Nutr* 2001;40:200–13.
7. Ibid.
8. Frassetto LA, Todd KM, Morris RC Jr, Sebastian A. Worldwide incidence of hip fracture in elderly women: relation to consumption of animal and vegetable foods. *J Gerontol A Biol Sci Med Sci* 2000;55:M585–92.
9. Van Staa TP, Dennison EM, Leufkens HG et al. Epidemiology of fractures in England and Wales. *Bone* 2001;29:517–22.
10. Grady D, Rubin SM, Petitti DB et al. Hormone therapy to prevent disease and prolong life in postmenopausal women. *Ann Intern Med* 1992;117:1016–37.
11. Dennison E, Mohamed MA, Cooper C. Epidemiology of osteoporosis. *Rheum Dis Clin N Am* 2006;32:617–29.
12. Berger C, Langsetmo L, Joseph L et al. Change in bone mineral density as a function of age in women and men and association with the use of antiresorptive agents. CMAJ 2008;178:1660–8.

13. Massey LK. Dietary animal and plant protein and human bone health: a whole foods approach. *J Nutr* 133:862S–5S.

14. Sebastian et al. *Am J Clin Nutr* 2002;76:1308–16.

15. Jenkins DJ, Kendall CW Vidgen E et al. Effect of high vegetable protein diets on urinary calcium loss in middle-aged men and women. *Eur J Clin Nutr* 2003 Feb;57(2):376–82.

16. Sebastian et al. *Am J Clin Nutr* 2002;76:1308–16.

17. Denton D. *The Hunger for Salt*. New York:Springer-Verlag, 1962.

18. Sebastian et al. *Am J Clin Nutr* 2002;76:1308–16.

19. American Association of Orthopedic Surgeons. Facts on Hip Replacements, at http://www.aaos.org/research/stats/Hip_Facts.pdf.

20. Sacks JJ, Luo YH, Helmick CG. Prevalence of specific types of arthritis and other rheumatic conditions in the ambulatory health care system in the United States, 2001–2005. *Arthr Care Res* 2010 Apr;62(4):460–4.

21. Katz JD, Agrawal S, Velasquez M. Getting to the heart of the matter: osteoarthritis takes its place as part of the metabolic syndrome. *Curr Opin Rheumatol* 2010 June 28.   [Epub ahead of print]

22. Dumond H, Presle N, Terlain B et al. Evidence for a key role of leptin in osteoarthritis. *Arthr Rheum* 2003 Nov;48(11):3118–29.

23. Wang Y, Simpson JA, Wluka AE et al. Relationship between body adiposity measures and risk of primary knee and hip replacement for osteoarthritis: a prospective cohort study. *Arthr Res Ther* 2009;11:R31.

24. Toda Y, Toda T, Takemura S et al. Change in body fat, but not body weight or metabolic correlates of obesity, is related to symptomatic relief of obese patients with knee osteoarthritis after a weight control program. *J Rheumatol* 1998 Nov;25(11):2181–6.

25. Christensen R, Astrup A, Bliddal H et al. Weight loss: the treatment of choice for knee osteoarthritis? A randomized trial. *Osteoarthr Cart* 2005 Jan;13(1):20–7.

26. Anderson AS, Loeser RF. Why is osteoarthritis an age-related disease? *Best Prac Res Clin Rheum* 2010;24:15–26.

27. Meyer D, Stavropolous S, Diamond B et al. Osteoporosis in a North American adult population with celiac disease. *Am J Gastroenterol* 2001;96:112–9.

28. Mazure R, Vazquez H, Gonzalez D et al. Bone mineral affection in asymptomatic adult patients with celiac disease. *Am J Gastroenterol* 1994 Dec;89(12):2130–4.

29. Stenson WF, Newberry R, Lorenz R et al. Increased prevalence of celiac disease and need for routine screening among patients with osteoporosis. *Arch Intern Med* 2005 Feb 28;165(4):393–9.

30. Bianchi ML, Bardella MT. Bone in celiac disease. *Osteoporos Int* 2008;19:1705–16.

31. Fritzsch J, Hennicke G, Tannapfel A. Ten fractures in 21 years. *Unfallchirurg* 2005 Nov;108(11):994–7.

32. Vasquez H, Mazure R, Gonzalez D et al. Risk of fractures in celiac disease patients: a cross-sectional, case-control study. *Am J Gastroenterol* 2000 Jan;95(1):183–9.

33. Lindh E, Ljunghall S, Larsson K, Lavö B. Screening for antibodies against gliadin in patients with osteoporosis. *J Int Med* 1992;231:403–6.
34. Hafström I, Ringertz B, Spångberg A et al. A vegan diet free of gluten improves the signs and symptoms of rheumatoid arthritis: the effects on arthritis correlate with a reduction in antibodies to food antigens. *Rheumatol* 2001;1175–9.

CHAPTER 9

1. Bengmark S. Advanced glycation and lipoxidation end products—amplifiers of inflammation: The role of food. *J Parent Enter Nutr* 2007 Sept-Oct;31(5):430–40.
2. Uribarri J, Cai W, Peppa M et al. Circulating glycotoxins and dietary advanced glycation endproducts: Two links to inflammatory response, oxidative stress, and aging. *J Gerontol* 2007 Apr;62A:427–33.
3. Epidemiology of Diabetes Interventions and Complications (EDIC). Design, implementation, and preliminary results of a long-term follow-up of the Diabetes Control and Complications Trial cohort. *Diabetes Care* 1999 Jan;22(1):99–111.
4. Kilhovd BK, Giardino I, Torjesen PA et al. increased serum levels of the specific AGE-compound methylglyoxal-derived hydroimidazolone in patients with type 2 diabetes. *Metabolism* 1003;52:163–7.
5. Monnier VM, Battista O, Kenny D et al. Skin collagen glycation, glycoxidation, and crosslinking are lower in subjects with long-term intensive versus conventional therapy of type 1 diabetes: Relevance of glycated collagen products versus HbA1c as markers of diabetic complications. DCCT Skin Collagen Ancillary Study Group. Diabetes Control and Complications Trial. *Diabetes* 1999;48:870–80.
6. Negrean M, Stirban A, Stratmann B et al. Effects of low- and high-advanced glycation endproduct meals on macro- and microvascular endothelial function and oxidative stress in patients with type 2 diabetes mellitus. *Am J Clin Nutr* 2007;85:1236–43.
7. Goh S, Cooper ME. The role of advanced glycation end products in progression and complications of diabetes. *J Clin Endocrinol Metab* 2008;93:1143–52.
8. Uribarri J, Tuttle KR. Advanced glycation end products and nephrotoxicity of high-protein diets. *Clin J Am Soc Nephrol* 2006;1:1293–9.
9. Bucala R, Makita Z, Vega G et al. Modification of low density lipoprotein by advanced glycation end products contributes to the dyslipidemia of diabetes and renal insufficiency. *Proc Natl Acad Sci USA* 1994;91:9441–5.
10. Stitt AW, He C, Friedman S et al. Elevated AGE-modified Apo B in sera of euglycemic, normolipidemic patients with atherosclerosis: relationship to tissue AGEs. *Mol Med* 1997;3:617–27.
11. Moreira PI, Smith MA, Zhu X et al. Oxidative stress and neurodegeneration. *Ann NY Acad Sci* 2005;1043:543–52.
12. Nicolls MR. The clinical and biological relationship between type 2 diabetes mellitus and Alzheimer's disease. *Curr Alzheimer Res* 2004;1:47–54.

13. Goh et al. *J Clin Endocrinol Metab* 2008;93:1143–52.

14. Bengmark. *J Parent Enter Nutr* 2007 Sept-Oct;31(5):430–40.

15. Seftel AD, Vaziri ND, Ni Z et al. Advanced glycation end products in human penis: elevation in diabetic tissue, site of deposition, and possible effect through iNOS or eNOS. *Urology* 1997;50:1016–26.

16. Stitt AW. Advanced glycation: an important pathological event in diabetic and age related ocular disease. *Br J Ophthalmol* 2001;85:746–53.

17. Uribarri. *J Gerontol* 2007 Apr;62A:427–33.

18. Vlassara H, Cai W, Crandall J et al. Inflammatory mediators are induced by dietary glycotoxins, a major risk for complications of diabetic angiopathy. *Proc Natl Acad Sci USA* 2002;99:15596–601.

19. American Diabetes Association, at http://www.diabetes.org/diabetes-basics/diabetes-statistics.

20. Sakai M, Oimomi M, Kasuga M. Experimental studies on the role of fructose in the development of diabetic complications. *Kobe J Med Sci* 2002;48(5):125–36.

21. Sarwar N, Aspelund T, Eiriksdottir G et al. Markers of dysglycaemia and risk of coronary heart disease in people without diabetes: Reykjavik prospective study and systematic review. *PLos Med* 2010 May 25;7(5):e1000278.

22. International Expert Committee. International Expert Committee report on the role of the HbA1c assay in the diagnosis of diabetes. *Diabetes Care* 2009; 32:1327–44.

23. Khaw KT, Wareham N, Luben R et al. Glycated haemoglobin, diabetes, and mortality in men in Norfolk cohort of European Prospective Investigation of Cancer and Nutrition (EPIC-Norfolk). *Brit Med J* 2001 Jan 6;322(7277):15–8.

24. Goldberg T, Cai W, Peppa M et al. Advanced glycoxidation end products in commonly consumed foods. *J Am Diet Assoc* 2004;104:1287–91.

25. Negrean et al. *Am J Clin Nutr* 2007;85:1236–43.

26. Gerstein HC, Swedberg K, Carlsson J et al. The hemoglobin A1c level as a progressive risk factor for cardiovascular death, hospitalization for heart failure, or death in patients with chronic heart failure: an analysis of the Candesartan in Heart failure: Assessment of Reduction in Mortality and Morbidity (CHARM) program. Arch Intern Med 2008 Aug 11;168(15):1699–704.

27. Khaw et al. *Brit Med J* 2001 Jan 6;322(7277):15–8.

28. Swami-Mruthinti S, Shaw SM, Zhao HR et al. Evidence of a glycemic threshold for the development of cataracts in diabetic rats. *Curr Eye Res* 1999 Jun;18(6):423–9.

29. Rowe NG, Mitchell PG, Cumming RG, Wans JJ. Diabetes, fasting blood glucose and age-related cataract: the Blue Mountains Eye Study. *Opththalmic Epidemiol* 2000 Jun;7(2):103–14.

30. Sperduto RD, Seigel D. Senile lens and senile macular changes in a population-based sample. *Am J Opththalmol* 1980 Jul;90(1):86–91.

31. Stitt et al. *Mol Med* 1997;3:617–27.

32. Ishibashi T, Kawaguchi M, Sugimoto K et al. Advanced glycation end product-mediated matrix metalloproteinase-9 and apoptosis via renin-angiotensin system in type 2 diabetes. *J Atheroscler Thromb* 2010; 17(6):578–89.

33. Vlassara H, Torreggiani M, Post JB et al. Role of oxidants/inflammation in declining renal function in chronic kidney disease and normal aging. *Kidney Int Suppl* 2009 Dec;(114):S3–11.

CHAPTER 10

1. Lamarche B, Lemieux I, Després JP. The small, dense LDL phenotype and the risk of coronary heart disease: epidemiology, patho-physiology and therapeutic aspects. *Diabetes Metab* 1999 Sep;25(3):199–211.
2. Packard CJ. Triacylglycerol-rich lipoproteins and the generation of small, dense low-density lipoprotein. *Biochem Soc Trans* 2003;31:1066–9.
3. De Graaf J, Hak-Lemmers HL, Hectors MP et al. Enhanced susceptibility to in vitro oxidation of the dense low density lipoprotein subfraction in healthy subjects. *Arterioscler Thromb* 1991 Mar-Apr;11(2):298–306.
4. Younis N, Sharma R, Soran H et al. Glycation as an atherogenic modification of LDL. *Curr Opin Lipidol* 2008 Aug;19(4):378–84.
5. Stalenhoef AF, de Graaf J. Association of fasting and nonfasting serum triglycerides with cardiovascular disease and the role of remnant-like lipoproteins and small dense LDL. *Curr Opin Lipidol* 2008;19:355–61.
6. Zambon A, Hokanson JE, Brown BG, Brunzell JD. Evidence for a new pathophysiological mechanism for coronary artery disease regression: hepatic lipase-mediated changes in LDL density. *Circulation* 1999 Apr 20;99(15):1959–64.
7. Ginsberg HN. New perspectives on atherogenesis: role of abnormal triglyceride-rich lipoprotein metabolism. *Circulation* 2002;106:2137–42.
8. Sniderman AD. How, when, and why to use apolipoprotein B in clinical practice. *Am J Cardiol* 2002 Oct 17;90(8A):48i–54i.
9. Otvos JD, Jeverajah EJ, Cromwell WC. Measurement issues related to lipoprotein heterogeneity. *Am J Cardiol* 2002 Oct 17;90(8A):22i–9i.
10. Stalenhoef et al. *Curr Opin Lipidol* 2008;19:355–61.
11. Ford ES, Li C, Zhgao G et al. Hypertriglyceridemia and its pharmacologic treatment among US adults. *Arch Intern Med* 2009 Mar 23;169(6):572–8.
12. Superko HR. Beyond LDL cholesterol reduction. *Circulation* 1996 Nov 15;94(10):2351–4.
13. Lemieux I, Couillard C, Pascot A et al.) The small, dense LDL phenotype as a correlate of postprandial lipemia in men. *Atherosclerosis* 2000;153:423–32.
14. Nordestgaard BG, Benn M, Schnohr P et al. Nonfasting triglycerides and risk of myocardial infarction, ischemic heart disease, and death in men and women. *JAMA* 2007 Jul 18;298(3):299–308.
15. Parks EJ, Hellerstein MK. Carbohydrate-induced hypertriacylglycerolemia: Hisotrical perspective and review of biological mechanisms. *Am J Clin Nutr* 2000; 71:412–23.
16. Hudgins LC. Effect of high-carbohydrate feeding on triglyceride and saturated fatty acid synthesis. *Proc Soc Exp Biol Med* 2000;225:178–83.
17. Savage DB, Semple RK. Recent insights into fatty liver, metabolic dyslipidaemia and their links to insulin resistance. *Curr Opin Lipidol* 2010 Aug;21(4):329–36.

18. Therond P. Catabolism of lipoproteins and metabolic syndrome. *Cur Opin Clin Nutr Metab Care* 2009;12:366–71.

19. Centers for Disease Control 2010, Dietary intake for adults 20 years of age and over, at http://www.cdc.gov/nchs/fastats/diet.htm.

20. Capeau J. Insulin resistance and steatosis in humans. *Diabetes Metab* 2008;34:649–57.

21. Adiels M, Olofsson S, Taskinen R, Borén J. Overproduction of very low-density lipoproteins is the hallmark of the dyslipidemia in the metabolic syndrome. *Arteroscler Thromb Vasc Biol* 2008;28:1225–36.

22. Westman EC, Yancy WS Jr, Mavropoulos JC et al. The effect of a low-carbohydrate, ketogenic diet versus a low-glycemic index diet on glycemic control in type 2 diabetes mellitus. *Nutr Metab (Lond)* 2008 Dec 19;5:36.

23. Temelkova-Kurktschiev T, Hanefeld M. The lipid triad in type 2 diabetes—prevalence and relevance of hypertriglyceridaemia/low high-density lipoprotein syndrome in type 2 diabetes. *Exp Clin Endocrinol Diabetes* 2004 Feb;112(2):75–9.

24. Krauss RM. Atherogenic lipoprotein phenotype and diet-gene interactions. *J Nutr* 2001 Feb;131(2):340S–3S.

25. Wood RJ, Volek JS, Liu Y et al. Carbohydrate restriction alters lipoprotein metabolism by modifying VLDL, LDL, and HDL subfraction distribution and size in overweight men. *J Nutr* 2006;136:384–9.

CHAPTER 11

1. Hadjivassiliou M, Sanders DS, Grünewald RA et al. Gluten sensitivity: from gut to brain. *Lancet* 2010 March;9:318–30.

2. Holmes GK. Neurological and psychiatric complications in coeliac disease. In Gobbi G, Anderman F, Naccarato S et al., editors: *Epilepsy and other neurological disorders in coeliac disease*. London: John Libbey; 1997:251–64.

3. Hadjivassiliou M, Grünewald RA, Sharrack B et al. Gluten ataxia in perspective: epidemiology, genetic susceptibility and clinical characteristics. *Brain* 2003;126:685–91.

4. Cooke W, Smith W. Neurological disorders associated with adult coeliac disease. *Brain* 1966;89:683–722.

5. Hadjivassiliou M, Boscolo S, Davies-Jones GA et al. The humoral response in the pathogenesis of gluten ataxia. *Neurology* 2002 Apr 23;58(8):1221–6.

6. Bürk K Bösch S, Müller CA et al. Sporadic cerebellar ataxia associated with gluten sensitivity. *Brain* 2001;124:1013–9.

7. Wilkinson ID, Hadjivassiliou M, Dickson JM et al. Cerebellar abnormalities on proton MR spectroscopy in gluten ataxia. *J Neurol Neurosurg Psychiatry* 2005;76:1011–3.

8. Hadjivassiliou M, Davies-Jones G, Sanders DS, Grünewald RA. Dietary treatment of gluten ataxia. *J Neurol Neurosurg Psychiatry* 2003;74:1221–4.

9. Hadjivassiliou et al. *Brain* 2003;126:685–91.

10. Ibid.

11. Hadjivassiliou M, Kandler RH, Chattopadhyay AK et al. Dietary treatment of gluten neuropathy. *Muscle Nerve* 2006 Dec;34(6):762–6.

12. Bushara KO. Neurologic presentation of celiac disease. *Gastroenterol* 2005;128:S92–7.
13. Hadjivassiliou et al. *Lancet* 2010 March;9:318–30.
14. Hu WT, Murray JA, Greenway MC et al. Cognitive impairment and celiac disease. *Arch Neurol* 2006;63:1440–6.
15. Ibid.
16. Hadjivassiliou et al. *Lancet* 2010 March;9:318–30.
17. Peltola M, Kaukinen K, Dastidar P et al. Hippocampal sclerosis in refractory temporal lobe epilepsy is associated with gluten sensitivity. *J Neurol Neurosurg Psychiatry* 2009 Jun;80(6):626–30.
18. Cronin CC, Jackson LM, Feighery C et al. Coeliac disease and epilepsy. *QJM* 1998;91:303–8.
19. Chapman RW, Laidlow JM, Colin-Jones D et al. Increased prevalence of epilepsy in celiac disease. *Brit Med J* 1978;2:250–1.
20. Mavroudi A, Karatza E, Papastravrou T et al. Successful treatment of epilepsy and celiac disease with a gluten-free diet. *Pediatr Neurol* 2005;33:292–5.
21. Harper E, Moses H, Lagrange A. Occult celiac disease presenting as epilepsy and MRI changes that responded to gluten-free diet. *Neurology* 2007;68:533.
22. Ranua J, Luoma K, Auvinen A et al. Celiac disease-related antibodies in an epilepsy cohort and matched reference population. *Epilepsy Behav* 2005 May;6(3):388–92.

CHAPTER 12

1. Smith RN, Mann NJ, Braue A et al. A low-glycemic-load diet improves symptoms in acne vulgaris patients: a randomized controlled trial. *Am J Clin Nutr* 2007 Jul;86(1):107–15.
2. Cordain L, Lindeberg S, Hurtado M et al. Acne vulgaris: A disease of Western civilization. *Arch Dermatol* 2002 Dec;138:1584–90.
3. Miyagi S, Iwama N, Kawabata T, Hasegawa K. Longevity and diet in Okinawa, Japan: the past, present and future. *Asia Pac J Public Health* 2003;15 Suppl:S3–9.
4. Cordain. *Arch Dermatol* 2002 Dec;138:1584–90.
5. Bendiner E. Disastrous trade-off: Eskimo health for white civilization. *Hosp Pract* 1974;9:156–89.
6. Steiner PE. Necropsies on Okinawans: anatomic and pathologic observations. *Arch Pathol* 1946;42:359–80.
7. Schaefer O. When the Eskimo comes to town. *Nutr Today* 1971;6:8–16.
8. Fulton JE, Plewig G, Kligman AM. Effect of chocolate on acne vulgaris. *JAMA* 1969 Dec 15;210(11):2071–4.
9. Rudman SM, Philpott MP, Thomas G, Kealey T. The role of IGF-I in human skin and its appendages: morphogen as well as mitogen? *J Invest Dermatol* 1997 Dec;109(6):770–7.
10. Cordain. *Arch Dermatol* 2002 Dec;138:1584–90.
11. Franks S. Polycystic ovary syndrome. *N Engl J Med* 2003;13:853–61.

12. Tan S, Hahn S, Benson S et al. Metformin improves polycystic ovary syndrome symptoms irrespective of pre-treatment insulin resistance. *Eur J Endocrinol* 2007 Nov;157(5):669–76.

13. Cordain L. Implications for the role of diet in acne. *Semin Cutan Med Surg* 2005 Jun;24(2):84–91.

14. Frid H, Nilsson M, Holst JJ, Björck IM. Effect of whey on blood glucose and insulin responses to composite breakfast and lunch meals in type 2 diabetic subjects. *Am J Clin Nutr* 2005 Jul;82(1):69–75.

15. Adebamowo CA, Spiegelman D, Danby FW et al. High school dietary dairy intake and teenage acne. *J Am Acad Dermatol* 2005 Feb;52(2):207–14.

16. Abulnaja KO. Changes in the hormone and lipid profile of obese adolescent Saudi females with acne vulgaris. *Braz J Med Biol Res* 2009 Jun;42(6):501–5.

17. Smith RN, Mann NJ, Braue A et al. A low-glycemic-load diet improves symptoms in acne vulgaris patients: a randomized controlled trial. *Am J Clin Nutr* 2007 Jul;86(1):107–15.

18. Abenavoli L, Leggio L, Ferrulli A et al. Cutaneous manifestations in celiac disease. *World J Gastrolenterol* 2006 Feb 16;12(6):843–52.

19. Junkins-Hopkins J. Dermatitis herpetiformis: Pearls and pitfalls in diagnosis and management. *J Am Acad Dermatol* 2001;63:526–8.

20. Abenavoli et al. *World J Gastrolenterol* 2006 Feb 16;12(6):843–52.

21. Kong AS, Williams RL, Rhyne R et al. Acanthosis nigricans: high prevalence and association with diabetes in a practice-based research network consortium—a PRImary care Multi-Ethnic network (PRIME Net) study. *J Am Board Fam Med* 2010 Jul-Aug;23(4):476–85.

22. Corazza GR, Andreani ML, Venturo N et al. Celiac disease and alopecia areata: report of a new association. *Gastroenterol* 1995 Oct;109(4):1333–7.

23. Gregoriou S, Papafragkaki D, Kontochristopoulos G et a. Cytokines and other mediators in alopecia areata. *Mediators Inflamm* 2010;928030.

CHAPTER 13

1. Trepanowski JF, Bloomer RJ. The impact of religious fasting on human health. *Nutr J* 2010 Nov 22;9:57.

2. Kendall CW, Josse AR, Esfahani A, Jenkins DJ. Nuts, metabolic syndrome and diabetes. *Br J Nutr* 2010 Aug;104(4):465–73.

3. Astrup A, Dyerberg J, Elwood P et al. The role of reducing intakes of saturated fat in the prevention of cardiovascular disease: where does the evidence stand in 2010? *Am J Clin Nutr* 2011 Apr;93(4):684–8.

4. Ostman EM, Liljeberg Elmståhl HG, Björck IM. Inconsistency between glycemic and insulinemic responses to regular and fermented milk products. *Am J Clin Nutr* 2001 Jul;74(1):96–100.

EPILOGUE

1. Diamond J. The worst mistake in the history of the human race. *Discover* 1987 May;64–6.

INDEX

Underscored references indicate tables or boxed text.